D1222105

MUSIC IS HISTORY

I dedicate this book to all scientists of sound.

MUSIC IS HISTORY

Questlove
with Ben Greenman

ABRAMS IMAGE, NEW YORK

CONTENTS

INTRODUCTION

As long as I can remember, I have been listening to music, and that means I have also been collecting it, categorizing it, building bridges between songs I loved from one era and songs I loved from another era, songs from one genre and songs from another. In retrospect, I was practicing a kind of history, though I wouldn't have used that word then, and I'm a little reluctant to use it now.

Why? Because I remember how I approached history as a student back in school. I memorized what I was supposed to memorize and was lucky enough to have a good enough memory to get by, but I wasn't always sure what I was learning, other than how to memorize. What if history wasn't just a few big events keyed to a few big dates and a long list of names? What if it was everything else? People say that history was written by the winners, but what if it was written by the simplifiers. Or is that too simple?

● ● ●

A few years back, I was asked to contribute an original song to Kathryn Bigelow's movie *Detroit*. I was aware of the events the film related, more or less. It was set during the Long Hot Summer of 1967, which saw a number of American cities fed up with police violence erupt with civil unrest: Atlanta, Boston, Cincinnati—and that's just the beginning of the alphabet. Then came Detroit. I knew Detroit had burned, and that it was the site of a disproportionate amount of the violence in America that summer. But, at the time, I didn't know much about the specific story at the heart of the movie, the Algiers Motel incident, in which a group of young Black men at a Detroit motel were brutally beaten by police.

Kathryn screened the movie for me. Near the beginning, there was a scene inside a concert hall. A group was about to go onstage. Just before they could, the cops shut down the hall and sent the group packing. No show tonight. I got up out of my seat and found the projectionist. "Is this the Dramatics?" I asked. He nodded. I knew the Dramatics from history, or at least music history. In the mid-'60s they had released a song called "Bingo" by a small label under the control of Golden World, a Detroit indie operation owned by a man named Ed Wingate. A few years later, Motown took over Golden World, and the Dramatics released a regional hit, "All Because of You." That night in 1967, they were scheduled to perform the song at a showcase. But events overtook them, and they got into their vehicle to head home.

As the movie went on, I learned that the Dramatics weren't just incidental to the plot. They were central to it. As they drove away, they were surrounded by protestors and had to split up. Some of them, including the vocalist Ron Banks, found their way home. Others, though, didn't. Another of the group's singers, Cleveland Larry Reed, and a young man named Fred Temple—a friend of the band who is sometimes called a bodyguard, sometimes a valet—instead ended up in a local motel, at which point they were pulled into the darkest heart of history. I won't say more. I don't want to ruin the suspense of the movie. Is that strange, to worry about suspense in a story from fifty years ago? Or is suspense more dependent upon what is known than what happened?

That's what happened. The Dramatics changed the way I watched the movie. They didn't make it more dramatic, ironically, but they made it more real. There was something about watching two strands of history intertwine, about watching the large textbook narrative ("Detroit, 1967") intersect with this very specific set of sense memories (hearing the Dramatics on the radio when I was a kid—though most of their songs were sung by Banks, who stayed with the group, rather than Reed, who was so shattered by his night in the Algiers that he left secular music for the church). There was the official record, and then these other records, which were actual records. The song that the Roots wrote for the movie, "It Ain't Fair," with Bilal singing, made it more real all over again—it was a song about pain and injustice that we recorded at Diamond Mine in New York, where I thought we could get a sound like Motown's Studio A. I was trying to join up with the past in my own way. “It Ain’t Fair” went on the movie’s soundtrack album next to songs by Marvin Gaye, Brenda Holloway, Martha Reeves, and others. The song, about history, was placed in music history, and became both. (The entire soundtrack pays off that idea of the present overlaid on the past, sometimes in surprising ways. I’m thinking of “Grow,” where the actor Algee Smith, who plays Cleveland Larry Reed, duets with the man himself.) Despite my overall discomfort with the execution of the film—when is Black pain art, and are there times when depictions of it cross the line?—we managed to turn the song around and get a frame around the film.

• • •

Detroit was an especially explicit version of something that had always been implicit. When I think about history—what I’ve learned, how I’ve learned, when in my life I’ve been ready to learn—it’s always connected to music. It’s not too much of an exaggeration to say that I think of the America we live in as a series of songs, partly because I think of everything that way. When I remember my own childhood, almost every event is keyed to a song. My parents were touring musicians, which meant that they would go away for stretches and leave me and my sister with my grandmother, and that meant that songs I heard, whether on the radio or my small 8-track player, were not only burned into my brain but time-stamped. Rufus’s “Egyptian Song” reminds me of the nights before they went away. Deniece Williams’s *Song Bird* reminds me of when the loneliness of being at my grandmother’s started to sink in. Those moments of personal history hang from those songs like banners.

Maybe the best metaphor isn’t individual songs, but record albums. Back in the 1920s and ’30s, when music was recorded on 78 rpm discs, companies would sell binders for storing a set of them. They came to be called record storage albums—like photo albums. Later on, after the LP was invented in 1948, multiple songs could go on the same round platter. When the record album was born, the record storage album died. But I still approach history the same way. When I go back through the past in my mind, I imagine flipping through pages.

What I have tried to do in this book is to move year by year through modern history—and by modern history, I mean the slice of the planet, and specifically America, that coincides with my life. I'm starting in 1971. For each year, I am selecting a song that represents some idea connected to history: how it was experienced at the time, or how it is learned and understood, or what figures surface within it, or how different versions of it are reconciled, or how they cannot be. Sometimes I'll look at actual music history—who made which records when, and how the circumstances of their creation can teach us all about the art form and the society that defined (and redefined) it. And sometimes I'll use ideas about music to illustrate ideas about history. Why do some moments surge up the charts while others fall away? Are some events A sides, while others are B sides? What is history's equivalent of liner notes? In the Roots, when we thought of titles for our albums, we wanted them to have three layers of meaning: to refer to something that was happening within the band, something that was happening in the hip-hop world, and something that was happening in the world in general. I have tried for a version of that here.

Like many children of the '70s, I first came to know the band Chicago through their monster radio hits, like "Saturday in the Park" or "25 or 6 to 4." As time went on, I came to know them by their albums, too. For a little while, I was drawn to *Chicago III*, which came out the year I was born—and, even closer than that, the month I was born (it was released on January 11; I was released on January 20). That's the Tattered Flag cover, which shows the band's logo on a distressed American flag, which itself illustrates a moment in history—the Vietnam War was still going, and the record came with a poster of the band standing in front of a field of crosses that represented those lost in the war. But the song I gravitated to was about a larger kind of history. It was "Mother," which was about birth, but not mine or the album's—it was about the way that the planet birthed us all, and why we should be more respectful of our time with it.

Now skip forward slightly to September 1971, the same month as John Lennon's *Imagine*, the debut album by Labelle, and Aretha Franklin's *Greatest Hits* (since supplanted by a million other collections, but if you've seen the cover image once, you've never forgotten it—it's the one where she's standing on a red staircase, between two escalators, wearing a dress that perfectly/unfortunately blends in). Not to mention the Jackson 5's *Goin' Back to Indiana*, their sixth album and the soundtrack of a TV special that had aired only two weeks earlier and showed what big stars the Jacksons had become by putting equally big stars next to them: Bill Cosby, Diana Ross, Tommy Smothers, Bobby Darin, Rosey Grier, Bill Russell, and more.

I looked at all that in the context of history. What did September 1971 mean? What did it contain? The big event was the Attica prison riot. It took place in upstate New York from September 9 to 13, which people know mostly because "Attica!" was chanted in *Dog Day Afternoon* as a way of getting the crowd outside the bank riled up. But it's a much more complex, bloodier story than that: Prisoners, demanding better conditions, took over the prison, and initially had most of their demands met but were at loggerheads regarding a guarantee of amnesty. At that point, Governor Nelson Rockefeller sent in state police to seize back control of the prison. Forty-three people were killed: ten guards and employees, thirty-three inmates.

Attica wasn't an isolated incident, but a rebellion that grew out of the George Jackson situation. Back in January 1970, Jackson, then an inmate at Soledad Prison, witnessed a white guard, Opie G. Miller, respond to a fist fight in the yard by opening fire on the mostly Black prisoners, killing three. Three days later, a grand jury cleared Miller, citing justifiable homicide, and within an hour another Soledad guard, John Vincent Mills, was beaten and thrown from a third-floor window. He later died. Jackson and two other inmates were charged with Mills's murder. The three became known as the Soledad Brothers, and were a cause célèbre among Black Power and leftist activists. Over the months, tensions between the mostly Black inmates and the mostly white guards in the California prison system escalated. Two guards were held hostage. One more was killed. In August 1970,

George Jackson's seventeen-year-old brother Jonathan interrupted a trial at the Marin County courthouse, held Superior Court Judge Harold Haley at gunpoint (later taping a road flare, which he pretended was a stick of dynamite, to Haley's neck), took more hostages, and demanded the release of his brother and the two other Soledad Brothers. Jonathan Jackson intended to get them to an airplane so they could escape. A van carrying the kidnappers and the hostages left the courthouse and encountered a police roadblock, at which point there was a volley of gunfire. Jonathan Jackson was killed, as was Judge Haley.

The guns that Jonathan Jackson used had been purchased by the activist and former philosophy professor Angela Davis, who was jailed and later tried on charges including conspiracy to commit murder. She was acquitted. George Jackson went on to publish *Soledad Brother*, a collection of letters from prison. He died in August 1971, a year and two weeks after his brother, during an attempted escape from San Quentin that also claimed the lives of three officers and two inmates.

The events spun into pop culture, specifically pop music. Bob Dylan had a song out about George Jackson by November 1971, in two versions: one "Big Band," one solo acoustic. One of the backup singers on the Big Band version was Jo Armstead, who had been an Ikette, a backup singer for Ike and Tina Turner, and gone on to write hits with Nick Ashford and Valerie Simpson, including "Let's Go Get Stoned." Later in life, after leaving the music industry, Armstead managed a boxer named Alfonso Ratliff, who in September 1986 lost by TKO to a twenty-year-old Mike Tyson, six months away from becoming the youngest heavyweight champion in history, and five and a half years away from going to prison himself. History.

In picking both events and songs, I have allowed the same spirit to guide me, which is to say that I have not made the biggest deals of the biggest deals. I have sometimes gone for the fattest fish, of course. I'd be crazy not to. But just as the largest hits are not always the most important songs, or the most enduring, the biggest events in a year are not always the ones that lodge in the head and the heart.

So that's the charter, to chart history through music and to trace music through history, all the while trying to look more closely and more critically, trying to unpeel and uncover, and to encourage readers (that's you!) to do the same. Because the issues are difficult, they may also be messy, and I am willing to leave that mess intact. Behind it, there are even messier issues. Why do some people turn away from verified history, from facts and documentary proof, and allow themselves to drift into conspiracy? What authorities should we respect, conditionally or unconditionally? How can we protect ourselves against conspiracy theories and other flawed thinking? How much history can we truly know—and how much do we have to admit can never be known? Those questions have been especially important in recent months, but they have been there forever.

• • •

Before I wrap up the introduction and roll into the rest of the book, I want to talk a little bit about lists. A few years back, I worked on a movie that Chris Rock was making called *Top Five*. It was a romantic comedy with a conceit: people keep lists. So along with the essays about songs and years, this book includes some lists. Restraining myself on the list front was not easy. I love lists. I love playing with them. I love playlists and playful lists. To me, lists are a game that will never end: sort of like history. But I tried, for the purposes of this book, to build lists that are natural outgrowths of the ideas in the essays, lists that reflect and reiterate historical principles.

So there it is: music as seen through history, history as seen through music. Before the journey begins, one more instruction. Do not keep your arms and legs inside the vehicle at all times. I am not a trained historian and I am not pretending to be one. I have tried for accuracy in all things, but I can say without hesitation that I am sure I have fallen short here and there, or fallen off to the side: a fact that requires explanation, an interpretation that provokes disagreement. That's why I urge you to read critically. When you see something that seems suspect, go look it up. When there's an argument that doesn't convince you, write out a counterargument. Be an active participant rather than a passive one, both because it's more fun to read that way and because active participation is a vital skill that's being lost as our culture falls more to echo chambers and social-media sniping. Most important, don't let this be your last book. Get a stack going on the table next to your bed, and another stack going on the counter in your kitchen. Always have something within arm's reach that makes you consider and reconsider, agree and disagree, follow someone else's train of thought and then switch it onto your own track. In the words of George Clinton (who was in Detroit that fateful night in July 1967 with the Parliaments, in fact on the same bill as the Dramatics at the Fox Theater for *The Swingin' Time Revue*), "Think—it ain't illegal yet."

1971

The Supreme Court rules that the Pentagon Papers can be published ○ Evel Knievel jumps nineteen cars at the Ontario Motor Speedway in California ○ President Nixon announces the War on Drugs ○ The Negro League star Satchel Paige is inducted into the Baseball Hall of Fame ○ *All in the Family* debuts on CBS ○ The United States bans cigarette ads from radio and television ○ *The Ed Sullivan Show* goes off the air ○ The Congressional Black Caucus is established, after which Richard Nixon refuses to meet with the group, after which the caucus boycotts his inauguration ○ Walt Disney World opens ○ *Willy Wonka & the Chocolate Factory* comes out ○ Jesse Jackson founds Operation PUSH ○ Johnson Products becomes the first Black-owned company listed on the NYSE ○ *Soul Train* debuts ○ Beverly Johnson is the first Black woman on the cover of a major fashion magazine (*Glamour*)

STRETCHED ON HISTORY'S WHEEL

Everything has to start (and end) somewhere.

I want to start with a song by Tony Williams, or rather by his group the Tony Williams Lifetime—a song called "There Comes a Time," from the 1971 album *Ego*. My relationship with this song starts deep in my past. For starters, it was released the year I was born. It came into the world within months of when I did. But it came into my life as I was being born as a musician, as the Roots were just beginning. At that time, Tariq and I used to listen to a DJ up at WRTI at Temple play all this avant-garde jazz. Little did we know—how could we have known?—that that DJ, Richard Nichols, would come to manage the Roots and steer us through more than two decades of our career. Rich passed away in July 2014 of leukemia. I will mention him often in this book, and in a sense he's always being mentioned in my life. His influence is massive, both in terms of my career, but also in terms of how I think about culture, society, history, and the human place within those giant tapestries. What is power? What is time? What determines who defines those things? Those were the kinds of questions that Rich's mind put into everyone else's mind.

All that is to say that I already had a nostalgic connection to "There Comes a Time," even before I started listening to it closely. When I did, I realized that the song, in addition to having personal currency, was musically singular. It was mind-bending, both in its strange time signature (a cracked 5/4) and in Williams's vocal. He sings like the sonic version of the Grady twins from Stanley Kubrick's *The Shining*; his vocals are inviting, eerie, not straightforwardly part of life, edging just beyond it.

As it turns out, this wasn't Tony Williams's first time visiting that strange intersection of being and not being. For most of the '60s, he was the drummer for Miles Davis, which meant that he was a central part of Miles's second great quintet, alongside Wayne Shorter, Herbie Hancock, Ron Carter, and of course Miles. That band kicked off with *E.S.P.* in 1965 and bowed out with *Filles de Kilimanjaro* in 1969. Toward the end of that run is *Nefertiti* (1968), which I consider to be Miles's last true jazz release. It almost feels like a contractual obligation album. You can hear it in Miles's playing and the way he structures the record. He's bored and wants to move further, to discover newer New Directions in Music. This restlessness, and the resentment that he had to stand in place for a little while longer, is most apparent on the title cut. In jazz, the drums and bass are supposed to be the anchor, with the keyboard and horns dancing around them. That's the conventional thinking, at least. Miles turns the whole thing inside out. He and Shorter repeat the central figure, without soloing, ad nauseam, for almost eight minutes, while Ron Carter and Tony Williams literally go full Tasmanian Devil (or Yakko, Wakko, and Dot, depending on your Looney era) for the duration of the ballad. Each time Miles and Shorter repeat the line you can hear the dread and the boredom, the sarcasm, the defiant exhaustion. They do it eleven times, I think, and by the fifth or sixth it almost feels like an Andy Kaufman move. It tries your patience. What takes the edge off is that Tony Williams and Ron Carter are running amok, a cat and dog playing tag inside a china shop. As a kid I was forced to listen to lots of jazz: you know, education. That was the first time I heard a jazz record and didn't consider it punishment. On "Nefertiti," Tony Williams got to represent life, (not so) plain and (not so) simple: energy, entropy, chaos, charge. On "There Comes a Time," he visits the other end of the spectrum of existence, especially in his vocals, that Black male deadpan holding hands with itself in the Overlook corridor. There is an eerie comfort hearing him sing in unison with himself, getting sharper in tone each time he returns to the phrase. (I can't think of another case of having this much fun with someone singing off-key, unless it's the house classic "Follow Me" by Aly-Us, from 1992). I sang and performed that song at Rich Nichols's memorial service. D. D. Jackson wrote a string arrangement. There were solos by David Murray on saxophone and Vernon Reid on guitar. When we got to the lyric "I love you more when it's over," the music stopped short but the sense of the music carried forward.

History operates similarly. It resists sameness. It embraces change. Sometimes it forces change.

The process dramatized in this song, the process of leaving behind modal jazz, is also the process of leaning into something else, even if that something else is not yet known. Every time there comes a time, it is both a time for ending and a time for beginning. It also hints at a paradox. The farther away an event gets, the more we can potentially know about it—the more we've been able to read about it, think about it, process various theories about it. The things that are still in process, the things that aren't over, can't yet be history. Can they be fully understood? Or do they have to end before any true thinking about them can begin?

This song, then, is a starting point for the book but also a way of starting to talk about endings. Rich's death was an end, and it ended a certain way of looking at things, in a sense. But it also started a new way, in another sense. He was immensely analytical and peerlessly brilliant, and he made me think about those things every day. The song makes me sad, but it's bracing and clarifying and helps bring the world into focus. Tony Williams illustrates the ways that ideas can be slow to change while people are impatient for them to change. In 2020, we saw lots of both of those things.

1972

Five Republican operatives are arrested for burglarizing the headquarters of the Democratic National Committee ○ *Blacula* is released ○ Eleven Israeli athletes are murdered by terrorists at the Munich Olympics ○ Intel invents the single-chip microprocessor ○ Al Green releases *Let's Stay Together* ○ Hurricane Agnes ravages Pennsylvania, killing more than a hundred people ○ *The Godfather* is released ○ Shirley Chisholm becomes the first Black woman to campaign for the Democratic presidential nomination ○ The Equal Rights Amendment is passed by the Senate ○ The first issue of *Luke Cage: Hero for Hire* is published ○ A smallpox epidemic, the latest to date, breaks out in Yugoslavia ○ Roberto Clemente dies in a plane crash while delivering supplies to victims of an earthquake in Nicaragua

MUSIC IS THE MESSAGE

Culture shines a light on the world around it.

Just because two periods of time are the same length doesn't mean that they merit the same amount of consideration in history. There might be a single day (say, April 15, 1865, for example, when Lincoln was shot) that has hundreds of thousands of pages written about it, while there might be another day (June 16, 1911, say) where nothing happened. Is that possible, even? That there are days, or weeks, or months that were entirely devoid of events, and that as a result are not in history? The absence of history would be pretty historical.

Even if there isn't a day when nothing happened, there are days when less happens—and months, and years. In our lifetime, some years seem absolutely packed with events. The year 2020 was one of those, and when people try to compare it to anything, they compare it to 1968. Those are the newsiest years, but they're not the longest. What's the longest? The longest year in history was 1972. It was already longer than the years around it because it was a leap year, and it got a little extra push when, because of the slowing rotation of the Earth, two leap seconds were added. I don't think that people reset their clocks or slept through meetings, but officially, as part of Coordinated Universal Time (which, for some reason, is abbreviated UTC), 1972 stretched out longer than any other year. Time didn't fly. But it did *Super Fly*.

On August 4 of that year, the same day that one of the largest recorded solar flares in history knocked out cable lines across the United States (I can't speak to whether that's related to the longest-year thing), *Super Fly*, starring Ron O'Neal as the Harlem drug dealer Youngblood Priest, appeared in theaters. It was also the day that Arthur Bremer was sentenced to sixty-three years in prison for his attempted assassination of the Alabama governor and Democratic presidential candidate George Wallace. Bremer inspired the character of Travis ("You talkin' to me?") Bickle in *Taxi Driver*, who in turn inspired John Hinckley to shoot Ronald Reagan, in part to impress Jodie Foster, who had starred in the movie back in 1976. (Or is it ahead in 1976?)

● ● ●

Today we think of *Super Fly* as a blaxploitation classic. Back then, as the genre was being born, it was just a movie following on the heels of other movies. That's another thing about history. Categories get created after events, and those events (and more) are retroactively loaded into those categories.

To understand the category around *Super Fly*, you have to go back a year, to another movie, *Shaft*. *Shaft* was the Big Bang of Black movies. Before that, of course, there were other Black directors. There was Oscar Michaux. There was Spencer Williams. There was the experimental director William Greaves (*Symbiopsychotaxiplasm*), and the versatile and surprisingly commercial indie director Melvin Van Peebles (*Watermelon Man*, *Sweet Sweetback's Baadasssss Song*).

And then there was *Shaft*. Gordon Parks, who directed the movie, was already a Black Renaissance man. "Renaissance man" makes me laugh in this context, because it defines not just a specific kind of person, but a specific period in history. What would a Black man from America have done back in the real Renaissance? How would he have been received? Parks probably would have appreciated the irony. He had been a pioneering photographer with *Life* magazine in the 1950s and '60s, had written a memoir, and had made a movie based on it. *Shaft* was based on a detective novel by a man named Ernest Tidyman, who turned it into a screenplay with a man named John D. F. Black. Black was white, as was Tidyman, as was the Shaft in Tidyman's novel. Onscreen, though, Shaft turned Black, in the person of Richard Roundtree, and the co-stars included Moses Gunn, a classically trained actor with perhaps the coolest name in history, and Camille Yarbrough, a performance poet and stage actress , the sultry voice that holds the word "Shouuuuuuuuuuuuuuuu uuuuuuuuuld" for thirty seconds in Fatboy Slim's "Praise You."

The movie was an undeniable hit. Theaters in New York showed it around the clock ("Shaft! 24 Hours a Day!" said the ads—sounds exhausting).

And then there was the soundtrack. Isaac Hayes had been one of the staples of the Memphis-based Stax label for a decade. He did everything there: he was a session player, a producer, and (with his partner, David Porter) a songwriter who fed material to Stax's top acts. Toward the late '60s, the label went through changes. Otis Redding died in a plane crash. Atlantic took control of Stax. Hayes reemerged as a performer, and a specific kind of performer, delivering albums filled with long, orchestrated versions of pop songs like "By the Time I Get to Phoenix" and "Walk On By," not to mention originals like "Hyperbolicsyllabicsesquedalymistic." He was the label's savior, and he looked like one, with his big bald head, his big gold chains, and his big dark sunglasses. Hayes was actually considered for the lead role in *Shaft*, but instead he got the soundtrack gig. Based on the dailies that Parks was supplying, he wrote a number of compositions, including a song called "Soulsville" and an instrumental called "Ellie's Love Theme." The third piece was the Shaft theme.

You know it, right? Who doesn't! Hi-hat skims along on sixteenth notes, drums played by Willie Hall. Then there's the immortal wah-wah guitar played by Charles "Skip" Pitts, who only a year or so before had played an equally immortal part on the Isley Brothers' "It's Your Thing." Then the rest of the band, flute, horns, piano. It takes almost three minutes for any vocals, and they're more spoken than sung. The lyrics mostly just describe Shaft. Above all, he's a bad mother . . . fucker. (There—I said the unsayable after five decades of denial.)

The album stayed on the chart for more than a year and became the bestselling release in Stax history. It was the first double album by a soul artist, and Hayes won four Grammys for it and was nominated for two Oscars. He won Best Original Song for the title track, the first Black composer to do so.

• • •

Shaft was so big that everything else was in its wake. For starters, it had sequels. Two, in fact, one where Shaft had a big score (*Shaft's Big Score*—Hayes was busy so Parks did the music himself, but in a "What Would Hayes Do?" spirit—the cues are so derivative), the other where Shaft went to Africa (*Shaft in Africa*—music by Johnny Pate, including a loop that Jay-Z later used on "Show Me What You Got" to usher in the "gospel chops" wave). *Super Fly* was not a sequel, though it was in a sense a direct descendant of *Shaft*—it was directed by Gordon Parks, Jr.

The movie was a qualified hit. O'Neal was mainly a stage actor—he had picked up an Obie back in 1969—but people took exception to the Youngblood Priest role. Especially Black people. Junius Griffin, who ran the Hollywood branch of the NAACP—there's a job—worried that it was glorifying violence, drug use, and a life of crime. He didn't just worry. He spoke out against it: "We must insist that our children are not exposed to a steady diet of so-called black movies that glorify black males as pimps, dope pushers, gangsters, and super males." The organization, along with CORE (the Congress for Racial Equality), tried to keep it from reaching theaters, or to pull it out of the theaters it had already reached. Other organizations argued that it was, if not an overt tool of white control, a perfect example of the way that the white hegemony had forced Black people to internalize stereotypical ideas of themselves. Others found the film exciting, thrilling, and even inspirational. Rick Ross—not the rapper, who was born William Leonard Roberts, but the guy he took his stage name from, the legendary California drug trafficker "Freeway" Rick Ross—has said that he was motivated to take up a life of crime specifically because of *Super Fly*. There is a fascinating discussion here about the influence of culture on society, about the seductive power of negative role models and the way that they can fill a vacuum that isn't otherwise occupied by positive options. I want to focus that discussion by speaking not about the movie, but about the soundtrack.

Recorded by Curtis Mayfield as his third studio solo album, after *Curtis* in 1970 (that's the one where he's in the foreground of the cover photo wearing yellow pants) and *Roots* in 1971 (brown jacket, sitting at the base of a tree), *Super Fly* was, from the looks of the album cover, a collision of messages. The left side, apart from Curtis's name at the top, is given over entirely to the movie, to the hand-lettered red-and-yellow logo of the title and a photo of Ron O'Neal, the star of the film, gun in hand, standing over a barely clothed woman (Sheila Frazier). The right side of the cover is all Curtis, his face hovering thoughtfully like a moon. That's the tension of the cover, and of the album: Would it continue that "steady diet" of "pimps, dope pushers, gangsters, and super males," or would it reflect Mayfield's history of incisive social commentary, mixing uplifting messages of justice and Black empowerment with warnings about what might happen if those messages weren't heeded? Would the artist be able to salvage ethical content from a movie that seemed at times unwilling to control its message?

It was a battle, and from the first seconds of the album, Mayfield won the war. "Little Child Runnin' Wild," the opener, nods to the Temptations' "Runaway Child, Running Wild," which had been released back in 1969, moving further into the hardening (and darkening) counterculture of the '70s. "Pusherman" was a lightly funky, deeply seductive portrait of a drug dealer. And then there was "Freddie's Dead," the album's lead (and highest-charting) single. Freddie was a character in the movie played by Charles McGregor, a veteran Black actor and a staple of blaxploitation movies. McGregor had been in prison often as a young man, and after his release specialized in playing streetwise characters. He was in *The French Connection* before *Super Fly*, and in a number of blaxploitation classics (*Across 110th Street*, *Hell up in Harlem*, *Three the Hard Way*) after it. You might also know him from Mel Brooks's *Blazing Saddles*, where he played Charlie, the railroad worker who is sent with Bart (Cleavon Little) on a hand cart up the tracks to find some quicksand that the surveyors have reported. The joke is that when the railroad bosses realize they have to figure out the extent of the quicksand situation, the crew boss suggests sending horses. The big boss smacks him on the head. "We can't afford to lose horses, you dummy!" Who can they afford to lose? See you later, Bart and Charlie. Brooks's movie was both as brutal and as empathetic an act of Jewish articulation of Black pain as "Strange Fruit" (and not in a carpetbagging way—the movie was famously co-written by Richard Pryor), but it wouldn't come out until 1974. So from the perspective of *Super Fly*, it didn't yet exist. At that point, Charles McGregor was only Freddie. And while in the movie his death followed the code of the streets—he was picked up by the cops and snitched, though only after being beaten, and then was killed by a car while trying to escape—the song works wonders, converting Freddie, and his memory, into both a vessel of empathy and a cautionary tale. We discover right at the beginning that "Everybody's misused him, ripped him up and abused him." He's "pushing dope for the man," Mayfield sings, "a terrible blow" (which is also sort of a terrible pun), but also "that's how it goes." Matter of life and death, matter of fact. And then "Freddie's on the corner," or maybe "a Freddie's on the corner," a new one, getting ready to start the same cycle all over again.

History repeats itself, especially when people don't remember that Freddie's dead.

Charles McGregor would continue acting throughout the '70s, with his final role coming in *Andy Warhol's Bad*, the last film that Warhol produced in his lifetime. Gordon Parks, Jr., went on to make three more films—the blaxploitation/action movie *Three the Hard Way*, the Black-Western *Bonnie and Clyde* update *Thomasine & Bushrod*, and the multiracial *Romeo and Juliet* update *Aaron Loves Angela*—before dying in a plane crash in Nairobi in 1979, at the age of forty-four. I'm not even sure that Freddie was that young. Mayfield, too, fell victim to tragedy: in the summer of 1990, while performing at an outdoor show at Wingate Field in Brooklyn, he was struck by stage lighting that had been knocked down by a sudden wind. He was paralyzed from the neck down. He continued to record, but under extraordinarily difficult circumstances—vocals had to be recorded line by line while he was on his back. He heroically managed one more record, *New World Order* in 1996, and died in 1999.

Mayfield's album ends with the classic title track, but for me its signal song is the next-to-last, a longish instrumental called "Think." The title is audacious, in its own subtle way. By 1972, there were already two classic soul songs called "Think." There was the Lowman Pauling version, recorded by the Royals and then the "5" Royales and famously covered by James Brown in 1960. And then there's of course the Aretha Franklin version, which first burst out of the gate in '68 and was back for the Blues Brothers (not to mention a 1989 cover by the Queen herself). But those two songs are in the tradition of soul songs. They are direct messages to recently departed (in the sense that they have left, not that they have left us) lovers urging them to reconsider. The "Think" of *Super Fly* is thinking in the Mayfield sense: social consciousness, the levers of class and race, history. It's wordless, so it's open-ended, but it's also surrounded by messages that direct that thinking. And the feel of the instrumental is meditative in the best sense, endlessly peaceful. It gives you a sense not only of knowing, but of being. He thinks, therefore I am.

Falling Out of History

***Shaft* has two meanings, at least. It's the title of the movie, of course. It can also mean "to get the shaft," to be undervalued or treated unfairly. This list collects songs from across the years, not just 1972, that not only weren't given proper appreciation at the time they were released but weren't given any attention in the wake of that. As a result they were allowed to fade from communal memory. The songs are all worthy of being reinstated.**

"SAY AHA"
Santigold

Santogold, 2008 [Downtown/Lizard King]

Santi's pop-writing zone was masterful, as she proved on the 2001 Res album *How I Do*. Had Res been white, that would have been a knock out of the park. I feel the same about this record. It's perfect pop that got rejected because it was by a thirty-year-old Black woman.

"I NEED YOUR LOVING"
The Human League

Crash, 1986 [A&M]

I asked Jimmy Jam why he didn't save this song for Alexander O'Neal—he would have torn it out the frame. He said that they had written "Fake" for O'Neal, and that this was practically the same song. It remains one of their funkiest, and it's moderately okay, but the pop audience that leaned into the Human League wasn't that deep into funk.

"MR. KNIGHT"
John Coltrane

Coltrane Plays the Blues, 1962 [Atlantic]

I know the world thinks mostly about *A Love Supreme*. Even my radio show is named after it. But this is my go-to Coltrane album. Sometimes you want to touch down just before the moment of supreme genius, because it sets up the later story.

"WHISPER SOFTLY"
Kool and the Gang

Open Sesame, 1976 [De-Lite]

I study no band harder than Kool and the Gang. And unlike James Brown, what was perceived as their down period (1975–1979) was in some cases even more adventurous. All over this album, there are opportunities for them to show how smart they are without turning off the dumb jocks. Khalis Bayyan told me about their battles with the label, and how in this case they took Coltrane's scale theory and applied it to a four-on-the-floor beat.

"GIRL I THINK THE WORLD ABOUT YOU"
Commodores

Hot on the Tracks, 1976 [Motown]

There was a time period on albums by Black artists where the hits were the songs that didn't scare middle America and the filler was showing off how good your report card was. To me, the fillers were always more of an attraction.

"SOUP FOR ONE"
Chic

Soup for One, 1982 [Mirage]

Probably my all-time favorite Chic song and underrated because it's on a soundtrack. It's the Chic song that I play to let my fellow nerds figure that I know the deep cuts. Of course, the other nerds use it too.

"REACH YOUR PEAK"
Sister Sledge

Love Somebody Today, 1980 [Cotillion]

It's really hard to capture an understated compelling keyboard performance, especially in the post-disco period. On songs like this, I immediately tune in to Raymond Jones's funky keyboard work in the chorus instead of what Nile Rodgers's guitar is doing. Which is an achievement in itself.

"MY OLD PIANO"
Diana Ross

Diana, 1980 [Motown]

I'm probably the only listener of this song who doesn't see this as "Diana's Chic song," even though they are all over her entire album. She's way more present in it than people think. Another rare example of Rodger's masterful rhythm ax getting upstaged (this time by Bernard Edward's basswork).

"SING A HAPPY SONG"
War

Youngblood: Original Motion Picture Soundtrack, 1978 [United Artists]

Think of the irony of the whole presentation: a band called War singing "Sing a Happy Song" on a soundtrack called *Youngblood*. This song was brought to my attention as a Brand Nubian sample (see 1977). After I saw Fishbone do a Sunday morning show just for kids, I started a three-month quest to find what songs could work with kids today without pandering to them. This is definitely in my top five.

"SHORTBERRY STRAWCAKE"
Sheila E.

The Glamorous Life, 1984 [Paisley Park]

Prince breezed through this instrumental in maybe forty-five minutes. As much as his DNA is all over this song, I can't imagine this being on a Prince album or a B-side. However, on Sheila's album this is damn near a funk miracle.

"(IF YOU WANT MY LOVE) PUT SOMETHING DOWN ON IT"
Bobby Womack

I Don't Know What the World Is Coming To, 1975 [United Artists]

Rod Stewart gave this song the shaft by stealing its melody for "Da Ya Think I'm Sexy?" But Rod was smart about knowing exactly which part to elevate. Years later the Roots did a version of Gershwin's "Summertime" with Bobby Womack, and he incorporated part of this and explained the lyrics, how they're about putting something on layaway until you can pay for it in full.

1973

The United States signs the Paris Peace Accords in January, officially ending the Vietnam War ○ Maynard H. Jackson is elected the first Black mayor of Atlanta ○ The United States Supreme Court rules on *Roe v. Wade*, guaranteeing abortion as a federal right ○ Two men, Calvin Parker, Jr., and Charles Hickson, are allegedly abducted by a UFO on the banks of the Pascagoula River in Mississippi ○ OPEC pulls back on oil production, increasing the price by more than double and sending Europe into recession ○ Tom Bradley becomes the first Black mayor of Los Angeles ○ More than two hundred members of the American Indian Movement occupy Wounded Knee ○ The Sears Tower is completed in Chicago and becomes the tallest building in the world ○ Billie Jean King defeats Bobby Riggs in the Battle of the Sexes, an exhibition tennis match ○ Mao Zedong suggests to Henry Kissinger that China might give the United States ten million Chinese women as a gift ○ Secretariat wins the Triple Crown

PAST IS PROLOGUE—AND PROTEST

When you put your foot down, are you taking a stand?

Music can reflect social reality, as blaxploitation did—though it reflected it through a kind of funhouse mirror, where exaggeration in the service of entertainment was a top-line priority. And over the course of reflecting on it, music can challenge that reality. Is society sending the wrong messages? Is it creating equal opportunities? Does it have the right priorities? In that, it's doing its job as art.

But sometimes these kinds of questions aren't even mediated by fictional scenarios. That leads directly to another set of questions, just as surely as 1972 leads into 1973. What is a protest song? Where did the idea come from? Can music truly change minds?

To answer those questions, we can't stay in 1973. We're going to have to hop in the Questlove time machine, which isn't really a time machine but a series of paragraphs in which I'll be returning to the past to further explore an idea.

Way back at the beginning of America, people were talking about a revolution. Think of a song like "Yankee Doodle." It started life not as a protest song but as a British song mocking Americans: you know, look at that foolish Yankee, that hopeless doodle, sticking a feather in his cap and calling it macaroni. Soon enough, Americans turned the song back around, using it as a source of pride ("Say that about our cap again!") and adding verses about the fledgling nation. They reclaimed the "Yankee Doodle" idea until it became more than a song of resistance to the British, but a legitimate anthem of new-nation pride. It's like when Prince took Jesse Johnson's title *Shockadelica* and recorded a song under that name to show him up. Nice flex. Where was I? Right, Yankee Doodle. Let's jump again, this time to early-nineteenth-century America, where much protest centered around slavery, the injustice and inhumanity of it, and one of the ways to illustrate that was to draw on biblical motifs. Is that someone singing "Go Down Moses," an African-American spiritual? Got to get out of here. Now I'm in a seder in Brooklyn in 2011 or so. They're singing "Let My People Go." Similar song, safer environment.

On my way from there to here in my time machine, I stopped briefly in 1843, where I witnessed the Hutchinson Family Singers, a New England–based group whose close harmonies and socially oriented material helped them become what people consider to be the first American protest singers. They really were family, organized around the core of four brothers, John, Jesse, Judson, and Asa, and they included as many as thirteen siblings, male and female. The year I touched down, the Hutchinsons, then nicknamed the Tribe of Jesse, were in the midst of becoming fervent abolitionists, and also singing about causes like women's rights and temperance. I didn't talk to them. I only saw them perform. They were good. They didn't yet know that when the Civil War began, they would split into two groups, the Tribe of John (which would stay in the eastern part of the United States) and the Tribe of Asa (which would go west). They certainly didn't know that Judson, one of the founding brothers, would hang himself in John's basement in 1859.

I also stopped in 1872, at what I think was the home of a prosperous Black family in Baltimore. I can't be sure. I didn't make much noise because how do you explain showing up in someone's house unannounced, wearing a T-shirt that says "Hall & Oates"? I am assuming it was a prosperous Black family because I saw a family portrait, and also because the bookshelf included Thomas Wentworth Higginson's *Army Life in a Black Regiment.*

Higginson, who was white, was a captain in the 51st Massachusetts Infantry in the Civil War and then, after an injury, commanded the first Black regiment made up of freedmen, the South Carolina Volunteers. His book, written as a journal, was a fairly documentary look at the lives of the Black soldiers, and it included some of the first recorded spirituals. Here is his entry from December 5, 1862.

> Give these people their tongues, their feet, and their leisure, and they are happy. At every twilight the air is full of singing, talking, and clapping of hands in unison. One of their favorite songs is full of plaintive cadences; it is not, I think, a Methodist tune, and I wonder where they obtained a chant of such beauty.

> "I can't stay behind, my Lord, I can't stay behind!
> O, my father is gone, my father is gone,
> My father is gone into heaven, my Lord!
> I can't stay behind!
> Dere's room enough, room enough,
> Room enough in de heaven for de sojer:
> Can't stay behind!"

• • •

Poetry, song, and how they combine in acts of social justice are part of American society, and they lead directly to one of the most famous protest songs in American history, "Strange Fruit." (I'm not getting back in the time machine and setting dials. They're talking about it at this seder.) Back in the late '30s, there was a man named Abel Meeropol who taught English at DeWitt Clinton High School in the Bronx, which is, I feel safe saying, one of America's most important public high schools. Meeropol, who was an alumnus before returning to join the faculty, taught James Baldwin, among others. (Baldwin, during his time there, worked at the school newspaper with a classmate of his, Richard Avedon.)

In 1937, Meeropol saw a picture of a lynching in a newspaper and was moved to write a poem. The original, titled "Bitter Fruit," was published in a Teachers' Union magazine in January 1937. It offered a stark picture, with bursts of shocking lyricism, with references to "blood on the leaves," "blood at the root," and a "Black body swinging in the Southern breeze." It's lush, sensual, and brutal.

The poem made the rounds, and then Meeropol recognized that it might work better as a song. With his wife, he set it to music, and it started to make the rounds again. It was performed in and around New York, and in 1938 the Black singer Laura Duncan sang it at Madison Square Garden. From there, the story gets a little murky, or at least there are conflicting versions. Some people say that Meeropol got the song to the legendary jazz vocalist Billie Holiday, who was performing regularly at Café Society, New York's first integrated nightclub. Others say that it made its way to Holiday through Barney Josephson, who managed Café Society, or Robert Gordon, who was directing Holiday's show. This is one of the cases where precise history may be unrecoverable in a pure sense. Without a time machine, DeLorean or otherwise, we can't be absolutely certain. Even if we were to suddenly meet a hundred-year-old woman who was, as a much younger Café Society waitress, an eyewitness to the moment, we couldn't guarantee that she wasn't remembering wrong, or grinding an eighty-year-old ax, or inflating her own importance. What we do know is that once Josephson saw that Holiday had the song in hand, he set about preparing his club and his audience for what he knew would be a kind of cultural bomb going off. He made some rules. For starters, it had to be the last song in her set. All food and drink service would end before she started. The room would be entirely dark save for a spotlight on her face. Holiday began to perform the song. The rest is (somewhat recoverable) history.

I'm back in my time machine now, surveying other protest singers and songs of the twentieth century. There's Joe Hill, who sang about the rights of the working man in songs like "The Preacher and the Slave." There's

Woody Guthrie, who wrote "This Land Is Your Land" as a kind of ragamuffin version of "God Bless America," and "Deportee" when he was bothered that a newspaper article about a plane crash dehumanized the migrant farm workers who died in the wreck. There's Pete Seeger in the Almanac Singers, and then Pete Seeger and the Weavers. There's Mahalia Jackson, singing in Montgomery in 1956 against a backdrop of death threats, resetting the moral and spiritual agenda with songs like "I've Heard of a City Called Heaven." There's Bob Dylan, who started in the blues tradition and moved into explicit protest, with songs about Emmett Till (left unreleased at the time) and Medgar Evers ("Only a Pawn in Their Game," which was first performed in Greenwood, Mississippi, at a voter registration drive, only a few weeks after Evers was assassinated there).

Most of my travel through the century was at a high speed and high altitude, though I slowed down when I got to the downbeat and possibly even cynical edge of '70s soul. Curtis Mayfield, as we have seen, blazed through the late '60s with optimistic anthems written for the Impressions. "We're a Winner" is more than just a title. This same attitude was echoed by Sly and the Family Stone, at least while the '60s were still a going concern: "Stand" and "I Want to Take You Higher" supercharged this pose.

But the late '60s passed through without bringing on Utopia, and artists began to downshift. The big player here, of course, is Marvin Gaye. For years, Gaye had been straining at the limits of Motown, which wanted him to record commercial hits. He had something else in mind. He went into semi-hiding with his band and a group of friends and put together an album, *What's Going On*, that looked at the busted promises of America. The album is a stone-cold classic, any way you slice it, with beautiful vocal arrangements and passionate lyrics about everything from war to poverty to drugs to the destruction of the environment. Stevie Wonder, more kaleidoscopic in his talents and more abstract in his message, was doing something similar at the time, and would continue to.

But I want to look elsewhere, and where I want to look starts at the beginning of 2020, with the death of Bill Withers.

Withers was my first true idol. I think of his history as intertwined with mine somehow: His debut album, *Just as I Am*, came out in May 1971, four months after I was born. When I first heard his songs, either on the radio or from my dad's record collection, I knew that I was hearing something different. His music, and his vocals, were as down to earth as the earth itself. Too often, Black artists get classed as otherworldly talents who are almost alien in their strangeness (Michael Jackson, Prince) or gritty, up-from-the-streets hustlers who are barely overcoming animal instincts (see: hip-hop). Withers was something else: a Black everyman, a superb, sensitive, soulful singer-songwriter who understood, and was able to communicate, simple truths about ordinary lives.

When people talk about the singer-songwriter era, they usually mean white acts, but Withers was doing the same thing: singing and songwriting. His biggest hits—"Ain't No Sunshine," "Lean on Me," and "Use Me"—found him writing about human emotions with a directness that was simple without being simplistic. When I have spoken or written about him, I have called him "the Black Springsteen," which is both a glib joke but also somewhat true. Look at the cover art from his first album. He's holding the lunchbox he took to work at the mechanic's job he didn't give up even after he was signed.

Bill's studio albums were great. I'll even go to bat for the late ones that no one (including Bill himself) liked. But let's talk about his live album. It's called *Live at Carnegie Hall*, and it's a document of a show there from late in 1972, though it wouldn't be released until the following April. Though it's not usually mentioned among the best live albums in soul music history, it should be. Withers delivers intense versions of his hits, sometimes leading into the songs with extended commentary (called "raps" in the liner notes). I memorized that record down to the last second. To this day, I can re-create the two-and-a-half-minute spoken intro that leads into "Grandma's Hands."

Brief digression: I want to pause here for one moment and talk about live records, and the degree to which they represent real history. When I was a kid, I assumed they were just documents of actual events. A concert happens. Some people are running tape. Tape is released as album. Done and done.

But as I've gotten older and learned how many live albums were sweetened in the studio—applause added, instrumental parts replayed, vocals resung—it's made me kind of cynical, or at least driven in a level of skepticism. What does it mean to deliver a historical record that isn't actually that? And should I take the same approach to documentary film footage, or to photographs? When the past comes to us in the form of so-called primary sources, should we accept them on their own terms? This is a question I can't fully answer, but my partial answer is that we should not. The process of remaking the past begins the second that it becomes the past.

One of the highlights of the live Withers record is "I Can't Write Left-Handed." There was no shortage of anti-Vietnam music, Black or white. You've heard Edwin Starr's "War," of course (covered by the non-Black Springsteen), and Jimi Hendrix's "Star Spangled Banner," and Jimmy Cliff's "Vietnam," and there are others that you should hear if you haven't: Roy C's "Open Letter to the President," Freda Payne's "Bring the Boys Home," the Dells' "Does Anybody Know I'm Here," even Funkadelic's peerlessly creepy "March to the Witch's Castle." Withers's protest song, like Withers, takes a very specific tone: intimate, subtle, and devastating, telling the story of a young soldier who has suffered an injury on the field of battle. The intro rap notes that between the time the song was recorded and released, the war had officially ended (though it would drag on through reality for a few more years). It's not clear to me if Withers was working on it for an official album release or not, but it didn't get one. It is clear that the song is from the perspective of an injured soldier: just before he starts singing, Bill says, "Maybe he cried, maybe he said . . ." and then the song bursts out.

I don't want (or maybe even need) to do a deep reading of the song, but it's filled with honest and unpretentious wisdom (unsurprisingly) and (maybe surprisingly) manages to compress so much of the Black experience of serving in the armed forces into a few brief moments. The young soldier in the song asks the Reverend to pray for him and tells the family lawyer to get a deferment for his younger brother. And it ends with a consequence that might seem trivial compared to what people have seen in movies—mines blowing up with men atop them, endless rat-a-tat gunfire, helicopters brought down—but that is just as crippling in its own way because it interferes with his writing a letter to his mother: a shot-up right shoulder.

• • •

After the death of J Dilla (in 2006), I became less interested in producing artists other than the Roots. Life is short. At the same time, I became more aware that I had a list of production projects that if I never did I'd regret it forever, until the end of life and beyond. Bill was at the top of that list. He hadn't recorded since the mid-'80s, and his recording career didn't end on a high note (his last record, *Watching You, Watching Me*, was a source of frustration both for him and for the label). I approached Withers, or at least approached people who knew him, and word came back that he wasn't interested. While I waited for Bill to change his mind, I did a record with Al Green that won three Grammys. That would hook Bill, right? It didn't. I did the same thing with Booker T.—he knew Bill and had produced his first record back in 1971. Again, Grammy. Again, no Bill.

My last-ditch attempt revolved around "I Can't Write Left-Handed." It's a song that always cut deeper than some of the others for me, maybe because it never made its way onto a regular album, maybe because its message is still sadly relevant. The Roots recorded it with John Legend for *Wake Up!* in 2010. John swapped out Bill's original intro, obviously, with a new one that ruminated on the persistence of war and the consistent importance of songs like "I Can't Write Left-Handed." I think what we were trying to say was that certain protest songs are perennials, because human behavior doesn't change from generation to generation. You could say that they are protesting in vain, but you could also say that they are simply documenting the way that people behave no matter when and where you touch down in history. People couldn't write left-handed in Vietnam, and they couldn't write left-handed in the Gulf War, and they couldn't write left-handed in the Civil War, and they couldn't write left-handed twenty-two hundred years ago in the Chu-Han Contention.

And the relationship between soldiers, especially minority soldiers, and countries, the relationship between battles waged in faraway places and the failed barrios and ghettos closer to home, has continued through time and also through song. Public Enemy's "Black Steel in the Hour of Chaos" picks up that thread almost sixteen years later (and picks up the stitch with a sample from Isaac Hayes's Vietnam-era "Hyperbolicsyllabicsesquedalymistic"), as does Tricky's cover of the Public Enemy song, as does the Pharcyde's low-comedy rewrite "Officer" (where the letter comes from the DMV). This is one of the ways that history works, when it works—great art enters the ether, but rather than etherize us, it sharpens us, keeps us looking.

Our cover brought him out of hiding (or at least hiding from us). Bill Russell, one of Bill Withers's friends— they must have met in the Bill Club—heard our version in a Starbucks, inquired after us, and passed the intelligence along to Bill Withers. "Who is this?" he said. Then Bill Withers got his hands on our version and wrote us an amazing email, and all of that culminated with a show we did in Los Angeles where he came out to see us play. Afterward, backstage, he appeared. He was in his early seventies then but looked like he was ten years younger. He was quiet at first, but then he started to tell us stories. The whole time, I was thinking only two things: 1) This is Bill Withers, right here in front of me, and 2) This is Bill Withers, who has thus far resisted working with me. He paused between stories. I rushed in. I told him how important his work had been and how important it still was. I told him that it was wrong of him to let his work pass into history, because there was a danger that he would pass out of history. I don't remember exactly what I said. But I made my pitch.

He watched the pitch come in. He was quiet, poised, careful.

"No," he said.

1974

Richard Nixon resigns as president of the United States ○ Muhammad Ali and George Foreman fight the Rumble in the Jungle in Kinshasa, Zaire ○ Hank Aaron hits his 715th home run, passing Babe Ruth ○ Duke Ellington dies ○ *Good Times* premieres on CBS ○ Patty Hearst and members of the Symbionese Liberation Army rob a branch of Hibernia Bank in San Francisco ○ The national 55-miles-per-hour speed limit is imposed to conserve gas ○ Late in the year, President Gerald Ford pardons Richard Nixon ○ Coleman Young is inaugurated as the first Black mayor of Detroit. He will be reelected four times and serve as mayor for twenty years

COOL LIKE THAT

Living on the edge of history helps you see the center more clearly.

Whenever there's a history happening, there's more than one history happening. To tell the story of the American colonies, you have to tell the story of seventeenth- and eighteenth-century Great Britain, not to mention the Middle Passage or the indigenous tribal cultures in North America that were violently displaced by the new arrivals. To tell the story of the Ulster Protestants, you have to tell the story of the Irish Catholics. It's not quite right to say that these are parallel histories, because parallel lines never cross. They are nonparallel histories, messily intertwined, multiply interdependent, and they remind you both that you can't learn one without the other and also that anything you're seeing is also something that you're not seeing.

A while back, I wrote a series for *New York* magazine about the evolution of hip-hop, how the genre grew, changed, triumphed, and stumbled over its first three decades. Whenever there's a history happening, there's a prehistory happening, and to look at the way that hip-hop helped (re)construct Black identity, I had to look at the way that Black identity was constructed in the decades before hip-hop.

Soon enough, it became clear to me that at least part of my thinking had to be about Black Cool. You know about Black Cool, right? It used to be a legitimate phenomenon in American culture, not just a label or a sales strategy but a quality that Black artists employed to move through a society that hemmed them in, that they embodied to justify the specificity of their bodies. That's a heady definition, maybe too much to take in all at once, so rather than go Big Philosophical, let's make a list. Forget "What was Black Cool?" for a minute and think, "Who was Black Cool?" That's what I did when I started to sketch out my *New York* piece. I thought it would be fairly easy, and at first it was. I jotted down a list of names I assumed that no one could possibly dispute. It included Angela Davis, Betty Davis, Jimi Hendrix, Sly Stone, Lena Horne, Marvin Gaye, and Richard Pryor. When I shopped it around to friends, acquaintances, and others, via email, via social media, I received a lot of feedback, not all good. "You are wrong," said one email, and then said nothing else, not even a name or two to tell me where I was wrong. Thank you for the constructive criticism. Another email started with a fake-out—"Hi! I love your work!"—before descending into a long diatribe that attacked Jimi Hendrix for absorbing too much of "hegemonic white masculinity" to be cool at all, let alone Black Cool. Opinions continued to fly in, birds on a wire. Marvin Gaye was cool but too sensitive. Richard Pryor was parodying cool. I don't remember every response, but I do remember that only four people managed to run the gauntlet and arrive at Peak Black Cool unbowed and untouched: Miles Davis, Muhammad Ali, Pam Grier, and a fourth figure that I will withhold until later in this chapter.

One of the second things I did was read an anthology edited by the writer Rebecca Walker called exactly that. Not *Exactly That*—it was called *Black Cool*. The seed for the book was a photo of Barack Obama coming out of a limousine. But the water and sunshine that grew that seed were the feeling on the part of Walker and the writers she edited that it was important to go looking for the concept. Why? It seemed to me that the search was for a concept that once had currency but had inflated itself out of existence. More on that a little later. "You can tell something's missing when you see people trying to find it." I wrote that back then, and then I rewrote it just now.

Walker and the writers in the anthology approached the topic from a variety of angles. Some were demographic: Mat Johnson wrote a piece about Black geekdom, and how that did or did not reupholster traditional ideas of Black Cool. Others were personal: Rachel M. Harper wrote about her father, an artist, and how she learned from his example that personal pain could be transformed into cool. The essay that stuck with me the first time I read through the book was called "Reserve." Written by Helena Andrews, it investigated the way that Black women learn to behave, and particularly the way they learn to wear a mask in their interactions with others. At one point, she imagined a Black woman on a subway. Here's the passage that stuck the most:

> She seems to be doing more than everyone else by doing so much less. Your eye is drawn to her. She acknowledges your presence by ignoring it. She is the personification of cool by annihilating your very existence.

Those four sentences are not universal. They are gender-specific, certainly, and they depend upon a certain kind of urban experience. But they summed up what is, for me, at the heart of Black Cool. It doesn't exist on its own. As I said at the beginning of this essay, history never does. Black Cool belongs to American society, which means that it belongs alongside—and beneath, and above, and inside, and tangled all around—white society. If there is an iceberg of the ways that Black people and white people interact in our society, Black Cool is the tip. Let's go back to the scene for a second. The woman on the subway gets attention, which she rejects, which leads to more attention, along with the additional bonus of making the observer value her attention at a higher level. She's also buying time, which is immensely useful in a situation where making the wrong move can have serious consequences. Cool is staying just enough behind the beat to make an intelligent decision without sweating the fact that you're slowing the pace for your own benefit.

The idea of withholding attention runs throughout human relationships, and not just on the basis of race. If you're dating someone and you show less interest, that's one way to feel like you have the upper hand. But when you widen the shot and see that the human relationships are not between individuals but between segments of the culture, and that those segments of culture are strongly correlated with race, then the picture complicates. Go back to the canonical figures of Black Cool above (Miles, Ali, etc.) and think of them in terms of the woman on the subway, both drawing the gaze of the mainstream while at the same time refusing to allow that gaze to penetrate too deeply. In these cases and others, the word *cool* is a bit of misdirection. It doesn't refer to a lack of temperature, but rather a high temperature held in check.

And that contained and controlled high temperature, that self-possession of never letting them see you sweat, defined not just a certain approach, but a certain way of being approached. I'll quote from the earlier piece one more time: "Certain African-American cultural figures—in music, in movies, in sports—rose above what was manifestly a divided, unjust society and in the process managed to seem singularly unruffled. They kept themselves together by holding themselves slightly apart, maintaining an air of inscrutability, of not quite being known. They were cool."

● ● ●

When did Black Cool start? Opinions vary. Was it in Louis Armstrong's Hot Fives and Sevens in the mid-'20s? (Probably not by the contemporary definition.) Was it in Jackie Robinson? (He demonstrated an awesome amount of grace under pressure, but when you're trailblazing under such intense public scrutiny, Dignity can be more important than Cool.) Was it in the first-wave rock-and-rollers like Little Richard and Chuck Berry? (Hmm.) Was it in the jazz players of the early '60s? (Getting closer, definitely, since it's hard to imagine a definition that didn't extend to Thelonious Sphere Monk: coolest first name, even cooler middle name.) By 1974, Black Cool was a foundational part of American culture, which means that it was a foundational part of American history. Maybe the signal event that year was the Rumble in the Jungle, the fight in Kinshasa, Zaire, between Ali (the former heavyweight champion, who had lost his title to Joe Frazier back in 1971) and George Foreman (the champion at the time, who had taken the title from Frazier in January 1973, at the "Sunshine Showdown" in Kingston, Jamaica—a nickname I'm fairly certain I'd never heard). It was, among other things, a perfect demonstration of Black Cool. From the second the fighters arrived in Africa, Ali established himself as the quick wit, the high hand, the relentless ironizer. He made Foreman look square, slow, old-fashioned, even old, despite the fact that the champ was seven years his junior. And while it's true both that Ali shifted the definition slightly (if Black Cool had a don't-look-at-me component, Ali didn't) and that Foreman brought some of it on himself (he came to Zaire with his pet German shepherds, the same dogs that the Belgians had used as guard/attack animals when the country was the Belgian Congo), it was also clear that while both fighters were Black, only one was Cool.

And that was just in the moments leading up to the fight. Once the two of them were in the ring, things got even cooler. Ali knew that he was no match for Foreman when it came to brute power. What he had was superior speed and, in his mind, superior intelligence, the combination of which allowed him to rewire expectations around approach, retreat, and exertion. He hung back and let Foreman punch, seemingly at will. Rather than move around the ring, he backed himself against the ropes and took the punishment. And not just took it—he invited it, continually baiting Foreman into attacking. "They told me you could punch, George," he said after the sixth round. After the seventh, he reportedly got up close to Foreman and whispered, "Is that all you got?" It was, more or less. In the eighth round Ali came off the ropes and threw a series of efficient punches. A left hook straightened up Foreman's head and set the table for a right hand that shot straight out, caught Foreman in the face, and dropped him to the canvas. The fight was over. The rope-a-dope had restored the title to Ali. Or, in subway terms, he had done more than everybody else by doing so much less.

● ● ●

When the Rumble in the Jungle was first announced, it was scheduled for late September. It was a busy month. On one day alone, Evel Knievel failed to jump the Snake River Canyon, Gerald Ford pardoned Richard Nixon, and TWA Flight 841, going from Tel Aviv to New York via Athens, crashed into the Ionian Sea when a bomb exploded in the cargo hold. That was the 8th—a Sunday, no less. The Foreman-Ali fight was set for the 25th (or the night of the 24th if you were planning to watch it on pay-per-view from the States), but about a week before that, Foreman was sparring and caught an elbow to the head that opened a cut above his right eye. In the time it took to give him eleven stitches, the entire international community was in a panic. What if the fight was canceled? Was that a real possibility? If it had to be postponed, who would handle rearranging the pay-per-view contracts and all the entertainment organized around the main event?

The fight was postponed to October 30 to give Foreman time to heal. But the concerns were well-founded. What couldn't be postponed was the three-night-long music festival, Zaire 74, that had been planned to precede and promote the fight, which would include performances by Celia Cruz, B. B. King, the Spinners, Bill Withers, and Manu Dibango. The headliner was the fourth figure on the Mount Rushmore of Black Cool that came together as I was beginning my *New York* magazine piece. It's no mystery: James Brown. Brown extends and revises the idea of cool sketched out above. He never did more by doing less. He was a maximalist. But at the same time, he made audiences come to him. In *The Night James Brown Saved Boston*, the documentary about his Boston concert of April 7, 1968, in the wake of Martin Luther King, Jr.'s assassination, Al Sharpton, who later worked and traveled with Brown, explains it succinctly. The Black artists with white audiences before Brown, from Nat "King" Cole to Sam Cooke to Motown's stars, crossed over into the mainstream. Brown made the mainstream cross over into Black music.

A few chapters earlier, I wrote about blaxploitation. The genre was many things, including a way of telling stories about Black characters in Black environments, a staging area for soul stars attempting to extend their stardom into a new decade, and an efficient delivery system for Black Cool. In fact, you could make the argument that blaxploitation films were a perfect example, since they were at their root take-offs of genre films (detective movies, prison movies, horror movies) that imitated the mainstream while also keeping their distance from it. You'd think that Brown and blaxploitation would have been a perfect mix. But Brown's entry into the genre was slow going. In 1970, he had put together one of the hottest bands of his career, the original J.B.s, which included the brothers Bootsy (on bass) and Catfish (on rhythm guitar) Collins, along with Bobby Byrd as hypeman/vocalist, Jabo Starks and Clyde Stubblefield on drums, Johnny Griggs on congas, and a horn section of Clayton "Chicken" Gunnells, Darryl "Hasaan" Jamison, and Robert "Chopper" McCollough. Within a year, though, that band would disband. Bootsy and Catfish would decamp for George Clinton's P-Funk empire. Brown would get a true funk band back together in time for albums like *There It Is* and *Get on the Good Foot*. But before that, he would go off on a strange excursion, incorporating rock music and rock rhythms into his music. His 1971 album *Sho Is Funky Down Here*, for example, was recorded with a backing group of younger musicians led by the keyboardist, pianist, and arranger David Matthews. When Matthews wasn't with Brown, he was leading a group of his own with the completely ridiculous name of the Grodeck Whipperjenny. That is not a typo. I did not fall on my keyboard. That's the name of the group.

Matthews didn't last long. Brown regrouped again. By 1973 he was back in the pocket enough to finally connect with blaxploitation. And connect he did. In February, he released the soundtrack album for *Black Caesar*, which starred Fred Williamson in a (very) loose remake of James Cagney's *Little Caesar* and told the story of a lifelong gangster working his way up through the Harlem crime world. In September, he released the soundtrack album for *Slaughter's Big Rip-Off*, which starred (a little confusingly) Jim Brown as a Vietnam vet who is trying to live a quiet life in Los Angeles after murdering the crime boss who murdered his parents but finds that he can't stay out of the old life, especially when a World War I biplane shoots into a picnic and kills his best friend. (If I had a nickel for every time a movie used that plot.) And then, in December, he was slated to provide the soundtrack for *Hell up in Harlem*, the *Black*

Caesar sequel, again starring Williamson. The producers rejected it as "that same old James Brown shit." What that meant, evidently, was that the songs Brown had recorded for the first record earlier in the year were considered too long. They weren't, really, except maybe the lead track and single, "Down and Out in New York City," and "Mama's Dead," which ran almost to five minutes. But the producers had made up their minds. They went to Motown instead and secured a soundtrack from Edwin Starr. Brown's music was released as a standalone record called *The Payback*.

If the producers were wrong that Brown's previous Williamson soundtrack had stretched the limit of the song form, they were righter than right here. Of the eight songs on the album, only one ("Forever Suffering") is under six minutes, and the last three ("Time Is Running Out Fast," "Stoned to the Bone," and "Mind Power") go on for more than ten minutes each! (I should add here that my father sided with the producers. He was a James Brown fan, of course, but he also wanted value for his entertainment dollar, and only eight songs on a record, no matter how deep their grooves, meant that this was the moment when he and the Godfather parted ways.)

The first single from the album was "Stoned to the Bone," trimmed down from its marathon running time to a four-minute radio edit. It was released in November 1973, and went Top Ten R&B, though it didn't get to the Top Fifty on the pop charts.

The second single was the title track, which contained one of the most indisputable grooves in Brown's career. The intro is deep funk, with an otherworldly wailing background vocal from Martha High and oddly articulate horns that almost sound like lyrics. Brown starts off with a clear statement of the theme of the song: "Revenge! I'm mad! Got to get back! Need some get back! Pay back!" (It's also the theme of the movie, of course, but there's no movie here anymore, just the song, which is movie enough.) The intro builds and crests with a horn part by Fred Wesley and the three trumpets: Hasaan was still there, but instead of Chicken and Chopper, he was now joined by Jasaan (Jerone Sanford) and Ike (Isiah Oakley). At the forty-second mark, the intro parts to let in the rest of the song, which consists mostly of Brown's explanation of what he can and cannot abide: he can do wheelin' and dealin' but not no damn squealin'; he can dig rappin' and scrappin', but he can't dig that backstabbin'. Right around the halfway mark, Brown delivers one of his most famous lyrics. Some people think he's saying "I don't know karate, but I know ka-razy." He's not. The actual line is "ka-razor." Brown is saying that since he doesn't know martial arts, he has to come with a blade. Either way, the lyric, and the way he enunciates it, is ka-razy. And either way, it's an archetypal moment of cool: heat in check, threat in reserve. Don't test me, because it's a test you can't pass. Watch me but don't look at me.

The opener of the Zaire show? "The Payback." I should have mentioned that sooner, but what's the rush? Be cool.

● ● ●

My *New York* essay wasn't about James Brown. It was about the way that Black Cool had dissipated in the hip-hop era. The argument, in short, was that Black culture in general had defaulted into the idea of hip-hop, which had in turn robbed hip-hop of its ability to be a source of Black Cool. From where I was standing, decades into hip-hop, most artists weren't acting out of individuality or idiosyncrasy, but rather following a script, because a script led to a destination, and that destination contained certain rewards. There was no unpredictability anymore, and without unpredictability, there was no reason to keep an eye on the scene or the figures in it. And that resulted not in a mainstream acceptance of Black culture, but in a kind of invisibility. I didn't mention James Brown explicitly in the final piece, though he featured in a paragraph in a draft. This paragraph:

> Quentin Tarantino, in *Django Unchained*, scores a scene to a blaxploitation mashup of "The Payback" and Tupac's "Untouchable." It's a brutal anachronism, but entirely intentional, his way of linking the Black Cool of the movie, which is set in Texas in the late 1850s, with the Black Cool of 1970s James Brown and the 21st century cool of Tupac. But do they link, or line up at all? Tupac was killed in 1996.

> That particular song was never released during his lifetime. It was pulled from the vaults repeatedly, for a Lisa "Left Eye" Lopez album, for the Pac's Life record, for the *Django* soundtrack. Definitely cool or deathcult? You be the judge.

About a month after I published the article, someone pointed me to a piece on the internet written by a Brooklyn author and photographer named Angel E. Fraden.

Fraden's piece engages with the original essay in an exceptionally intelligent way. Not because it agrees with me or doesn't. Because it's a close read and then a close write. That's something else that I want to insist upon when it comes to the reading and writing of history. Give other reading and writing the respect that they deserve. I'm not saying that this is what Angel E. Fraden did for me, though that's maybe true. It's what I did for Angel E. Fraden.

Fraden proposes that Brown, for a time, was a paragon of Black Cool—in fact, that I was thinking of James Brown in the back of my mind but didn't come right out and say it. "Although he never mentions Brown by name the exposition is absolutely riddled in subversive head nods to the JBE."

Brief note: That's the James Brown Experience, which is how James Brown refers to himself on "Mind Power," the closing track on *The Payback*. It's the only time he refers to himself that way, as far as I know. The abbreviation is a homage, as he (James Brown, not Angel E. Fraden) explains, to "the GBE," the show of the New York radio personality Imhotep Gary Byrd. "I dug this from a young man out of New York," Brown says. He says lots of other things in "Mind Power," too—from door to door, it's one of the all-time great stream-of-consciousness monologues, with detours into ESP, astrology, the Bible, and Brown's own hardscrabble upbringing.

> See I know where it's coming from
> Like the fellow sang, "having catfish head stew"
> And then like the catfish went in there with his head and come out very quick and didn't leave nothing else!

The fellow in question is not identified.

Fraden agrees that Black Cool waned in the wake of this moment, though he has a different explanation as to why. In his mind, Brown began to give ground through the late '70s, to come forward into mainstream expectations in a way that prevented him from keeping his cool.

> Further in the essay Questlove writes, "Taken to the extreme, cool can be sociopathic; taken to the right levels, it's a supremely intelligent mix of defense mechanism and mirroring." Here, in analyzing James Brown, the three words "sociopathic," "defense" and "mirroring" speak multitudes. The entertainer experienced several distinct stylistic phases in the manner he presented himself (i.e. hot pants and mustache era J.B., afro and bellbottoms era J.B.) What's ceaselessly interesting about James Brown, as Questlove elaborates, is how figures of Black cool "simultaneously drew the gaze of white cultural observers and thwarted that gaze." With the ascension of James Brown, Black America was no longer submitting to the cultural constructions of White America; instead the latter was adamant in thoroughly studying the former. By 1979, though, Mr. Brown was no longer thwarting this gaze but actively and wholly submitting to it.

Did it take that long? Little did I know that James would trade in his rebel cool for a double-down far-right conservative stance, starting with that weird mustache. Sometimes when you look closer and closer, you see that cool has a short leash. But the questions remain: Do ideas run their course because the people who embody them run their course? Or do the ideas run their course all on their own, leaving the people who embodied them stranded, in search of new ideas to embody but without the energy that let them find their way to the earlier ideas? Maybe it's both at the same time. Whenever there's a story happening, there's more than one story happening.

1975

Jimmy Hoffa goes missing ○ *Jaws* opens ○ *The Jeffersons* premieres ○ Gerald Ford survives two assassination attempts within three weeks, one from Lynette "Squeaky" Fromme, the other from Sara Jane Moore ○ *Saturday Night Live* premieres; Richard Pryor, who hosts the seventh episode, is the show's first Black host ○ The Jackson 5 depart the Motown label for CBS Records, at which point they are forced to change their name to "the Jacksons" ○ Elijah Muhammad, founder of the Nation of Islam, dies ○ *Wheel of Fortune* premieres on NBC ○ Jackie Wilson has a heart attack onstage in Cherry Hill, New Jersey, and never performs again ○ Arthur Ashe becomes the first Black person to win the men's singles title at Wimbledon ○ Frank Robinson becomes the player-manager of the Cleveland Indians and the next spring becomes the first Black manager of any Major League Baseball team

THE POV LANE

If history is only what's seen, what do we call the rest?

History is only what is seen. Does that seem like a controversial statement? It shouldn't.

Historians are people, and people can only know what they know, and they only know what they have seen—I mean "seen" here in all its forms, not necessarily eyewitnessed, but also encountered in old films, in photographs, in the library, in the memory of an interview subject. Historians can rediscover previously unknown events, though to do so, they have to see them. (In addition to being self-evident, this is a kind of paradox. Previously unknown? In most cases—maybe beginnings-of-the-universe discoveries are the exception—those events were known to the people who they happened to, and the people around those people, so maybe it is more accurate to say that those events have discovered previously unknowing historians.)

But the process is ongoing. When a person sees things they haven't seen before, there are still more they aren't seeing. And more after that. And after that. As we've established, things are happening all the time. But historians are people, and people know that they have a limited capacity, so they pick a place to pause and stop looking for more events. It's a process that

I've been through a billion times as a DJ, as a director, as an author. When you're researching an artist or a year, how do you know when you've seen enough, when you've unearthed enough facts, when you've made enough connections? Short answer: you don't. And especially if you are a person in a position of some authority, if your research isn't just for personal edification, that question lands with added weight, because your limited seeing works as an immensely effective filter. History gets told one way because what has been seen paves that path, installs the directional signs, and so on. Those who are present for the telling may or may not suspect that there are things that they (the told) are not seeing, and they may or may not understand that this is because there are things that you (the teller) haven't seen. Without any suspicion, there's passive and uncritical learning. With too much suspicion, there's a refusal to accept any portion of the truth. How do we wrap our heads around the fact that the story we're being told isn't the whole story, and that that means the lessons we extract from it, the truths we build upon it, are at least partly unfounded?

There's a book called *Unseen*, which is a provocative title all on its own. Once you see the book, how can it be unseen? But the subtitle is even more provocative: *Unpublished Black History from the New York Times Photo Archives*. The fact that it's a photo book redoubles the central paradox. Far from being unseen, the subjects of the photos were most specifically seen—framed by a lens, captured. But seen for a moment doesn't mean seen for the next moment. History has a way of mislaying most of its images. And this book, as the subtitle explains, focuses on a specific category of images, photos of Black people taken for *The New York Times* that were for whatever reason not run in the paper. I came to the book not because I bought it in a bookstore, but because I read a review of it. A somewhat negative review, or at least a pained one. In, of all places, *The New York Times*. The review, written by Tobi Haslett, takes the *Times* to task, not only for neglecting these images in the first place, but for resurfacing them in a fashion that sometimes feels more like a showy mea culpa than any attempt to remedy the narrow thinking that caused the problem in the first place.

> To survey some of the forthrightly "political" pictures here is to reckon with the fact that by declining to publish them, the paper's editors refused a chance to shape, and not simply record, political discourse.

The question of whether a newspaper should always seize the chance to shape discourse seems possibly misguided (should the paper of record do more than record?) and definitely beside the very point that the review is making. Declining to publish something does in fact shape discourse. Seeing (or not-seeing) is not passive. It's active. Sometimes it's even activist. The larger question, of course, is how any one act of seeing or not-seeing privileges one perspective over another. Back in 2015, in *The Atlantic*, Michael Conway wrote a piece where he lamented that much of the debate over how history is taught gets reduced to whose story is being told, rather than how we see the process of storytelling. This is no way to teach history. Conway discusses the then-debate over Ava DuVernay's *Selma*, and particularly the way the movie depicted the relationship between Lyndon B. Johnson and Martin Luther King, Jr. Depicted or distorted? Joseph A. Califano, Jr., who served as Johnson's top aide for domestic affairs during the late '60s, believed that the portrait of Johnson as a reluctant backer of the Voting Rights Act was so inaccurate that the movie should be "ruled out [for] awards season." Ava then tweeted that "the notion that Selma was LBJ's idea is jaw dropping."

Conway stands in the middle, not drawing conclusions so much as advancing an idea about how conclusions are drawn.

> A history is essentially a collection of memories, analyzed and reduced into meaningful conclusions—but that collection depends on the memories chosen. Memories make for a risky foundation: As events recede further into the past, the facts are distorted or augmented by entirely new details . . . An individual who marched across the Edmund Pettus Bridge probably remembers the events in Selma differently than someone who helped Johnson advance legislation in

> Washington. Both people construct unique memories while informing perfectly valid histories. Just as there is a plurality of memories, so, too, is there a plurality of histories.

It's not, Conway argues, that one side or the other has more of a claim to being told—or, in our terms, to being seen—but that the only true history tells all those stories simultaneously and then equips those who are hearing those stories with the skills necessary to sort through the competing versions.

It's not an academic issue, of course. The filtering process Conway describes, "the memories chosen," cannot be separated from the way we experience history, but it also cannot be separated from how we experience the world around us. Back in the 1971 chapter, I mentioned Rich Nichols, who passed in 2014. In the 1972 chapter, I mentioned *Shaft*. Rich used to tell me a story about when he first went to see the movie. He was maybe twelve or thirteen, growing up in Philadelphia. His sister took him. Various scenes showed New York's housing projects. When they were leaving the theater, Rich turned to his sister and asked her where the projects were in Philly. "You live in them, dummy," she said. The buildings in the movie, the buildings in New York, were taller. Philly had low-rises. Rich hadn't seen them in that light before, and in a sense he hadn't seen them at all. He certainly had never seen New York in the way the movie showed it. And he was suddenly aware of how much else was being overlooked.

● ● ●

But how easy is it to see many things all at once, either in the past or the present? How easy is it to get outside of the perspectives that limit us, which have been established and reinforced over the course of our lives? There are studies in early child psychology that demonstrate that children have only their own perspective. If you put a doll across the table from them and ask them what the doll sees, they will tell you what they see. They know the doll is across the table, but they cannot imagine a perspective other than their own. How different are we?

Back in 1975, Al Jarreau was just coming into the national consciousness as a jazz vocalist with crossover potential. By now, at the conclusion of a nearly half-century career, people have a certain picture of Jarreau, and it tends toward the nice-guy, easy-jazz, lots-of-smiling side of the spectrum, mostly because of hits like "We're in This Love Together," or the *Moonlighting* theme, or maybe that McDonald's commercial he did with Vesta back in 1996. The song, "You Don't See Me," shows us something unseen. It's a virtuoso vocal performance, of course, but it's about a more difficult subject—in this case, an unhappy relationship. In the song, Jarreau, or his character, begins with a scatted low vocal in which he says, over and over, "It has occurred to me / That you don't see me." Sometimes it turns into "You don't want to see me." When the song moves out of the intro, it moves into a place of frustration, pain, and victimization. He tells her she didn't see him when he was trying to do right, when he was an upstanding citizen and a lover making his case—and, worse, that she didn't advocate for him, "stand up and speak out in [his] favor."

He wants to know why he wasn't represented properly, or at all. He wants to know why she failed to advocate on his behalf or to advance his point of view. This seems like a legitimate question. It's a question that echoes some of the questions in Michael Conway's piece about *Selma*, or in *Unseen* (or Haslett's review of *Unseen*). But at some point, the song takes a dark turn. Jarreau's narrator doesn't just ask why she's not seeing him, but starts to see right back at her, and not in a favorable way. He calls her "a devil in bed, scratching 'til [his] bones are bare."

It gets worse. His shoes are wearing thin. He's demented, he says, "burned unto a cinder." His only recourse is to find a pistol, which he does, and that's followed by accusations that she's running from him, that she's ducking and hiding, and that's followed by him threatening to "beat [her] mama" and "beat [her] daddy," and even "go to jail," because "It don't make no motherfuckin' difference what happens to me." (Now we're in the same territory as Prince's "Bob George," from *The Black Album*, where Prince, voice electronically deepened, plays a jealous man who threatens his girlfriend with escalating violence. It's also the song where Prince, in character, dismisses

Prince as "that skinny motherfucker with the high voice"). Within the span of minutes, "You Don't See Me" has gone from the story of a man who laments that he isn't being seen to the story of a man who is desperate to be seen at any cost. This fills in the rest of the principle above: not seeing people, or parts of society, isn't always a one-way street. Sometimes it is. Sometimes they just slip from the record entirely. But sometimes those people who aren't seen, who know that they're not being seen, will take matters into their own-hands.

Interestingly, the song exists in multiple versions, multiple lengths, and they change the way that the character is seen. The original studio version was released on the *We Got By* LP back in 1975. That one is the one I've been talking about: it's track four of nine, five minutes long, sandwiched between "Susan's Song" and "Lock All the Gates." On the live album *Look to the Rainbow*, from 1977, it's longer, more than six minutes, but that's fine. Live can be longer. But when we entered the streaming era, I found that the *Look to the Rainbow* version was originally even a little longer than that, by more than thirty seconds, and what was added was an intro that gave context to the rest of the song. I'm sure that it was edited off the LP for length. But when you hear it now, it puts back a moment of preparation, explains that this is an account of a relationship gone bad. Without it, the character sounds even more unhinged, damn near presenting the O.J. murder scenario in song.

Not seeing can have serious consequences. On January 29, 1975, a bomb went off inside the State Department in Washington, D.C. There had been a warning, a few minutes earlier, when a woman called the *New York Times* to notify them that the bomb was about to blow. She identified herself as part of the Weather Underground, a domestic political terror organization. The reasons the bomb had been placed, she said, had been written up and stashed in a phone booth near the *Times* office. It was not found, but another similar statement was, in another phone booth. That was how they delivered messages, very cloak and dagger, no seeing necessary. The statement explained that the Weather Underground did not agree with the United States' continuing to send money to South Vietnam to fund the regime of President Thieu, especially when the money could be better spent helping hungry people around the world. They had made their opinion known over and over again, but no one had listened, and the lack of attention paid to their perspective had forced them into extreme measures. If Al Jarreau turned that into a song, it would have been called "You Don't See Me, by My Own Choice, but I Want You to See What I Can Do, and Then I Want You to Read a Letter That Explains That I Can See You, and That What You're Doing Is Wrong Because It Neglects a Much Larger Group of People Who Remain Unseen, and You Should Start to See Them, or Else You'll See More of Me."

This was not the Weather Underground's first bombing. They had bombed the headquarters of the New York Police Department in 1970, the U.S. Capitol in 1971, and the Pentagon in 1972, and along the way even bombed themselves—an accidental explosion of a nail bomb being assembled in a Greenwich Village townhouse in 1970 killed three members of the group. And it wasn't their last appearance on the national stage: the Weather Underground surfaced as a conservative talking point during the 2008 presidential election, when commentators like Sean Hannity tried to tie Bill Ayers, the group's former leader, to Barack Obama.

My account of this 1975 event—both events, the bombing and Jarreau's song—intentionally evades the question of who is right and who is wrong. I have my own theories. (It's the guy!) But does that matter? Or rather, how does it matter? If you're standing on a street corner and you see this guy coming toward you, unsteady on his feet, eyes burning, that's one thing. Maybe you should stop him. But when you process this song, you should at least imagine withholding your conclusion until you have heard all other versions of the story: the woman's version, her father's, her mother's, the version of the pawnshop owner who sold him the pistol. History should be a latticework of cross-references and cross-currents, and seeing one story, one event, one name, should encourage you to see others, too. Back to Conway's piece from the *Atlantic*:

> And rather than vainly seeking to transcend the inevitable clash of memories, American students would be better served by descending

into the bog of conflict and learning the many "histories" that compose the American national story.

Teach the conflict, they say. But first you've got to see it.

• • •

The same year Jarreau recorded this song, Shelton Brooks died in Los Angeles. Brooks was an Afro-Canadian composer, raised in Detroit, who became a fixture as a ragtime piano player and then a songwriter. He had success with "Some of These Days," which became a hit for the world-famous singer/comedian/vaudevillian Sophie Tucker. It was a frustrated breakup song, like "You Don't See Me" without the pills and needles. But Brooks's most enduring song was "Darktown Strutters' Ball." Written in 1917, it was a spirited, vivid portrait of upscale Black social life that starts with a predate reminder ("I'll be round to get you in a taxi, honey / Please be ready 'bout half past eight") and imagines the big night to come: dancing, high spirits and "high-browns," the man in his "silk hat and frock tail coat," the woman in her "Paris gown and new silk shawl." The tone is elegant and joyful. Tucker immediately recognized the song's potential and rushed it into her act, and soon after that the Original Dixieland Jazz Band recorded it (some people consider it the first commercial jazz recording, others the first jazz recording made in New York City). It was covered over the years by dozens of acts including the Six Brown Brothers (a troupe of Canadian clowns, actual brothers, who performed in both whiteface and blackface), the Boswell Sisters (actual sisters, no clowning), Fats Waller, Bing Crosby, and even the Beatles (who supposedly performed it in Hamburg). As a crossover hit, it made Brooks's portrait of his Black protagonists visible to white audiences, and without the voyeuristic appeal of, say, a Carl Van Vechten novel (great black-walled city . . . sorry, Countee Cullen).

The key modern cover was recorded by Alberta Hunter, a Memphis-born singer who had achieved some fame in the first half of the century in Chicago (she had a regular gig at the Dreamland Ballroom), recorded blues staples like

"Downhearted Blues" and a version of "Cake Walking Babies (from Home)," toured in Europe, and appeared on the Broadway stage. When Hunter's mother died in 1954, she left showbiz. But she didn't leave without plotting an escape route. She cheated down her age by more than a decade, faked a high school diploma, and became a nurse. And that's what she did for twenty years, at Goldwater Hospital on Roosevelt Island, singing occasionally, but mostly remaining tucked out of sight.

In the mid-'70s, with the end of her nursing career in sight—mandatory retirement age was seventy, even though she was actually over eighty at the time—Hunter started to make her way back into the music world. Through her friend, the singer Mabel Mercer, she was connected with the pianist Bobby Short, who connected her to Barney Josephson, who was still running Café Society (see 1973). And then, through Josephson, she was connected to John Hammond, the legendary Columbia Records scout who had helped launch the careers of everyone from Benny Goodman to Count Basie to Aretha Franklin to Bob Dylan to Bruce Springsteen. Hammond signed her, and she put out two records in quick succession. The first was a soundtrack to a movie called *Remember My Name* (that's step two, after seeing someone) that starred Geraldine Chaplin (Charlie's daughter), Anthony Perkins (Mrs. Bates's son), and Moses Gunn (see 1972). The second was *Amtrak Blues*, which opened with a life-affirming cover of "Darktown Strutters' Ball" by the then-eighty-five-year-old singer. Her backing musicians, history all on their own, included Doc Cheatham, who had played with Cab Calloway; Frank Wess, who had played with Count Basie; and Norris Turney, who had played with Duke Ellington (see 1976).

Hunter's "Darktown Strutters' Ball" hadn't happened yet when Brooks passed. But a few months before he did, there was a blaxploitation musical comedy in theaters called *Darktown Strutters*. Produced by Roger Corman's brother Gene, it tells the story of Commander Cross (Norman Bartold), a chicken-and-ribs tycoon (think Colonel Sanders, I guess) who pretends to be an ally of the Black community but is actually, in the secrecy of his mansion, creating replicas of famous Black leaders as part of an evil plan to get them to eat more of his food. He's foiled by the leader of an all-girl motorcycle gang played by Trina Parks (no relation to Gordon or Gordon Jr., I don't think). It's like a food-themed cross of *Invasion of the Body Snatchers*, *The Muppet Movie* (Doc Hopper, anyone?), and *Get Out*.

There's even an appearance—in an underground dungeon, surrounded by lit torches, lip-synching their 1971 hit "Whatcha See Is What You Get"—by the Dramatics, the Detroit soul group whose entanglement in the 1968 Algiers Motel incident got me into this mess in the first place (see Introduction). The title now lands entirely as a caution.

The Part or the Whole

Hip-hop has trained me to dissect songs differently, to see them in parts and pieces, where a section can be extracted and turned into a work of its own. So I don't always hear songs as whole things, but rather as segments that fit together. I am aware that they are more than that, and even more than *that*—songs go onto albums, which become chapters in careers. This question of the atomic level versus the molecular and beyond is an interesting one for historians: Once you have studied an event and understood it, how much context do you need? If you study a campaign, do you have to study the battle? How about the war? How about the events around the war? At some point, have you lost your appreciation for the unique texture and details of the smallest event? The easiest way I can think about it is songs where I like one piece or part, strongly and truly, but can't get behind the entire thing.

"HOLLYWOOD"
Chicago

Chicago VI, 1973 [Columbia]

That intro and verse is everything, so strong. It has a Stevie Wonder feel. I feel like it could have been the white "You've Got It Bad, Girl." (In fact, now that I check, it's so close in time that I'm sure this was their take on it, with the same repeated lyric tags: "where they are" or "anywhere" instead of Stevie's "on the shelf.") The problem is when the chorus appears. The beginning is so beautiful and then the song never returns to it.

"SEE THE LIGHT"
Earth, Wind & Fire

That's the Way of the World, 1975 [Columbia]

Unlike "Hollywood," everything here is beautiful: the 7/8 intro in D minor, with horn arrangements running around like wild elephants especially. But it has lots of pieces (it's Charles Stepney flexing his Rotary Connection prowess) and they're not all equal. On long car drives, this makes you really feel the scenery.

"MANGO MEAT"
Mandrill

Just Outside of Town, 1973 [Polydor]

The hip-hop purist in me loves the ending, where the band repeats "mango—yeah." I borderline think it's a loop. But I can't get past the opening guitar riff, not because of what it was originally but because of what it became. Just Blaze showed me how he used it as the basis for a song, and it blew my mind.

"T.L.C."
Average White Band

Person to Person, 1976 [Atlantic]

Hamish Stewart's bass solo is a monster. But one of the best things about funk is limited musicianship. You have to hold back and work as a team. Here, it borders on busy. After Jaco Pastorius's "Portrait of Tracy," this became the new mountain to climb for bass players in 1976 (six years after the last mountain Sly left us). Jaco's take on limitations (certain notes on the fret give a distinguishable, hard-to-achieve sound) was melodic art. Stewart's take on the same process felt more like African percussion.

"MISS ME BLIND"
Culture Club

Colour by Numbers, 1983 [Epic]

This is their third single, and it's the one that got me. Specifically, the instrumental breakdown right before the last verse. Roy Hay is killing it on acoustic guitar, which is rare for a funk song. Usually you just go for it, all electric. The acoustic is very rare: maybe the Jackson 5's "Mama I Gotta Brand New Thing (Don't Say No)" and this.

"CALYPSO"
Herbie Hancock

Mr. Hands, 1980 [Columbia]

When D'Angelo was recording *Voodoo*, he made a bridge out of the intro of this song, though the song with it didn't make it onto the album. Years after that I finally got *Mr. Hands*. It's the classic Miles lineup playing here (along with Sheila E. on percussion) and Herbie does something similar to what Miles did in "Nefertiti," stays stable and lets Tony and Ron run rampant. Great song, but the melody was so hypnotic I didn't want to leave it for the Brazilian coda, which kind of gets dropped on your head like an ACME anvil. When I hear it all I can think of is Tom Willis on *The Jeffersons*, and that little cha-cha dance he did.

"I'M AN ANIMAL"
Sly and the Family Stone

Life, 1968 [Epic]

This album is full of short songs, AM-ready. This is one of the longer ones, but I wish it was even longer. I want to know what happens in the fade to make sure no humans were harmed after whatever it was that was let loose in the studio. It feels like there are some jazz chops at work.

"IN MY TIME OF DYING"
Led Zeppelin

Physical Graffiti, 1975 [Swan Song]

Toward the end, right before the breakdown, there's a part that locks into an incredible rhythm. You don't know who's driving, whether it's Bonham or Page—I see it as a horse race, and they're neck and neck. It's like the song itself is having an orgasm, even without Robert Plant actually verbalizing the way he does.

"BREAKING THE GIRL"
Red Hot Chili Peppers

Blood Sugar Sex Magik, 1991 [Warner Bros.]

The song is fine but the chorus is great. For me, it's something about the background vocals ; the angelic singing stands bright—kind of the opposite of the punk-rappy in-yo-face funk they are known for. I tend to like the Peppers' quieter moments—I feel the same way about "Californication."

"CHOCOLATE"
The Time

Pandemonium, 1990 [Paisley Park/Reprise]

On D'Angelo records, we would program a click track and then drunkenly dance around the metronome to build up rhythm. Prince does the opposite. Everything is airtight but then he'll go for the human element on something as simple as handclaps.

"LOOK INTO HIS EYES"
Flora Purim

That's What She Said, 1978 [Milestone]

I mostly focus on the spiraling vocal turnaround at the end, because J Dilla used it as an interlude on one of his beat tapes. I will forever know it based on that, on the last minute thirty. The beginning of the song really doesn't matter to me.

"SO YOU'RE LEAVING"
Al Green

Let's Stay Together, 1972 [Hi]

Norman Whitfield did such an amazing job with the Temptations that I started to associate the vocal "boo-boo-boo"s with him rather than Sly, who he took them from. In this song, there's a little breakdown where Al Green modernizes his sound by going for that kind of vocal pattern. That's the only sign that he's current in the context of the Hi Records sounds.

1976

The United States celebrates its bicentennial ○ Jimmy Carter is elected president, defeating Gerald Ford ○ Isabel Peron is deposed in Argentina ○ The CN Tower in Toronto, at a height of 1,815 feet, becomes the tallest free-standing structure in the world ○ Clifford Alexander, Jr., is confirmed as the first Black secretary of the U.S. Army ○ An earthquake in Tangshan, China, kills hundreds of thousands of people ○ Nadia Comaneci wins three gold medals at the Olympics in Montreal ○ The Concorde supersonic aircraft begins commercial flights ○ Black History Month is celebrated for the first time ○ Barbara Jordan delivers the keynote address at the Democratic National Convention in Chicago ○ *Rocky* is released, creating an American icon and launching the career of writer/star Sylvester Stallone ○ Lorne Michaels offers the Beatles $3,000 to reunite on *Saturday Night Live* ("You divide it any way you want. If you want to give Ringo less, that's up to you. I'd rather not get involved") ○ Howard Hughes dies

HAVING TWO PARTIES

How you unlock history depends on which key you use.

Stevie Wonder's "Sir Duke" was the first time I understood that a song was teaching me about songs of the past. I was five, so maybe it's okay that I didn't figure it out sooner. Before that, I had a sense that songs could be connected to the past. When I was two or three and heard songs that sounded familiar, I knew that they were not coincidences but versions of other songs (like Eric Clapton's "I Shot the Sheriff"). And I guess I understood early enough that rock bands like the Beatles, the Stones, and Led Zeppelin had been inspired by the world of Black American artists, whether from Motown, Chess, or the Mississippi Delta.

But "Sir Duke" was different. It was an actual history lesson, an overt memorial, not the present using the past to inspire the future, but the present lamenting the pastness of the past.

At the time the song was recorded, Wonder was in his mid-twenties, but he had already been a recording artist for fifteen years. Rewind to 1961, and to the Detroit home of Ronnie White, who sang baritone in the Miracles, Motown's first star act. Ronnie had a brother, Gerald, who was ten years younger; Gerald and Ronnie had a cousin, Harold Foster, who would sometimes stay with the White family; in summers, Gerald and Harold would fish off a pier on the Detroit River. On the way there, they would stop by the house of a friend, Junior Glover, see if he wanted to fish too. Junior was also a guitar player, and he told Gerald and Harold about a young kid he knew who was a talented singer. The kid was blind, which explained why he wouldn't be joining them fishing. Junior wanted the kid to meet Ronnie. He thought that maybe there was a spot for him at Motown. Junior introduced the kid to Gerald and Harold, and then Ronnie, who invited the kid to the Whites' basement for a kind of informal audition. Ronnie was impressed enough to call Berry Gordy, the founder of Motown, and set up a formal audition. The kid was signed and put in the care of two Motown producers and songwriters, Henry Cosby and Clarence Paul, who steered his first album, which didn't showcase his singing at all but instead found him performing nine instrumentals and playing everything under the sun: piano, organ, drums, bongos, and harmonica. The kid was a star. The kid was Stevie Wonder.

That story, longish on the page but rapid in real life, is filled with names that have since slipped from history. What do you do about that? History is a filter. Not everyone gets to move forward. I guess that by telling the stories of those who do, we can bring along some of the others.

From the start, Wonder was positioned as a repository of musical history. His second album, *A Tribute to Uncle Ray*, cast him not just as a Ray Charles imitator but as a successor. In Wonder's first half-decade as a star, he touched on standards from the American songbook (*A Song in My Heart*), folk (he covered Bob Dylan's "Blowin' in the Wind" on *Up-Tight* in 1966; later that same year he released *Down to Earth*, more Dylan: "Mr. Tambourine Man"), country (Merle Travis's "Sixteen Tons"), and rock (Sonny Bono's "Bang Bang"). And the 1968 album *Eivets Rednow*, whose title is just Wonder's name backwards, consisted entirely of instrumentals. Hsac barg? By the turn of the decade, even though he could still produce classic covers (his version of the Beatles' "We Can Work It Out," from *Signed, Sealed & Delivered*), his own songwriting muse was starting to guide him.

After that, it was all originals. Wonder, coming into his own as a thinker, wanted more latitude at Motown. The label resisted. He wrote an album's worth of songs with his wife, Syreeta Wright, produced them on his own, and delivered them to the label with an ultimatum: if he didn't get full creative control, he'd walk. The label conceded, and Wonder entered a five-year glory period that is the equal of any stretch of any pop artist in history. Beginning with *Music of My Mind* in 1972, continuing through *Talking Book*, *Innervisions*, and *Fulfillingness' First Finale*, he produced some of the most vibrant, powerful, and fully realized records that anyone has ever made. And then, in 1976, he upped his game with *Songs in the Key of Life*. His fifth album in five years, it was more than just an album. It was a game-changing extravaganza of seventeen songs with an accompanying EP called *A Something's Extra* that contained four additional songs.

And yet Wonder's magnum opus was also a uniquely nostalgic album, and at times almost a sentimental one. The first single, "I Wish," found Wonder looking back at his own childhood, "when [he] was a little nappy-headed boy" and his main preoccupations were opening Christmas presents and avoiding getting whupped for bad behavior. It resonated with everyone, and the fact that it had an irresistible, almost stuttering funk groove didn't hurt.

The second single was "Sir Duke."

Through the late 1960s and early '70s, Wonder expressed an interest in collaborating with the jazz artists who had inspired him. They weren't free-jazz trailblazers like Albert Ayler or Ornette Coleman, but rather commercially successful traditionalists like the vocalist Dinah Washington and the guitarist Wes Montgomery.

Washington passed away in 1963 at the age of thirty-nine, accidentally overdosing on pills prescribed for her diet and her insomnia. She was discovered by the NFL defensive back Dick "Night Train" Lane, her seventh husband. In the months before her death, she had expressed an interest in meeting Wonder, but schedules couldn't get sorted. And Montgomery had a fatal heart attack in 1968 at the age of forty-five. Though he was a successful musician, he had six kids, and he worked as a welder to make ends meet. There are stories of him, in the years leading up to his death, blacking out between sets, probably from exhaustion and chain-smoking. This was another loss for Wonder, and another lost chance: *Eivets Rednow* had originally been envisioned as a collaboration between the two men.

Wonder's third great inspiration was Duke Ellington. Ellington, of course, was one of the most prolific jazz composers and bandleaders, partly because he was able to assemble groups filled with brilliant players who helped his musical ideas spring to life, partly because he was able to find the right collaborators (Ellington's main creative partner, Billy Strayhorn, worked with him from the late 1930s until Strayhorn's death in 1967). But Ellington's vast body of work existed mostly because he moved that body for parts of six decades, starting before the Depression (he made eight records in 1924) and lasting well into the'70s (the third of his Sacred Concerts premiered six months after *Dark Side of the Moon* came out). When Ellington passed away in May 1974, Wonder took the news not just as a source of sorrow but as one of inspiration.

"Sir Duke" went back before Montgomery or Washington: "There's Basie, Miller, Satchmo, and the king of all, Sir Duke / With a voice like Ella's ringing out, there's no way the band can lose." I knew of the people he was naming. I knew something of their legacies. But here was a song that was explicitly promoting them. There was nothing sad about the song, and in that sense it was less memorial than festival, nothing like the tribute songs I would hear in years to come, from "Missing You" (which Diana Ross recorded with Lionel Richie after the death of Marvin Gaye) to "I'll Be Missing You" (Puff Daddy and Faith Evans after the death of the Notorious B.I.G.). "You can feel it all over," he sang, but he didn't mean it was all over, exactly—he meant that it would keep going on and on.

The single was released in March and spent three weeks atop the chart in May. If you had asked me, even recently, I would have said that it was the third single, after "I Wish" and "Isn't She Lovely," the mid-tempo love song that Wonder wrote for his infant daughter, Aisha. But "Isn't She Lovely" wasn't even released as a single. Can you believe it? I can't. The problem, I think, was that when I first heard the album, it was played by a singer in my dad's band, a woman named Rose, who loaded the album's two discs on top of the record changer. The LP was configured so that one disc had side one and side four and the other had side two and side three. For whatever reason, she stacked the discs so that side three played first, which meant that "Isn't She Lovely" played first. I assumed that it was the lead song, and thus the single. The whole situation was further complicated by the fact that later on, I bought the album on an 8-track, and there the order was changed yet again. Rather than ending with "Another Star," the record proper now ended with "Joy Inside My Tears." What is the real album? I guess people would point to the LP as the official release, but it's not the one I remember best. The devil may be in the details, but history is in the formats.

● ● ●

Records can be replayed after they end. Lives can only be remembered. Ellington passed away in New York City, in Columbia Presbyterian's Harkness Pavilion, where he had been receiving treatment for lung cancer since March, where pneumonia took him in May. Two months after that, Wonder released *Fulfillingness's First Finale*, his sixth album of the decade and nineteenth overall (prolific, sure, but Ellington wrote more than six thousand pieces). The first single from the record was "You Haven't Done Nothin'," an explicit political attack on Richard Nixon, with backing vocals courtesy of the Jackson 5. Nixon has sunk to depths, but Stevie's not surprised, and though "it's not too cool to be ridiculed," it's a logical consequence of the way that Tricky Dick has behaved. Stevie demands truth.

He should have called it "We Can't Work It Out."

The album came out in July. The single was released on August 7. On August 9, Nixon resigned. That's service! It began to climb the charts immediately, reaching number one in November, the same week that the Democrats made big gains in the midterm elections against a Republican Party crippled by Watergate.

Songs in the Key of Life was not as topical as "You Haven't Done Nothin'," though plenty of its songs commented on the world as Wonder saw it. "Village Ghetto Land" and "Pastime Paradise" lamented life in the inner city or in the immoral modern world. There were broadly spiritual songs like "Have a Talk with God" and broadly humanistic ones like "Love's in Need of Love Today." And "Black Man" was a compressed course in America's racial diversity. Toward the back end of the song, there's an instructional breakdown in which Stevie calls out a series of names of prominent Americans, and a backing chorus of children identify the person's race. He moves freely through space and time, touching on Sacagawea, "a red woman," who helped Lewis and Clark; Benjamin Banneker, "a black man," who helped design the capital and wrote the first almanac; Harvey William Cushing, "a white man" and a pioneer of neurosurgery.

His racial color-coding (American Indian = Red; Asian American = Yellow) is very much of its time, meaning very much not of our time. And the call-and-response has a touch of Book Report Lyric Disease. On the other hand, Crispus Attucks, the first person killed in the Boston Massacre (Black Man!), is mentioned up high, fitting for an album released during the bicentennial. Even so, the sound of those Marva Collins kids with Imhotep Gary Byrd used to scare me. All that yelling and shit. (And I'm talking about the teachers in the call-and-response, not the kids!!) As soon as that breakdown happened, I knew it was time to pack up and run upstairs out of earshot or ask Mom to change the record real quick. The album's donut cover was scary . . . but not scarier than them "Black Man" teachers yelling all evil.

● ● ●

Duke Ellington didn't make it to the bicentennial, though Alvin Ailey paid tribute to him at Lincoln Center that summer with a pair of pieces, including a new work called *Pas de Duke*. Puns have gotten neither better nor worse in the years since.

For Ellington to be embraced as an archetypal Black American artist made sense, on an artistic level. Politically, though, it was more complicated.

Though his works always demonstrated a commitment to social justice and racial equality (his 1941 musical revue *Jump for Joy* was way ahead of its time), and though he had in his youth been involved with Communist causes, Ellington was also a lifelong Republican. Don't take it from me. Take it from Terry Teachout, who wrote the Ellington biography *Duke*: "It was not widely known, nor is it now, that he was in fact . . . a lifelong Republican." Thanks, Terry. Of course, we're talking about Republican back then, which would have overlapped with today's Democratic Party. People say "Republican" now, and the mind goes to MAGA. That's not where it was. When Ellington was at the height of his fame in the 1940s, '50s, and '60s, Democratic presidents kept their distance from him—and many other Black celebrities—because the Democratic coalition still depended on the South. Ellington made overtures to the Roosevelts regarding a White House performance in 1934 and was received coolly at best. He reached out to Washington again after Kennedy's assassination, suggesting that his orchestra perform a set of memorial pieces. The White House did not respond.

The strain between Blacks and Democrats came from both sides. Many educated Blacks shared Ellington's political leanings, viewing the Democratic Party as inseparable from the history of southern segregation. Ellington worked out some of the conflicts in his heart, and then in his art. In 1943, rather than go to the White House, Ellington went to Carnegie Hall to premiere his latest piece, *Black, Brown and Beige*. "We would like to say that this is a parallel to the history of the American Negro," Ellington said at the premiere. "And of course, it tells a long story." The colors referred not to different skin tones, but to the gradual lightening of the historical burden—the Black section was about slavery, while Brown was about emancipation and the African-American contribution to the military, and Beige about the present day (now the distant past), hopeful but still in some ways dire.

The reception was lukewarm—though even those reviewers with mixed feelings recognized the brilliance of the "Come Sunday" section, which focused on the centrality of the church in African-American life. Ellington submerged the piece for fifteen years, during which time he finally made a visit to the White

House to have a talk with Harry S. Truman, who was also a piano player but not a jazz aficionado. In 1958, Ellington brought out *Black, Brown and Beige* as an album, with Mahalia Jackson singing. And then in 1963, he repurposed "Come Sunday" (along with another section, "The Blues") for *My People*, a stage show that he wrote about African-American history. The show was performed as part of the Century of Negro Progress Exposition in Chicago, which celebrated both the hundredth anniversary of the signing of the Emancipation Proclamation and the growing civil rights movement. *My People* included a new song, "King Fit the Battle of Alabam'," which was an old song ("Joshua Fit the Battle of Jericho") rewritten to comment upon the Birmingham Campaign of April 1963. Ellington took up the story of Joshua at Jericho and refitted it for King.

Five years after *My People*, ten years after the *Black, Brown and Beige* album, Black Americans experienced one of their most important, traumatic, tragic, transformative turning points when King was assassinated at the Lorraine Motel in Memphis. Stevie Wonder heard the news in Detroit. Less than a week later, he was in Atlanta for one of the many King memorials, along with other luminaries like Harry Belafonte, Diana Ross, Aretha Franklin, and Mahalia Jackson, who sang "Take My Hand, Precious Lord." (Aretha would sing it at Mahalia's funeral four years later.) The Black congressman John Conyers immediately had the idea that King's birthday should be a national holiday. Doesn't seem too controversial, does it? But the topic was deemed too hot at first, and then it cooled, and though a handful of states (Illinois, Connecticut, and Massachusetts) declared holidays, there was no national declaration. Toward the end of the '70s, Coretta Scott King went to Capitol Hill with the backing of then-president Jimmy Carter, but the effort stalled in the House.

Stevie to the rescue. His 1980 album *Hotter Than July* included the singles "Master Blaster (Jammin')" and "Lately," but the emotional center was "Happy Birthday," which praised King and his legacy as a way of finally pushing the idea of a holiday across the finish line. And it did! Stevie and Coretta collected six million signatures, presented a petition to Speaker of the House Tip O'Neill, and in November 1983 Ronald Reagan signed the holiday into law.

• • •

I wonder how Stevie felt when Reagan finally came around on the King holiday, and I especially wonder how he felt when Richard Nixon presented Duke Ellington with the Presidential Medal of Freedom. That was on April 29, 1969, which also happened to be the Duke's seventieth birthday. Nixon, an accomplished pianist who had played on *The Jack Paar Show* in 1961—that's before Stevie ever had a hit—sat down at the Steinway grand in the East Room, the one with gilt American eagle supports, to lead an impromptu "Happy Birthday" (the traditional song, not the as-yet-unwritten King tribute).

A formal concert followed, with performances of Ellington's best-known compositions, "Come Sunday" among them. Then Ellington himself came to the piano and improvised a ballad that he dedicated to Pat Nixon. The night ended with a jam session that included guests like Dizzy Gillespie, Benny Goodman, and Earl Hines and ran long past midnight. A big blowout jazz party at the White House? With a Republican president, no less? Hard to imagine. Great to imagine.

Ellington and Nixon—or at least Nixon's America—danced together for a little while longer. In the fall of 1971, to support Nixon's policy of détente, Ellington and a seventeen-piece band traveled to the Soviet Union for a month-long concert series that included stops in Moscow, Leningrad, Minsk, Kiev, and Rostov-on-Don. By all accounts, the tour went well, though Ellington told the Associated Press that he was eating too many cheeseburgers, or at least cheeseburgers that were too large—his band had to teach Russian hotel cooks how to make them, and the results were "about ten times the size of normal cheeseburgers."

Nixon remained an admirer of Ellington. When Ellington died, Nixon released a statement: "The wit, taste, intelligence, and elegance that Duke Ellington brought to his music have made him, in the eyes of millions of people both here and abroad, America's foremost composer. We are all poorer because the Duke is no longer with us."

That is, I guess, a form of doing somethin'.

Roots is aired on ABC ○ Elvis Presley dies ○ Apple Computer is incorporated ○ New York City experiences a twenty-five-hour blackout ○ President Anwar Sadat of Egypt visits Israel ○ The United States relinquishes control of the Panama Canal to Panama ○ James Earl Ray escapes from prison and is captured three days later ○ *Lil' Abner* ends its forty-five-year run as a daily newspaper strip ○ Roy Sullivan, a park ranger in Shenandoah National Park in Virginia, is struck by lightning for the seventh time ○ The Dover Demon, a beast with large glowing eyes and tendril-like arms, is spotted in Dover, Massachusetts ○ Snow falls in Miami Florida ○ Patricia Roberts Harris becomes the first Black woman to hold a cabinet position when President Jimmy Carter appoints her to oversee Housing and Urban Development ○ Andrew Young is sworn in as the first Black American to become a U.S. ambassador to the United Nations, under President Jimmy Carter

FUTURE TO THE BACK

For there to be a present there has to be a past.

The year started with *Roots*, which is an irony.

For there to be a present there has to be a past. At the smallest level this might seem obvious. To make sense of the world, to exist in it in a way that's not consumed by chaos, we need more than just the here and now. When we read, we have to remember the sentence before this sentence, or even the beginning of this sentence, even as it disappears into the rearview mirror. When we listen to a song, we have to hold the first half of a rhyme in our minds so that the second half can complete the pair. When we watch a movie, the previous frame has to hang in our minds, or else we won't register the illusion of motion.

History has this same problem, or the same process. We are only here, doing what we're doing, working through the conflicts that we're working through, using the resources that we're using, because of what came before. And what came before was only possible based on what came before it. How we relate to the past, both as individuals and as a society, varies. There are periods when we are especially focused on it, periods of nostalgia when the present is characterized largely in terms of the past. I have (just) written about the bicentennial year, 1976, and though that chapter didn't focus primarily on nostalgia, I remember it clearly—kids in kindergarten dressing up like colonists, tiny Paul Revere on wooden-chair horses, lots of Yankee Doodling (see 1973).

But there are other years that seem to want to tear away from the past, that seem especially aggressive about announcing that they belong to the future. For the most part, 1977 had that feel. America had a new president who was going to help the nation move away from Watergate. *Star Wars* opened, both ushering in a period of copycat sci-fi filmmaking and shifting American movies away from the human-scale works of the first half of the decade.

It was a speed and space year in other ways, too. The Concorde, which had been banned in the United States late the previous year because of concerns over sonic booms, was cleared for landing, and the first Concordes started to jet their way across the Atlantic, from London or Paris to New York. *Enterprise*, the first space shuttle, had its debut flight, not launched off a pad but released off the back of a 747. That was on August 12. On August 15, the Big Ear, a radio telescope that was a key part of the SETI project—that's the Search for Extraterrestrial Intelligence—picked up a signal from outer space that was so unlike anything heard previously that it was nicknamed the Wow!, after a marginal note scribbled on the report by one of the researchers.

Old eras were ending as new vistas quickly opened up. The day after the Wow!, Elvis Presley died at his home in Memphis, rigor mortis on the bathroom floor after a heart attack. It was a sad death and also a symbolic one—at the same time, punk music was surging in London and New York, insisting to anyone who would listen that it was burying the old regime. "No Future" was the rallying cry, but No Past was the strategy. Of course, it's all a little more complicated than any list suggests. Take the SETI signal. Aliens are futuristic, but any signal that comes from so far away is ancient. For that matter, *Star Wars* took place "a long time ago." And Carter couldn't effectively suggest a new start if the recent memory of rot wasn't still clear.

Perhaps the best example of this tension comes from the year's first massive hit, long before *Star Wars*: *Roots*. The massive ABC miniseries about the history of slavery in America, based on the Alex Haley novel of the previous year, aired in January, just after Carter's inauguration, and was watched by an unprecedented audience—something like 130 million people out of a total U.S. population of 220 million. More than 80 percent of American households, and probably close to 90 percent, saw at least part of the miniseries. And maybe most amazingly, the last installment had the highest ratings of any of the episodes. At the time, it was—apart from Super Bowls—the most-watched television program in history, and even today, it remains third on the list, behind only the final episode of *M*A*S*H* and the "Who Shot J.R.?" episode of *Dallas*.

I was in one of those households. I saw all the episodes, and it wasn't just that I saw them. I was compelled to see them. Black families compelled their kids to watch and in some cases even give progress reports. I was six and couldn't fully comprehend what it was that I was seeing. But the extreme images stuck with me forever, and the show's impact has never lessened. I even named a rap group after it! I also remember the music, which was created by Quincy Jones and featured the vocalist Letta Mbulu. Years later, when I had my own Roots, Tariq and I were sourcing for records. I was going through my dad's collection and found the *Roots* soundtrack. When I put it on, I went right to the main theme, "Mama Aifambeni," which Jones co-wrote with the South African composer Caiphus Semenya. The first thing I heard in the song was wind-chime synthesizers. That surprised me. It more than surprised me. It bothered me. There's nothing that gets under my skin more than when people create soundtracks and get tripped up by anachronism. In the Tina Turner biopic *What's Love Got to Do with It*, there's nothing but chronological errors. The first time she records with Ike, in the late 1950s, she's singing a song from the early '70s. There's a sign promoting a 1960 show with Otis Redding, who wouldn't have been performing as a solo act until two or three years later. They set her "Proud Mary" performance in 1968, even though the song didn't exist until 1969. And then there's that part where they have Tina and Ike first practicing "A Fool in Love" in space suits after they watch Reagan's "Mr. Gorbachev, tear down this wall!" speech. That last one didn't happen. But that's how I felt when I heard synthesizers in the Gambian world of Kunta Kinte. But now I see it a little differently. I see that Quincy Jones was struggling with the same tensions as the rest of the year. How do you talk about the past without denying the inevitable future? How do you move forward aggressively without aggressing against the past?

In the last few years, we've seen that appealing overtly to the past—telling people that you're going to make things great again—can resurface old ghosts and demons. Ideas that were lurking in the shadows can step into the light. But the same thing can happen when you're pushing toward a new footing. People can be scared that the ground under them is moving, unsure what's next, and that can lead them to cling to old ways. One of the other things I remember from 1977 is that the Nazis tried to march in Skokie, Illinois. It's possible I am confusing that with a movie scene from a few years after, in *The Blues Brothers*, when Jake Blues said, "I hate Illinois Nazis," and someone explained to me that the whole subplot was based loosely on a famous Supreme Court decision. Or maybe it was years after that, when I read about the decision, and how it paved the way for the Nazis to march in by rejecting the idea that a displayed swastika was the equivalent of a physical attack. But it all led back to suburban Chicago in 1977. That same year saw a bunch of Ku Klux Klan rallies around the country: in Mobile, Alabama, where the Klan was met by a large group of Black counterprotestors; in Plains, Georgia, Jimmy Carter's hometown, where a thirty-year-old white man drove his car into the crowd (he had been drinking, though "no more than a six-pack" and also "didn't like what was being said"); even in New York, where almost no one attended except for the Klansmen and the press.

In years when the future's being insisted upon, there can be an ugly impulse to hold on to the past.

Or, if you'd prefer, sample and hold.

• • •

When you are heading into an exciting but uncertain future, anxious about keeping a piece of the past, there are several ways to remain connected: a historical TV miniseries, say, or a hate rally. Or technology. The late '70s were a great time for new machines that allowed people to preserve pieces of the old world. The VCR, for example, which had been hanging around for a few years but hit the market in force in June, when the VHS format was introduced at a press conference in Chicago. Its main competition was Betamax, a proprietary format of Sony, but VHS machines were made by a variety of companies, and the VHS had some other advantages, too: longer recording times, lighter machines. A year later, VHS had taken almost half of Sony's market share, and within a decade 90 percent of the VCRs used the VHS format.

Within a year or two, I was the recording jockey in my house, responsible for setting up tapings for soap operas. Not as many homes had samplers.

For decades, people had been revisiting old music. The way they did it was straightforward—they listened to recordings. But since music was recorded, it was also possible to take some of it—a piece of an earlier record, say—and incorporate it into a new work. This practice goes back as far as the 1920s, when French composers like Pierre Schaeffer practiced what came to be known as Musique Concrète. It was an acousmatic genre, which meant that it was produced not with instruments, but with speakers that were used to convey already recorded sounds, musical or otherwise. A wide range of compositional practices followed, some using purely electronic tones, some cutting and splicing pieces of existing tape.

And then in the mid-'70s, an Australian teenager named Kim Ryrie started looking into the possibility of a computer-based musical instrument, a synthesizer, that could store and reproduce analog sounds in digital format. Ryrie and his friend Peter Vogel founded a company to explore the idea, and named it after a ferryboat that passed by Ryrie's grandmother's house in Sydney Harbor—the Fairlight. Until that point, most synthesizers were analog with digital control, meaning that they used computers to access stored analog sounds. Ryrie and Vogel wanted something entirely digital. (There's a pre-history: Marvin Gaye's *What's Going On* was Black America's first time experiencing that technology—there's a preset vocal piece inserted into the song at the end of the choral outro to "Mercy Mercy Me," right before "Right On." [Randy Jackson and Greg Phillinganes told me they used that same device on "Your Ways," a song from the Jacksons' *Triumph* album in 1980. They tried to use it also on "Heartbreak Hotel," but it didn't feel right, so Michael Jackson just sang the part.] Trivia inside trivia, but it's amazing to think about this technique even poking its head out of the groundhog hole back in 1971.)

The road forward for this technology was long and filled with obstacles. Microprocessors of the time were not powerful enough. The digital sounds that could be created and stored were limited in length (they could be a second long at most). The device, even when it worked, was almost impossible for a casual musician to master. To make money along the way, Ryrie and Vogel designed home computers for Remington.

The first true sampling synthesizer, the Fairlight CMI, took a few years to finally appear. It was 1979, the future for us here in 1977—or let's call it the extended present. Scientists were intrigued. Orchestras were insulted and threatened. Vogel somehow found his way to Peter Gabriel, who by that point was working on his third solo album. (Keeping track of Peter Gabriel's solo albums is not my specialty, exactly, though I know that they were all called Peter Gabriel, up to a point, and that people put them in order based on their cover photos: car, scratched window, melting face. This was melting face.) Gabriel loved it so much that he had Vogel stay at his house for a week, during which he used the device to create sounds like broken glass. Within months, Gabriel was the co-owner of a company that distributed the Fairlight, and musicians in both Britain (Alan Parsons, Kate Bush) and America (Stevie Wonder, Joni Mitchell) took to it immediately.

By 1982, when the second version of the Fairlight was released, circumstances were even more favorable, from both sides. The music world was more open to technology, and the Fairlight had added sequencing technology, which let it not only create sounds but edit them. It wasn't the only machine available, but it was the leader, and it opened up an entirely new mental space, especially in genres that were in their infancy. The main one, of course, was hip-hop, which was already using drum machines to create beats. Some people date the birth of hip-hop sampling to 1982, when Arthur Baker and Afrika Bambaataa released "Planet Rock," which was built on a sampled Kraftwerk synthesizer line. Except that Bambaataa insists that the synthesizer was not sampled, but rather played by John Robie. The Jonzun Crew's *Lost in Space*, in 1983, used the

E-Mu Emulator, a digital sampling keyboard that stored its sounds on floppy disc. New, cheaper, more versatile technologies were released every year, then every month, and soon enough nearly every producer could flip a sample.

Sampling let rap artists practice their creativity economically, designing musical collages that both generated the same energies and moods as instrumentally performed music and also allowed them to re-present history. It put hip-hop into a different position with regard to soul and funk history. They could be effective conservators even as they faced accusations of not making "real music." I also believe those records bring a feeling of productive imperfection that is needed to convey that we are human. Something that humans (especially Black ones) aren't allowed to be. Which is why, although perfectly executed, sometimes today's music leaves me cold. Because there is no evidence that a human is in our presence. And with Black people I need every affirmation that we exist and that we are indeed . . . human. It's been written about endlessly. It's been written about by me. Let me sample an earlier work of mine. I'll credit it fully. *Creative Quest*, by Questlove with Ben Greenman (Ecco, 2018):

> I want to come back to hip-hop for a little while and stay there. More to the point, I want to think of it in light of all the things we've been talking about: stealing from others, stealing from yourself, making the old new, and discovering ways to jump-start and sustain your creativity through all of these behaviors. The earliest hip-hop singles, like "Rapper's Delight" and "The Breaks," used studio bands, though those bands were just re-creating music from existing records. Then hip-hop entered an era of sampling. Technology made it possible, and aesthetics followed technology. For a little while there, most bands bit pieces of existing songs, both melodic and rhythmic, and arranged them into sonic beds over which MCs would rap.

The technology lets sampling happen. But sampling is also a more complex story about how the present enters the past. Producers sample older songs because something about the earlier work speaks to them—interesting beat, interesting synthesizer texture, nice vocal hook. As creators, they see it as the right ingredient, the way a chef might a certain spice. But I want to dispel a myth. Hip-hop artists are always pretending that samples are familiar to them. They'll hear a chopped bit of an old song in a new song and act like it's always been part of their repertoire. ("I been had this, I been knew that!!") *Lyin' mofo, you didn't know about it until the year of the sample!!!!!!!* I'll cop to that right here and now. For example, I was unfamiliar with the legendary New Orleans funk band the Meters until Ice Cube sampled "I Need More Time" for "The Nigga Ya Love to Hate" in 1990. I read who the group was in the liner notes, and sure, I could have walked around pretending that I had the Meters in my hip pocket all along, but that's fronting, and smart sampling (and paying attention to the smart sampling that other people practice) is all about going back.

The Meters weren't the first time. To me, the most important come-awake moment in this regard dates back to 1989, when EPMD released its second album, *Unfinished Business*. Midway through the record, there's an autobiographical song called "Please Listen to My Demo" on which Erick Sermon and Parrish Smith reminisce about their earliest days in the rap game. "Funky fresh demo tape in [their] pocket," they walk into the studio "with grins on [their] chins." They are hopeful that they can impress the label, and they do. As Erick Sermon explains: "They liked it, and they was very kind."

During the song, there's one prominent sample: a kind of slow-wash synthesizer that sounds like a high human vocal (it's sort of the opposite of the Martha High vocal in "The Payback," a human that sounds like a machine). I was immediately taken by it, though I had no idea where it came from. To the liner notes! I discovered that EPMD was sampling a group called Faze-O. I had a vague memory of them. Were they from the early '70s? Detroit? I was wrong on both counts. Faze-O was a late-'70s band from Dayton, Ohio, one of the cradles of 1970s funk, and they were an offshoot of sorts from the Ohio Players, produced by their horn player Clarence Satchell. The song with the high wave was called "Riding High," and as it turned out, I was familiar with that song via Gary Dove, the next-door-neighbor DJ of my grandma's who was my first North Star.

Years later, I got to know James "Diamond" Williams, the Ohio Players' drummer. He sat in on a college class I was teaching at NYU. While I was talking to him, he filled in some of the Faze-O story. Back in those days, studio time was expensive, and thus valuable. Groups had a certain number of studio hours budgeted as part of the process of making their record. While they were taking a break, they would double down on their time and let another band sneak in, often a junior band from their same scene, an act that they were interested in launching. Faze-O was the during-the-break band the Ohio Players let in during the making of their *Angel* album. One of the strange phenomena of those sneak-in bands was that they often had to use the instruments and settings of their sponsors. They couldn't touch too much because the more senior band was mid-process. In this case, I think it benefited Faze-O. Sonically, I like *Riding High* more than I like *Angel*. (It can go the other way, too. Back in 2011, Sharon Jones and the Dap-Kings opened for Prince at Madison Square Garden. Because there was going to be a quick turnover from opening act to headliner, Prince wouldn't let the Dap-Kings use their own instruments. What we got was a sonically hilarious one-off Vegas version of the Dap-Kings.)

I wouldn't have learned any of those things, or understood them as part of the fabric of musical history, unless I had been led there by hip-hop, and by one specific sample. It shone a light on what came before, and that glow lasted all the way from the past to the present and on into the future.

● ● ●

The more I have thought about samples—and I've thought about them constantly running on thirty years now—the more I have developed a theory for how to handle them. At this point, my advice is fairly straightforward. When you discover the source of a sample, work chronologically. Once you have identified the artist who produced that sound originally, go back to the earliest available moment in his or her career and start listening from there. You'll encounter your sample along the way, but you'll also get a full sense of that artist's development. Return to Point A for access to the entire alphabet.

That creates a window, which creates a genre. If a record was released between 1967 and 1977, it was worth checking out. That was an authorized period of soul and funk, likely to yield the kind of sound that could resonate later. That kind of recycling felt right, partly because it respected historical rhythms—certain sounds and styles tend to resurface based on the memories and motivations of the creators (or the audiences they're imagining), who encountered them first in childhood and then felt a desire to reunite with them in adulthood.

I want to pause here and talk about the set of rules guiding sampling and resurfacing. There aren't any. Okay. All set. Unsatisfied? Me, too. The fact is that people, whether cultural critics or cultural practitioners, have all kinds of theories about the Nostalgia Interval, meaning how long we have to wait before cultural products (music, fashion, etc.) return to us as a source of new inspiration. I remember reading a *New Yorker* article about *Mad Men* that claimed that things returned in forty-year cycles, which seems ridiculously long to me. Other people say that it happens twelve to fifteen years later, which seems too short, though there are cases that support that theory, like the way *American Graffiti* in 1973 revived 1962 and music that was a few years older than that. This is clearly a larger issue for the overall metabolism of history, the complement of the old truism "Those who forget history are condemned to repeat it." It's something like "Those who repeat history are commended because they will not forget it." In this case, I'll locate the '90s sampling window with albums and songs released between 1967 and 1977.

This is for students, of course. Practitioners—that's what happens after you're a student—can bounce around. The legendary producer J Dilla went anywhere and everywhere, into the '80s, into other genres, where there were songs no one would have thought to mine. I learned to do that, too. I remember rediscovering the Who's "Eminence Front" in the mid-'80s. It had been in my family's collection of 45s for a few years—my father, and then later my sister, collected new songs so that the band could learn them—which meant that I definitely heard it, but I didn't pay too much attention, partly because I didn't like the MCA rainbow logo. Later, I latched on to it, though the way it was characterized confused me. The Who goes New Wave? Weren't they using synthesizers for a decade? If anything they were the proprietor of that sound.

Brief digression: "Eminence Front" has a backstory. In the early '80s, there was a song I heard constantly while I was playing Defender at the 7-Eleven down the street from my eighth-grade school, or while I was in a hotel with my parents. It just always seemed to be on. I didn't know the title or the artist. It was just a Generic Rock Song with Attitude. But everyone needs one of those, and I especially liked the "kick them in the shit" part in the lyrics. In my mind, that was conflated with "Eminence Front." Years later, I found out that it was Don Henley's "Dirty Laundry." I also found out that I had been mishearing the lyrics, that it was "kick them when they're stiff," which I guess means when they're dead (?). I don't know. It was a disappointing clarification. This song is also one of the best examples of another category. Before I knew it was Don Henley, I was looking for it forever under the title "Kick 'Em." That's what it should have been called. When I finally found out the actual title, I was furious. Sometimes when you delve into the past, it lets you down.

● ● ●

The History Channel rebooted *Roots* in 2016. There had been a sequel back in 1979 that picked up the last seven chapters of Haley's novel, but this was a full remake that covered much of the same ground as the original miniseries.

I was asked to score the show, which was an honor. I was careful not to put any modern sounds into the music. I composed a short theme, which I called "Binta's Theme" after Kunta Kinte's mother (played by the South African actress Nokuthula Ledwaba). It was a melody that would start deep in the past and recur throughout the life of the series. Kunta might be walking by a church and hear something that reminds him of it. Chicken George might hear Kunta whistling it, and then use the same melody to improvise a song during the Fort Pillow Massacre. I wanted it to resurface at various moments, and each time send people back into the earlier layers of the story. I wanted it to work like a sample.

Finding the Past in the Present

As I say, some hip-hop producers love to front that they knew everything about all the music behind their samples. I am happy to come clean about what I didn't know. Mainly, I'm happy because of the historical principle it illustrates, which is that the present is constantly sending us back into the past. Hip-hop, for a relatively recent music, carries decades. Here are some songs that I would never have learned were it not for sampling.

"RIGHT PLACE WRONG TIME"
Dr. John

In the Right Place, 1973 [Atco]

The first remix I ever heard, in the true hip-hop sense, where the 12-inch is better than the album version, was for Steady B's "Serious." KRS-One, who made it, had a weird in-song internal monologue ("I was listening to BDP when suddenly . . .") and then the song burst in like the Kool-Aid Man. The remix used an obscure song by the Turtles ("I'm Chief Kamanawanalea [We're the Royal Macadamia Nuts]") and Dr. John.

"AIN'T NOTHIN' WRONG"
KC and the Sunshine Band

KC and the Sunshine Band, 1975 [TK]

Black radio was very much aware of KC, but they had so many hits that this song somehow got overlooked. It's like KC's "Baby Be Mine." I never knew it existed until Digable Planets sampled it.

"YOU'RE GONNA NEED ME"
Dionne Warwick

Just Being Myself, 1973 [Warner Bros.]

After she was with Burt Bacharach, Dionne made an album with Holland-Dozier-Holland that was her Blackest record. This song was a big sample for a song on Usher's *Confessions*, "Throwback," that J Dilla then sampled for *Donuts*.

"FIGHTING FIRE WITH FIRE"
The Bar-Kays

Coldblooded, 1974 [Volt]

Lots of us tease the Bar-Kays for being so blatantly derivative, though that was part of their plan—better for them to record their own versions of songs than have to cover originals. This song has a magical eight-bar breakdown at the 3:03 mark. Chi-Ali used it—the Beatnuts sampled it for him—and I put it in the first remix I ever did, King Britt's "Gettin' Into It."

“I’M TIRED OF GIVING”
The Spinners

Spinners/8, 1977 [Atlantic]

I remember going record shopping with my dad and seeing this on the rack near the cashier. The album cover was nothing, just the band logo. I was a big fan of “Rubber Band Man,” but this record was underwhelming, sort of a sad orphan, and this song didn’t register until Mobb Deep sampled it for “Up North Trip.”

“IT’S ALL RIGHT NOW”
Eddie Harris

That Is Why You’re Overweight, 1976 [Atlantic]

When the Roots went to London, we had our Monday nights free, and I would go to Bar Rumba to watch Gilles Peterson spin rare soul. I recognized this song from the Young Black Teenagers’ record “Korner Groove.”

“I REMEMBER I MADE YOU CRY”
The Headhunters

Straight from the Gate, 1977 [Arista]

Lots of us just stopped at the Headhunters’ “God Made Me Funky” and didn’t truly investigate the follow-up. This is another Mobb Deep discovery, from “Drink Away the Pain.” (It’s a funny song because it speeds up as it goes. Same thing for “Sir Duke,” actually. Songs like that are interesting to use in a DJ set because they can invisibly accelerate things.)

“JAGGER THE DAGGER”
Eugene McDaniels

Headless Heroes of the Apocalypse, 1971 [Atlantic]

Supposedly, Spiro T. Agnew, Nixon’s vice president, was alarmed by the political power of this record and called on Atlantic to stop promotion. For me, it’s a great record from start to finish, full of nuggets and great songs. And it’s a go-to for A Tribe Called Quest on their debut album, a running gag in interludes throughout the entire album.

“THE WORST BAND IN THE WORLD”
10cc

Sheet Music, 1974 [UK]

I was eventually aware of 10cc because of “The Things We Do for Love” and as the former home of Godley and Creme (videos for “Cry,” Yes’s “Leave It,” and the Police’s “Every Breath You Take,” among many others). But I hadn’t heard this before Dilla’s *Donuts* sampled it.

“SPORT”
Lightnin’ Rod

Hustler’s Convention, 1973 [Celluloid]

On the original album, Kool and the Gang is the band backing Lightnin’ Rod. I heard this first when Melle Mel covered it as “Hustler’s Convention.” But the best use is on a brilliant, obscure ’80s hip-hop single, “Small-Time Hustler,” by the Dismasters.

“A CHANT FOR BU”
Art Blakey

Buhaina, 1973 [Prestige]

The start of A Tribe Called Quest’s “Excursions” on *The Low End Theory*, which is where I first heard this, is one of the most potent openings of any album. Post-1988, hip-hop always presented interludes as just as important (sometimes more important) than the songs itself. So for Tribe to deliver such an important record with no album intro or interlude was a statement as strong as anything else on the record.

“GENTLE SMILES”
Gary Bartz

The Shadow Do, 1975 [Prestige]

A straightforward sentiment can land too heavily if the artist doesn’t have subtlety or grace, or it can land in the sweet spot. People, including me, know this song from A Tribe Called Quest’s “Butter.”

Egypt and Israel sign the Camp David accords ○ *The Wiz* is released ○ The Japanese explorer Naomi Uemura becomes the first person to reach the North Pole in a solo expedition ○ The first test-tube baby is born ○ In *Regents of the University of Calfornia v. Bakke*, the Supreme Court bans racial quota systems in college admissions ○ Affirmed wins the Triple Crown ○ The first Unabomber attack occurs in the security department of Northwestern University ○ Pete Rose gets his 3,000th hit ○ *Dallas* debuts on CBS ○ *Hustler* publisher Larry Flynt is shot and paralyzed ○ Richard Chase, the Vampire of Sacramento, is arrested ○ Muhammad Ali is the first heavyweight champion to win the title three times, by defeating Leon Spinks in New Orleans ○ Faye Wattleton becomes the first Black woman to preside over Planned Parenthood Federation of America

DISCO TECH

Does the assembly line of history reduce meaning?

Disco is one of those magical words that conjures up an entire world: a mirror ball hanging from the ceiling, a dance floor lit up from underneath, women in big shoes, men in flared pants and big collars. It's specifically generic. When it appears in a movie, in a TV show, the rules are clear, and if you execute it properly, no one will misunderstand where and when you're directing their attention—an American city, most likely one with a sizable gay and Black population, late 1970s. What rises in their minds is less a setting than a sticker.

There's a story before that story, of course. Disco emerged from the European club scene of the 1960s, where live entertainment was replaced by records played over a sound system. Parties ensued. And while there were dance clubs everywhere and everywhen, the discotheque idea hung around long enough for it to be revived in America about a decade later, to massive effect.

By the mid-'70s, Black music had evolved away from the conscious funk and soul of the late '60s and early '70s. The end of the Vietnam War and, maybe more important, the end of the draft took the pressure off a bit where protest music was concerned, and the social messages that surfaced in the work of artists like Curtis Mayfield, Sly Stone, and James Brown hit the skids. It wasn't that all of society's problems had been solved. It was that they hadn't: A surge in crime, a rise in drug use, and a slackening of the economy reset people's needs. They didn't want to look closely at reality any longer. They wanted to feel better. Combine that with the advances in gay rights and women's rights, and you have the makings of a party.

The party broke out. And for a little while, it didn't break up. Other cultural landmarks came along to help push it higher and higher in the public consciousness—the movie *Saturday Night Fever*, released right at the end of 1977, was based on an article in *New York* magazine from the summer of 1976. The article, "Tribal Rites of the New Saturday Night," found Nik Cohn, a British journalist, trying to come to grips both with the disco culture in New York and with the very different non-disco lives of the young people who flocked to the clubs, particularly Italian Americans in Bay Ridge, Brooklyn. Cohn didn't know much about disco, so he worked his way through the scene by comparing the people he met with people from his youth in Derry, Northern Ireland. Most of the characters were composites: in fact, while the article was accepted as a work of journalism for decades, Cohn eventually revealed that it had been mostly a work of fiction.

But fiction can sometimes be true. The article turned into the movie, and the movie turned into a phenomenon, launching into the stratosphere the careers of its star, John Travolta, and its musical stars, the Bee Gees. Between January and July 1978, the *Saturday Night Fever* soundtrack was the nation's number one album, on the way to a 120-week stay on the charts and sales of more than $45 million worldwide. Other brands sprang up, most notably the Manhattan nightclub Studio 54 on West Fifty-Fourth and Broadway. Previously a radio and TV studio owned by CBS called Studio 52 (named not for the street on which it was located but for the order in which it was acquired by CBS), the space was bought by Steve Rubell and Ian Schrager and rapidly turned into a disco for the stars. Andy Warhol! Diana Ross! Liza Minnelli! Mick Jagger! Bianca Jagger! Calvin Klein! Everybody else! (Except of course, the nobodies—you had to be somebody.) Disco was glitz and glitz was disco. Done and done.

But the genre's mainstreaming, quick as it was, didn't tell the full story. The movie centered on the Bay Ridge disco 2001 Odyssey (named for what was at the time a ten-year-old movie, *2001: A Space Odyssey*), part of a network of clubs throughout the city that formed the real backbone of disco, from the Paradise Garage to the Loft, from Ice Palace 57 to Roseland. Each place had its own culture, though when *Saturday Night Fever* and Studio 54 swamped the national consciousness, they got reduced to subcultures: Hispanic disco, Black disco, gay disco, gay Black disco. GG's Barnum Room, which opened in 1978 on 128 West Forty-Fifth Street—the once (and future) site of the Peppermint Lounge, which had been the epicenter of the Twist dance craze back in 1960—was known as a trans club.

And it wasn't just New York. In Philly, where I grew up, places like Second Story and Catacombs, both owned by the Geftman Brothers, had top-flight sound systems that led to the creation of new dance-music genres like house and Philly Classics. Houston, Atlanta, Montreal—every city had its own scene.

But that's the live side of things. The recorded side is a little different. One of the criticisms of disco albums and singles was that they all sounded the same, and while that's a little reductive, it was also a little bit the point. Maybe it's more accurate to say that disco was happy to be a product, perfectly willing to keep cranking out song after song that fit a similar template. While rock and roll, or soul music, depended on stars who rose into view by virtue of their own strong personalities, disco deemphasized individual expression in favor of ruthless efficiency. There were stars, of course—the Bee Gees, as we've established, and Donna Summer, and Chic—but you didn't need stars to make a great disco record. Just as often, the architects of the disco sound were labels like Casablanca and SalSoul or DJs like Larry Levan and Tom Moulton. There's a debate over whether the first disco song to hit the top of the charts was "Rock the Boat" by the Hues Corporation or "Love's Theme" by the Love Unlimited Orchestra. (The first number one on the disco chart, once it existed, was Gloria Gaynor's "Never Can Say Goodbye.") What's not up for debate is that both acts had extremely generic names, almost as if they were zoned for a lack of personality. And "Rock the Boat" was additionally typical in that it described a motion that was repetitive, potentially sexual, and without any unnecessary additional details. "Rock the Boat." "Ring My Bell." "Knock on Wood." Pleasure sought, pleasure produced.

And many disco songs were even more generic than that: dance songs about dancing. Or, as the mid-'70s had it, boogieing. Remember the Sylvers? They were a Memphis-based family group that migrated west to inherit the bubblegum mantle of the ever-growing Jackson 5—they even had a youngest brother, Foster, who went solo as a preteen and had a Top Ten hit with "Misdemeanor." In the mid-'70s, they signed to Capitol Records, which deepened the Jackson connection by assigning them to the producer Freddie Perren, who had been part of the Corporation, the team responsible for hits like "I Want You Back," "ABC," and "The Love You Save." Perren was onto disco early, moving the Miracles into the genre with "Do It Baby" and "Love Machine," and when the Sylvers came to him, he was ready. He gave them "Boogie Fever," which went to number one and inspired a string of boogie songs: "I'm Your Boogie Man" by KC and the Sunshine Band (which had already had the earlier "Boogie Shoes"), "Blame It on the Boogie" by the Jacksons, "Boogie Wonderland" by Earth, Wind, & Fire, and more. (Group leader Leon Sylvers himself had a slightly different take. He said "Boogie Fever" was as if his favorite Beatles song, "Day Tripper," were a disco song seen through the eyes of the Jackson 5.)

"Boogie Oogie Oogie," which came out in the summer of 1978, followed in the fine tradition of disco singles, meaning that it had a familiar origin story. A Taste of Honey was a relatively faceless vocal group that had started out in Los Angeles and kicked around for years, including time on the USO circuit. They, too, were signed to Capitol Records, and they, too, were paired with producers who had done time with the Jacksons: Fonce and Larry Mizell, who had in fact started out co-producing with Perren, furnishing a song for the 1973 album *Skywriter* and for solo albums by Michael and Jermaine. "Boogie Oogie Oogie" differs from the story only in that it was written by two members of A Taste of Honey, Perry Kibble and Janice-Marie Johnson, rather than handed to the group by a producer. When it was released, it was an instant smash, becoming the first single in the history of Capitol Records to sell more than two million copies. At the Grammys the following year, the group won Best New Artist, beating out Chris Rea, Toto, Elvis Costello, and the Cars.

Disco was a great (if temporary) success story for groups like A Taste of Honey. It took singers who might otherwise have slipped into obscurity and elevated them to the top of the charts. But disco can also be seen as a tragedy, particularly for the musicians who were forced to live and work under its regime. As records were stamped out like assembly-line products, factory workers were needed, and those factory workers were guitarists, bassist, drummers, and more. The genres that preceded disco—soul, funk, rock and roll—required talented musicianship, and rewarded it. Sometimes those players became stars in their own right, like Bootsy Collins. Sometimes they remained anonymous, like the Funk Brothers at Motown. But they were playing at the top of their ability and making records that showed it. And the genre that preceded those genres, jazz, was nothing if not a showcase for Black Genius. Louis Armstrong was Louis Armstrong because of how he played, and because he played the best—and the same goes for Charles Mingus, or John Coltrane, or Cecil Taylor. Disco meant simpler songs and simple playing. Great talents were compelled to play the same mechanical beat over and over again, not just on one song but on song after song—the more that disco dominated the charts, the more it dominated their session work. People were placed into the service of a product, and a process, to the point where it compromised their humanity.

● ● ●

For a few years there, disco just grew and grew. And then, like all products, it fell out of fashion. People objected to it as inauthentic, the enemy of what true art should be. The most infamous articulation of this objection came in the summer of 1979, when Disco Demolition Night was held at Comiskey Park in Chicago, in the middle of a doubleheader between the Chicago White Sox and the Detroit Tigers. The DJ Steve Dahl, a self-declared enemy of disco and everything it stood for, burned disco records in the stadium's outfield. (Nile

Rodgers, the lead guitarist of Chic, one of the genre's few true virtuosos, likened the night to a Nazi book burning, and there's something to that. A night of fire might be a form of history, but it takes things out of history—permanently.) To me, the strangest thing about the stunt is that it didn't attack the genre so much as understand it. Disco was always designed to be disposable. It produced pleasure, which dissipated until there was a demand for it to be produced again. The end of the road was always part of the road.

Just before the sidewalk ended, though, one of the great innovators of Black music showed back up to take his cuts. In 1979, with the genre beginning to wane, James Brown released an album called *The Original Disco Man*. It was produced, and mostly written, by Brad Shapiro, who had started in Miami with Henry Stone before Stone's TK Records became a disco powerhouse, working with artists like pre-Blowfly Clarence Reid and Betty Wright. Shapiro went on to co-produce the first J. Geils Band records and oversaw Millie Jackson's classic pair of infidelity concept albums, *Caught Up* and *Still Caught Up*.

That impressive résumé brought him, in the last years of the 1970s, to the doorstep of the Godfather of Soul, who was nearing the end of his tenure with Polydor Records. Working alongside Randy McCormick, a veteran of the Muscle Shoals Rhythm Section, Shapiro wrote many of the album's songs, including the strange (and strangely documentary) title track, in which Brown claimed credit for inventing the genre. While female backing vocalists, largely devoid of personality, sang the chorus ("He's the original disco man / With the original disco band"), Brown taught a (selective) history lesson. He starts back in 1955 (when people were "dancing to all kind of jive") and then time-jumps to 1966 (when "you all got down with [his] funky licks").

The music behind him, appropriately mechanical, occasionally inserted one of those funky licks from a past James Brown hit, just to remind everyone who was singing.

Disco was narrow, and it was quick, but it's a mistake to say that it had no lasting impact. Hip-hop, for example, was at least in part a direct reaction to disco. In 1977 or so, punk had stood on top of what it claimed was the bloated corpse of rock and roll. Hip-hop did something similar with disco. When it appeared, it was a countermovement, a reiteration of the possibility of Black Genius. Hip-hop moved in directions that disco couldn't. The lyrics could be political or anthropological, philosophical or philological, gleefully surreal or crushingly real. Early hip-hop, especially, was all about discovery, doing something new, taking the risk. It was never a factory, and always a factor.

• • •

If disco is filled with release, this discussion of it is filled with tension. Thinking about disco as a formula that foreclosed individualism, and in thinking about other forces around its edges (hip-hop, say, or James Brown) as a way of challenging that foreclosure and trying to recapture that individualism, points to a larger question in history—or rather a larger question about history, about the way it's recorded and the way that those records are understood. Is history primarily about the actions of individuals or is it an account of events that have occurred and the causes of those events? In the case of disco, one answer (the latter) rises while the other falls. If we're asked to sketch out the causes of a genre like disco, we're more likely to talk about what we talked about before: the malaise and melancholy of the mid-'70s, and the need for a hedonism in music to offset them. There are other times and places in history where the answer would seem to lean more toward the former, toward intentional choices and behaviors. These two ways of thinking aren't entirely separate. They're not mutually exclusive. They're interwoven tightly like two instruments in an arrangement. Which one comes to the fore depends a little on how the musicians are playing, and a little on how you're hearing.

1979

The Shah of Iran flees to Egypt and Ayatollah Khomeini returns, leading to revolution and the November taking of hostages ○ Jimmy Carter and Leonid Brezhnev sign the SALT II treaty ○ Michael Jackson releases *Off the Wall* ○ The Pittsburgh Steelers win their fourth Super Bowl of the decade ○ Octavia Butler's *Kindred* is published ○ Margaret Thatcher is elected in Britain ○ The Soviet Union invades Afghanistan ○ Carter gives his "national malaise" speech ○ The Pol Pot regime in Cambodia collapses ○ Frank E. Petersen, Jr., becomes the first African-American general in the Marine Corps ○ Pink Floyd releases *The Wall* ○ Marxist Sandinistas take power in Nicaragua ○ "Rapper's Delight" is released ○ *The Muppet Movie* comes out ○ Franklin Thomas is named president of the Ford Foundation ○ The Nobel Prize in Economics goes to Sir Arthur Lewis of Princeton University, the first Black person to win the award in a category other than Peace

AN IDEA RUNS WILD

Is history a random set of events, or is it driven forward by big ideas?

Thinking about history can feel like waking up from a dream. You know that something complicated happened, and for a little while you think you have it all sorted out. But then you're not sure. Are you remembering things correctly? What was the order of events? How come it seems like it's slipping out of your grasp? What people do with dreams, usually, is seize on one detail. It was the dream where I was running on the surface of a river. It was the dream where I was inside a cylinder. That's the only way our memory of that dream can be a building block for more conscious thoughts about ourselves, the people we know, the day ahead of us. We're reductive so that we can be constructive.

History works similarly. Extremely complicated situations are simplified so that they can be communicated to others. Slippery and treacherous rock faces are given handholds and footholds. Events with no discernible meaning wait until they can be fitted into the puzzle. Think about the letter *E*. Think about it in a major way, and in a minor way. I'll explain.

• • •

Music nerd moment, for just a moment. Maybe two. Sly and the Family Stone's "Thank You (Falettinme Be Mice Elf Agin)" is one of the most important funk songs in music history, if not the most important. Partly that's because of Sly's deep, dark lyrics, which describe spiritual torture, the perils of stardom, and other happy topics with his usual brilliant compression: "Lookin' at the devil, grinnin' at his gun / Fingers start shakin', I begin to run." Partly that's because it was dropped as a bonus track on the *Greatest Hits* album in 1970, which isn't the usual way artists surface their most iconic material. Partly that's because Sly revisited the song on his next album, *There's a Riot Goin' On*, as "Thank You for Talkin' to Me Africa," a slowed-down and even murkier cover of his own song. But mostly it's because it's the E minor godhead.

E minor is the key of that song, and because of it, E minor is the key of a million others songs. Before it, there's not a dance song in that key. After it, there are not many that aren't. It makes sense. For beginning bass players, it's the easiest key. It's naturally funky. You can stay there, vamping to your hearts' content. But because of that, there's an inherent risk. It's not a straightforward flag that Sly planted. Many E minor songs aren't quite songs at all. They are riffs extended lazily, to diminishing effect, groove exercises that forget to find a melody. E minor is, for me, the *Thelma and Louise* cliff jump of keys. You can try it, but many of you are going to end up at the bottom of the canyon.

Not everyone will, of course. Sly wasn't the only one who figured it out. Sly's greatest heir and also closest contemporary, George Clinton, wrote a whole raft of songs in E minor for Parliament and Funkadelic: "Can You Get to That," "Super Stupid," "Up for the Down Stroke," "Ride On," "Give Up the Funk (Tear the Roof off the Sucker)," "Night of the Thumpasorus Peoples," "Gamin' on You," and that's only the beginning. There's even a song on *Chocolate City* called "What Comes Funky" that I sometimes hear as a rhetorical question ("What comes funk: E?"). Clinton's greatest Sly theft actually lies within "You Can't Miss What You Can't Measure," a 1973 Funkadelic song that is in a bass player's greatest nightmare key (E-flat minor, a half step down, which, according to Jimmy

Jam, has only one purpose: to leave the bass player feeling left out, because most E-flat minor jams are made for synth bass players to have fun, and most render four-string bass players silent—it's the one low note you cannot achieve on the instrument unless you have the uncomfortable five-string bass device). Other than the funk-derivative "Sledgehammer," by Peter Gabriel, I can't think of one funk staple in E-flat minor that has bass in it. I almost think George purposely keyed it half a step lower to deodorize the song of the scent of fandom, which is weird, considering this song would get an E-minor makeover three years later on Parliament's "Do That Stuff." The blueprint George was building from on "You Can't Miss . . ." was Sly's self-referential "Sing a Simple Song," another "funk E" monster that in its own way allowed "Elf Agin" to even exist.

Prince used it as well, though not on his most straightforward songs; predictably, it ended up in unpredictable places, like "Annie Christian," "Christopher Tracy's Parade," "Sexual Suicide," and "What's My Name." He never followed it into cliché. The closest he got, oddly, was "The Ballad of Dorothy Parker," from *Sign o' the Times*. You can hear the bass in there, funkin' away, but the rest of the song springs from his happy place in Joni Mitchell's *Hissing of Summer Lawns*, so the E minor–ness of it is minimized. And then there's "The Dance Electric," which Prince gave away to Andre Cymone, although the rumor is that Cymone was too embarrassed (or too proud) to ask for himself, so his mother made the request. Prince obliged immediately. It's almost like he was relieved to unload a song so straightforward.

My E minor epiphany came earlier than Prince, but later than Sly. I was too young to hear "Thank You (Falettinme Be Mice Elf Agin)" in its natural habitat. By the time I got to it, or it got to me, it was already a Stone-cold classic. As the Father went, so went the Son ("Shining Star," by Earth, Wind & Fire, which came out in 1975) and the Holy Ghost ("Give Up the Funk [Tear the Roof off the Sucker]," by Parliament, 1976). They passed me by before I even knew enough to know that's what was happening.

As I've explained, I came of age as a record buyer and radio listener around 1977, and the first funk classic that got to me was "Glide," by Pleasure, an Oregon-based band that was shepherded into fame by the saxophonist

Grover Washington, Jr. (best known for his duet with Bill Withers on "Just the Two of Us"), and the trombonist Wayne Henderson (of the Crusaders). Pleasure had a hit in 1977 with "Joyous," which was later sampled by Janet Jackson ("Joyous" got its bass DNA from James Brown, a creator who owned the key of D minor—33 Top Tens in that key—and who strangely enough made his greatest gangsta statement ["The Payback"] . . . in the very un-Brown-like B flat). But they first came to my attention two years later, with "Glide." I was there for it. It got me fully. Musically, I mean: I never understood the lyrics, which are about a guy who can't get to work no matter what vehicle he tries: car's out of gas, bus breaks down, cab's too expensive. The song then turns to philosophy: "Don't let that keep you behind / Glide, glide on by." When I say I didn't understand the lyrics, I don't mean that I wasn't yet driving so I didn't identify with their frustration. I mean that I literally didn't understand them. I thought they were singing "Glide, dynamite." I want to make clear, though, that the only version of this song that's acceptable is the radio edit: one verse, one chorus, then fade before you know what's hit you. The album version? Nah. It's an E minor casualty, too long, too repetitive, not enough energy.

Not everyone was in the grip of E minor. Some artists, including some geniuses, went in another direction. Stevie Wonder owns E-flat minor, which is half a step below. Why? Because it's the one key where there aren't any wrong notes if you play only the black keys. His first singles from an album have always been in E-flat minor, from "Superstition" to "Skeletons." In second place in the E-flat minor Olympics are Jimmy Jam and Terry Lewis, who produced a good twenty-song run of Black hits in that key. Jam and Lewis, of course, started out in the Minneapolis band Flyte Time, joined forces with Prince, where they were the backbone of the early Time, and then went on to produce for everyone from the S.O.S. Band to Janet Jackson. I asked Jimmy why they went in for E-flat minor, and he told me that they didn't want to play to the lowest common denominator, and that in order to separate their sound from the pack they had to get rid of the one key figure that signified Black, or funk. So they had to take the song into a key where the bass wasn't as welcome. They were Studio

54 bouncers. If you wanted to get into their music and play it, you had to get through the velvet rope.

• • •

Back to Duke Ellington for a moment. In Duke's *New York Times* obituary, there's an anecdote that may or may not be true—history alert!—but it's too good not to pass on. It's not about cheeseburgers or Pat Nixon. It's a claim that back in 1972, during an orchestra rehearsal in Madison, Wisconsin, he lost his temper when his musicians weren't playing a piece correctly.

> "No! E! E as in Ellington! E! E as in Edward! E! E as in Ellington! E as in excellence! E as in elegance! As in Edward and Ellington! E! E! E as in all good things! Edward, Ellington, excellence, elegance! E!"

The *Times* may have been picking up on an article in the *Detroit Free Press* from about a month earlier that opened with a scene of Duke asking his musicians to learn something new he had written overnight, and then blowing his top when they didn't get it immediately. But they have it a little different.

> "No, no, no," the maestro shouted. "I said E! E as in Ellington. E as in Edward Ellington. E as in excellence. E as in elegance. E as in endurance. E as in Ellington and E as in everything—everything that is fine and good, everything that is prime and fancy."

That story started on a bus—to a musician, that checks out. On the other hand, it ends by noting that after Ellington's outburst, "The men grimmed [*sic*] despite themselves." Typos aren't necessarily a reason to disbelieve everything around them, but they suggest a certain cearlssenss. So I'm not sure how much authority that anecdote demands. A decade later, in *Esquire*, it changed again.

> "E! E as in Ellington! E! E as in Edward! E! E as in Ellington! E as in excellence! E as in elegance! As in Edward and Ellington! E! E! E as in all good things! Edward . . . Ellington excellence . . . elegance! E!"

These are minor variations. E minor variations?

The *Esquire* piece, in the December 1983 issue, was an appreciation of the Duke written by Alistair Cooke. Yes, that Alistair Cooke: the super-British host of *Masterpiece Theatre*, who would have at the time been known by the eight-year-old me, if known at all, as the inspiration for "Alistair Cookie," the host of the *Sesame Street* segment Monsterpiece Theater. Reading around a little bit, I learned that Cooke was only yards away from Bobby Kennedy when Kennedy was assassinated, and also that his real name was Alfred. That revelation sent me right to "Cloreen Bacon Skin," an extended and extensively funky Prince track recorded the same year that Cooke wrote his piece for *Esquire*. The song seems to have grown out of a jam session with Morris Day, who plays drums while Prince plays bass. Prince is clowning, improvising, coaching Morris toward a possible song. and after inventing the title character (the narrator's first wife), he invents a second one, her brother, Alfred. "Alfred," he says, "Alfred, I need you to talk to me, son, come on, Alfred." From a Duke to a Prince.

That song, weirdly enough, is not in E minor. It's in A minor. Like Jam and Lewis, Prince was staking out his own ground. But it's more than that. The Time made it explicitly known that they were not funk, at least not in the way that people had come to think of it. In 1982, they released the first single from their second album, "777-9311," written and performed (like most everything from the early Time) by Prince, with Day on vocals. The B side was a song called "Grace," which takes the music of "777-9311" and overlays a fake interview between Day and a journalist—it's Bridgette Harrington, who worked with Prince's accountant, and she says her name, but Morris keeps calling her "Grace," which was a go-to move for him. (It lasted for the rest of the decade, at least. Check out the beginning of "Release It," from *Graffiti Bridge* in 1989.) Morris establishes his cool, insisting that he was born not in his birthday suit but in a zoot suit. Then the interviewer asks him how the Time manages such a funky sound. "Pardon me," Morris says. "I know you didn't just say 'funk.'" He goes on: "Let me just say one thing. Funk is dead. Funk is something you can learn in school. And ain't nothing funky about being cool."

This brings us back to the concerns of Day's once and future bandmates Jam and Lewis (who Prince would fire when a snowstorm prevented them from flying back from an S.O.S. Band session in Atlanta to rejoin the Time in San Antonio). History makes categories, sometimes simplistically, and if that's not the bag you want to be in, you have to fight your way out. History teaches lessons, sometimes reductively, and if those aren't the lessons you want to learn, you have to write your own curriculum. If you simply accept those categories and those lessons without critical pressure—without putting Grace under pressure—you're history.

Majoring in E Minor

E minor isn't just a way of life for funk songs, but a world unto itself. In grappling with the mass of E-minor songs, I have divided the E-minor theme into two camps, the songs that get over and the songs that underwhelm. One song is both: "Cool Joe," by George Clinton. George is the Michael Jordan of funk. His foul shots are more exciting than the tomahawk dunks of lesser players. But "Cool Joe" is a foul shot. To me, its errors come not from E-minor slackness only, but from a miscalculation regarding technology. If you're going to use synthesizers and other electronic instruments, you have to be careful about tone and texture. You can't surround your technology with studio sheen and antiseptic perfection, or it'll just wash out. Technology needs an inferior studio environment, or at least one that's muddied or scumbled, to truly shine. It's counterintuitive, I know, but there are so many examples. Again, *There's a Riot Goin' On*, one of the muddiest records imaginable; or Prince's earliest records, with their inferior equipment and superior tone; or LL Cool J's first hits. "Cool Joe" earns my admiration, but to me it's too neutered, too pristine. And yet, despite that, I can sense the life that's there, because it was written and performed by George, and George is all about life. I listen to this song the same way that I see the Bride in *Kill Bill* when she's in her coma. You know that inside her mind she's all there, but you also have to go on faith.

SONGS THAT MADE THE JUMP

"SURRENDER (A SECOND TO THINK)"
Saul Williams

Saul Williams, 2004 [Fader]

I don't know. I believe Saul Williams. I believe him. That's the thing. With one false move it could have easily fallen the other way.

"YOU CAN'T CHANGE THAT"
Raydio

Rock On, 1979 [Arista]

I didn't like "Jack and Jill," the Raydio hit before this. But "You Can't Change That" was different. I generally fell asleep during *Midnight Special*, but I remember them opening up the show with it. Summertime, I think. And this was right around the same time that I met KISS in Buffalo, at a hotel—a week earlier I had met Lynn Swann and the Pittsburgh Steelers in the same hotel, in the game room. I knew it had a good association for me.

"HOT STUFF"
The Rolling Stones

Black and Blue, 1976 [Rolling Stones]

My record collection started with the throwaway songs that neither my dad nor his band wanted to attempt. Every two weeks Dad would go to the record store and binge-shop every 45. I couldn't touch them at first, but as they found that certain songs couldn't be added to their show (which was more middle-of-the-road, Johnny Mathis, Shirley Bassey), certain 45s went back in the box. For me it worked as funk, overdone, repeated, but still. Mick Jagger has an inner black person. He's always been dying to express himself in that way, and he was already a bluesman caricature as it was. I didn't have any defenses up in listening to it when I was six years old.

"BOY"
Swamp Children

Little Voices 12-inch, 1981 [Factory]

This sounded underperformed and a little cheap, so there was something compelling about it. The band really performs together, like a unit. Later, this was tacked on to the *So Hot* album, but I like it in its original context, where it's a strange experimental funk song.

"WILD & LOOSE"
The Time

What Time Is It?, 1982 [Warner Bros.]

Prince wasn't even a star yet, but he was making music this amazing. In eight minutes he provides a documentary with some shady bad characters. Are they gangsters? Are they musicians? Are they the ones your mama told you about? Not to mention the genius way you can hear sexy socialites talk about Morris in one ear and you can hear Jesse, Terry, Jerome, and Morris talk about it in the other ear, hard panned. It's like Robert Altman. Another film reference: it's the *Citizen Kane* of '80s funk.

"UP FOR THE DOWN STROKE"
Parliament

Up for the Down Stroke, 1974 [Casablanca]

Or I could have picked "Ride On," or "What Comes Funky," or "Night of the Thumpasorus Peoples," or "Do That Stuff," or whatever. I celebrate their entire catalog.

SONGS THAT FELL A LITTLE SHORT

"SWEET GYPSY JANE"
The Temptations

Wings of Love, 1976 [Gordy]

Not great, though I'm not mad at this song. It first came to my attention on a *Soul Train* episode, and it's a really good vocal performance. This has to be the same house band that was on *A Song for You*.

"WHO REALLY ARE THE MONSTERS?"
Lenny Kravitz

Raise Vibration, 2018 [Roxie/BMG]

I don't know if he was trying to get Chromeo-ized or if he just challenged himself to make a song like this, a Talking Heads move, and I'll give him points for adding congas. But it goes a little far, though it's almost like he knew he was going to get caught out there.

"FEVER"
Ronnie Laws

Fever, 1976 [Blue Note]

Man. First of all it's "Fever." I don't trust any song with that vibration.

"WATCH OUT BABY!"
George Duke

Reach for It, 1977 [Epic]

I feel like a horrible Philadelphian, but I can't get behind Stanley Clarke here. Is it bad that the song from his solo work that touched me the most is the Bl(acht)Rockian (may I make up a portmanteau?) "Heaven Sent You," his bassless E-minor jawn with Shalamar's Howard Hewitt?

"YOU'RE A FOXY LADY"
Larry Graham and Graham Central Station

Star Walk, 1979 [Warner Bros.]

I remember this as one of the few records I panned as a nine-year old. Maybe it's because Mom got it for me out of the "cheap bin" on a Woolworth's trip two years after the fact, in 1981. However, I will also note that my band has taken a liking to "Scream" and "Sneaky Freak." Not to rabbit-hole, but I guess once Prince made it known to me that this era of GCS was his North Star (similar to his preference for the mustache-having, post-sample-ready James Brown hit-or-miss '74–'81 period), it made me hear this record with a fresh set of ears. But revisionist thinking can be tiring. Sometimes we need to cop to our original sense. And so here, officially, I will admit that I hated *Star Walk* as an album/song/creative direction for its first thirty-seven years.

"CREOLE/FEELING FUNKY"
The Crusaders

Chain Reaction, 1975 [ABC/Blue Thumb]

It's lazy. I'm not a fan of the Crusaders at all. And yet there's the fact that DJ Premier and all these cats find good samples. Maybe there's something to the melody. But the song doesn't work for me.

"KALIMBA SONG"
Bobby Caldwell

Bobby Caldwell, 1978 [Clouds]

I love the intro but it goes nowhere. It fools me every time.

Jimmy Carter loses the presidential election to Ronald Reagan ○ BET premieres ○ J.R. is shot on the prime-time soap *Dallas* ○ Pac-Man is released ○ Richard Pryor is burned while freebasing cocaine ○ *Voyager* 1 passes Saturn ○ The Mariel Boatlift sends more than 100,000 Cubans to the United States ○ Civil rights activist and Urban League president Vernon Jordan is seriously wounded in an assassination attempt, which becomes the first story covered by the new news network CNN ○ Rosie Ruiz wins the Boston Marathon, but is later discovered to have cheated ○ The Pennsylvania Lottery is fixed by a group of men that includes the live drawing's TV host ○ Candy Lightner of Fair Oaks, California, founds MADD (Mothers Against Drunk Driving) after her thirteen-year-old daughter Cari is killed ○ The Winter Olympics in Lake Placid includes the men's hockey team's Miracle on Ice ○ The United States boycotts the Summer Olympics in Moscow ○ In what is known as the "Canadian Caper," six U.S. diplomats pose as Canadians to escape from Tehran ○ *The Far Side* debuts

TEACH THE CHILDREN

Different people enter history at different points on the timeline.

As of this writing, I am happily involved with a woman who is roughly the same age that I am, and I can only assume that this relationship will last for the rest of my life. Good. It's been a year of strangeness, thanks to the pandemic, and it's been great to spend the year getting healthier (mind and body) in the company of someone who both wants that for me and has a sense of how to make it happen. But relationships haven't always been my history. For much of my forties, I tended to date younger women (yes, I was tempted to say "I tend to only get with young jawns," but alas). Very nice people, all, but given that so much of my life revolves around cultural references and touchstones, that could be a big gap to close. What it meant was that I ended up trying to close the gap with lots of playlists and movie recommendations, strategically displayed magazines and come-again moments. *You never heard of "Ashley's Roachclip"? Well, it was sampled by P.M. Dawn in . . . You never heard of P.M. Dawn?* My intent was sincere, but the women weren't always interested. Some didn't want to be in the student position, and when I sensed their resistance, it made me feel overly pushy, or overly picky, or overly pretentious. Some of that still happens now, because I'm a pop-culture and especially a music obsessive, but it's easier when you're dating someone who has more or less the same cultural touchstones. You can work in shorthand. I don't even have to say "P.M. Dawn." I can just put my left hand up to my chin and flick it outward, and she knows immediately: "Set Adrift on Memory Bliss" video, 1991, 1:19 mark. Okay, maybe she doesn't know that it's at the 1:19 mark, but you get my adrift.

All of this is to say that even though I was still in single digits when Steely Dan's "Hey Nineteen" came out, I'm right there with it. In the song, the narrator condescendingly tries to explain pop culture to his younger girlfriend. The key lyric in the song, of course, is "Hey Nineteen, that's 'Retha Franklin / She don't remember the Queen of Soul." I say the narrator, because I don't think of him either as Donald Fagen, who's singing, or Walter Becker, who co-wrote the song. Steely Dan does much too much character work for that. It's possible that something like this happened to them or to one of their friends, but it feels more like an invented dialogue.

I've been through the cycle with this song. At first, it made me laugh—at Hey Nineteen herself. Then I passed through a period where the song seemed like one of those stories that someone tells at a party that can't possibly be true. We're only talking about 1980, not 2280. Most nineteen-year-olds would have known 'Retha, though maybe not why knowing her mattered.

Then, when I got into the Narrator Zone myself, I rethought the entire thing. Let's assume that Hey Nineteen genuinely doesn't know who her older boyfriend is talking about. Why should she? We inhabit history in fits and starts. At a certain age, we sponge up everything around us. Then we process. Then we sift and sort. Then we re-present what remains so that it can be sponged up by a younger generation. That's an extremely rough account of the process. I only mean that we don't relate to all the segments of our culture the same way as we grow. There were years in my life where I didn't read the news part of the newspaper. It's not a source of shame: it's a function of being a self-absorbed teen, or a young man in his twenties trying to break into the record business. There are times now where I don't know every new music act, though I try. And whatever Hey Nineteen doesn't know, there's sure to be just as much coming back in the other direction that's in the narrator's blind spot. The Pretenders? Kurtis Blow? Jah Wobble? Prince's *Dirty Mind*?

• • •

Not only does "Hey Nineteen" have an internal target, it has an external one. Or at least that's how Aretha responded when she first heard the song. The rumor I have heard, from more than one source, was that she was angry to get the name-check, to the point where she even considered suing.

Her sister Carolyn didn't understand why. A discussion ensued. I wasn't there, but I assume that Carolyn tried to calm Aretha by explaining that there was nothing insulting about the mention, that the narrator—or at the very least, the song—was giving Aretha her due as a cultural icon. Aretha probably came right back by explaining that she had always made her living as a pop star, which meant that even though she was in part a conservator of the soul and vocal traditions, she was much more a commercial artist who tried to adapt to the newest trends. Why else would she have bounced from producer to producer, from Curtis Mayfield to Van McCoy to Luther Vandross to Narada Michael Walden? To be fair, not all of them had happened yet at the time of "Hey Nineteen," but Aretha stayed with each producer for an average of an album and a half or so, and if she wasn't getting the hits she wanted—and in the late 1970s and early '80s, she wasn't—she moved on. To Aretha, it would have been all well and good for the boyfriend in the song to hold her up as an example of authorized taste and talent, but if she wasn't reaching the younger girlfriend, she wasn't achieving her goals. Even worse: the boyfriend was propping himself up with Hey Nineteen, and what he insisted was his superiority to her, precisely because he was worried about fading away, so why shouldn't Aretha have that same concern?

I can't guarantee that this was the exact dialogue, but I feel I've gotten close. Carolyn eventually talked her out of legal action.

This episode of Franklin Sisters Theater illuminates an important principle in cultural history and history in general. They always say that history is written by the winners. Maybe. But who is history read by? If the winners write it up and the next generation simply dismisses the historical record—or, as in "Hey Nineteen," a historical record—that official version is in danger of being swept out. You can insist on a canon all you want, whether it's in pop music or film or milestones in military actions or political campaigns, but if you fail to pass it along, it'll be history, and not in a good way.

There can be more serious consequences. There's a movie, *How Stella Got Her Groove Back*. Do you know it? Angela Bassett, Jamaica, generation gap, Taye Diggs, Whoopi Goldberg deathbed scene. Stella, the forty-year-old woman played by Angela Bassett, is on vacation when she meets Taye Diggs's character, whose name I forget. Hold on. (Trivia-I-just-learned alert: it's Winston Shakespeare!) She worries that she can't be with W. Shakespeare, not just because she's old enough to be his mother (which she says constantly) but because he has an entirely different cultural context. When she's with her friends, she can talk about Marvin Gaye, and *Soul Train*, and the Skate, but not with Winston, who gets called "Mr. Jailbait Hip-Hopper."

There's also a novel, and like most books that are turned into movies, it has things that didn't exactly make it to the screen. In one, Stella is talking to her friend Vanessa, who is fed up with the urban violence she's witnessing. "Motherfuckers still dying left and right," Vanessa says. "I'm about tired of working in ER really. All these gangbangers killing each other. This shit is getting old. I can't take much more of it. I'm serious."

Stella's answer is a master class in the importance of history. "Well," she says,

> lots of their stupid-ass parents are baby boomers like the majority of adult Americans, which means they should've been hip to Malcolm and Martin and they should've had sense enough to teach their kids—especially their sons—what's up, and if they had, these kids probably wouldn't be out there blowing each other's brains out,

> stabbing each other like death is a joke, like they're going to get a chance to do this again, and if they like made an audiotape of *The Autobiography of Malcolm X* required listening—since they won't read anything—in say third grade maybe these kids would know that the war is outside not inside, don't you think?

This points to the necessity of moving history along in ways that are not condescending or boring, the necessity of demanding a certain level of awareness from younger people but also knowing how to respond with creativity and sensitivity when they do not immediately demonstrate that awareness, the importance of teaching their kids what's up. It's worth quoting from "Young, Gifted and Black," the title song of Aretha's 1972 album but originally recorded by Nina Simone (next-door neighbors with Malcolm X's family in the mid-'60s in Mount Vernon, New York), who wrote music to match lyrics by the composer and playwright Weldon Irvine. The song is all about teaching uplift to the younger generation, about spotlighting their gifts and using the knowledge of potential to push through the moments when they "feel really low."

What Irvine/Simone/'Retha are talking about is a larger educational imperative that applies whether you're an annoying older boyfriend speaking to a tolerant younger girlfriend or a baby boomer parent speaking to a gangbanger kid. In fact, it's larger than just an educational imperative. It's a historical one. Facts matter, but fortitude matters more. Information matters, but assurance matters more. Cultural references matter, but confidence and self-respect matter more.

Incidentally, Steely Dan did get sued for their *Gaucho* album, though not by Aretha. The jazz pianist Keith Jarrett felt that the title track plagiarized his song "Long as You Know You're Living Yours," and Donald Fagen not only conceded that he had been influenced by Jarrett but awarded him a co-writing credit to avoid legal action. Maybe Aretha backed down too soon.

Ronald Reagan is sworn in as the fortieth president of the United States ○ Marvin Gaye releases *In Our Lifetime?*, his final album for Motown ○ Iran releases the fifty-two hostages that have been held for 444 days hours after Reagan's inauguration ○ Two months after taking office, Reagan is shot by John Hinckley ○ Walter Cronkite retires from the *CBS Evening News* after nineteen years ○ Toni Cade Bambara's *The Salt Eaters* wins the American Book Award ○ A rare form of pneumonia is reported in Los Angeles, the first awareness of what will become AIDS ○ Wayne Williams is arrested and charged with the Atlanta child murders ○ MTV debuts ○ Donkey Kong debuts ○ The first American test-tube baby is born

INSIDE OUTSIDE LEAVE ME ALONE

History is taken personally, to the benefit of both history and the person.

In fourth or fifth grade, a kid who sat near me brought a Police cassette to school. I heard him playing the album and instantly loved it. It had so much energy, and a cool way of using (reusing?) reggae. It was *Zenyatta Mondatta*, the one with "Voices Inside My Head."

It wasn't the first time I had heard the band, though it might have been the first time I knew that I was hearing them. Who remembers VHF and UHF? Old people—people whose single digits ended in the early '80s, say—remember. Those were the two main frequency bands of American TV tuning, pre-cable. VHF stands for Very High Frequency (anything from 30 to 300 megahertz), while UHF is Ultra High Frequency (300 megahertz to 3 gigahertz).

You don't need to know that, but you might need to know this: VHF channels, the lower-numbered ones, were stronger and less vulnerable to atmospheric fluctuations, which means that they carried the three (at the time) major networks, the one local flagship station, and public TV. UHF was everything else: the higher-numbered channels with more limited range where you could find cheaper and stranger programming: the wrestling, the soccer, the old movies, the local music shows. Every city had one. When I was growing up in Philly, one of our UHF channels was WKBS, Channel 48, which actually originated in Burlington, New Jersey, just across the Delaware River. At night the station would run musical interstitials between programming, and mostly they would use the Police and Kraftwerk. When I heard that kid's cassette, I recognized it immediately: "That's the twelve seconds from WKBS just before *Soul Train*!" That's how the Police first entered my psyche. Again, for a few years it was all vague, something I liked but couldn't quite define. And then I could, thanks to *Reggatta de Blanc*, the group's second album. It came out in 1979 but I'm putting it in 1981. You'll see why.

In the summer of 1981, I shot a movie. Maybe that's a little grandiose. I went to a performing arts school, and the director visited our class and selected a few students to star in a movie he was making called *West Side Store* about a group of kids trying to open up a neighborhood bodega. Getting picked felt like a big deal, though I knew in the back of my mind that it wasn't a movie-movie, not like *Raiders of the Lost Ark* or *Stripes*, which were dominating theaters that summer.

Still, I had to be on set, and that meant that the production guy would pick me up each morning and drive me to the neighborhood north of Old City where we were filming. (Now, through the magic of gentrification, that neighborhood has been rechristened "Northern Liberties," but back then it was just regular Northeast Philly.) The driver had two cassettes in his car, Squeeze's *Argybargy* and the Police's *Reggatta de Blanc*. I heard them over and over again, the whole albums (the stereo had autoreverse—if you're under the age of me, that means that it would run to the end of the cassette and then play the other side). I was okay with the hits, but I was more drawn to the way the record balanced them with non-hits. This is a broad historical idea, so remember it: often, the most interesting things are not the things that everyone knows (that might be obvious), but you have to understand them in their original context, tucked between those things that everyone knows, serving as counterweights and commentary.

Side two of *Reggatta* is all about alternation. It starts with a Sting-written hit ("Walking on the Moon") and then moves to "On Any Other Day," a snotty Stewart Copeland–written tale of despair complete with self-critical studio chatter that could be on the Time's "Grace" ("The other ones are complete bullshit. You want something corny? You got it." [The song also contains some attitudes toward the sexual orientation of the narrator's son that wouldn't fly today. My once-perfect perception of that album now has a that-didn't-age-well asterisk.]). Then there's another Sting composition, "The Bed's Too Big Without You," and then another Copeland, "Contact."

Then, before Sting ends the record with the punky "No Time This Time," we get Copeland's "Does Everyone Stare." The first few million times I heard it, in the car on the way to the set, I liked the song for the strange harmonies and structure, the way it starts off as a demo and then blossoms into a fully fleshed-out song. Later, when I (re)joined Columbia House—or maybe I should just say some record or tape club where I may or may not have fulfilled the membership requirements—and bought all the Police records, I really dug into the lyrics, and found . . . myself? No song had ever expressed the insecurities I had about myself more accurately. It's a song about social anxiety. The man in the song starts out shaky ("I change my clothes ten times before I take you on a date") and only gets worse. The guy in the song is in a cold sweat, but not like James Brown. He's got the heebie-jeebies, but not like Louis Armstrong. Copeland also gets off one of the great pre-*Hamilton* shot lyrics ("My shots will always miss, I know / My shots will always miss"). Drummers know what he's talking about. As a ten-year-old, I responded more to the social anxiety in the lyrics than the romantic anxiety. The movie didn't make it better. I was excited to be asked, but it also separated me from the pack, and back then being separated from the pack only made people stare more.

There's one more musical footnote to "Does Everyone Stare" that has ensured that it's followed me around my whole life. Sting has made a glorious career out of harmonizing the wrong notes with himself. It's done so brashly, with such a Pee-Wee Herman–style I-meant-to-do-that defiance that it's actually how I craft my notes now for the rest of the Roots whenever we cover a

Police song on *The Tonight Show*. I hand out the parts like Sting did, and immediately I'm reminded that there must be a secret thread for the band that doesn't have me on it. I can tell that there's mad shit being talked and typed behind my back, but all I'm getting is a prolonged look from various members of the band. Does everyone stare the way they do?

• • •

That song attached itself to me at ten, and then stuck around. But it's about something that's bigger than me. It's about how it attached itself and then stuck around. It's about the process of assembling a personal history. How do you deal with the fact that you're at the center of some things, and not at the center of other things, and that both can feel like uncomfortable options if you're not comfortable in your own skin? That question means one thing when you're young, and your own skin feels like a new thing. But what about as you get old, and you've worn it awhile, and you start to think more about where it came from, and what happened to the skins that preceded it?

In the fall of 2017, I appeared on *Finding Your Roots*, a PBS show hosted by the historian, writer, filmmaker, and academic Henry Louis Gates, Jr. Each episode consisted of Gates sitting down with a celebrity and leading him or her through a book of genealogical history. The episodes that were most interesting to me were the ones featuring Black Americans, whose pasts were often more difficult to chart as a result of slavery, poverty, and other historical injuries. There's a great early episode with Samuel L. Jackson, Condoleezza Rice, and Ruth Simmons. That episode, and every one like it, made me think of an old interview with Nina Simone that I saw in the documentary *What Happened, Miss Simone?*, where she talked about how Black people in America were, in one important respect, deprived of something that Africans had, and that was a sense of their own past. In the movie, the interview about the unrecognized beauty of Black identity phased into a performance of "Ain't Got No," from *Hair*, which I hadn't thought of in that way before, and afterward couldn't think of in any other way. Taking a piece of the American

Tribal Love-Rock Musical and turning it into the deepest well in the meadow. That's art strong enough to bend the arc of history away from injustice, at least.

In the fourth season of the Gates show, I was invited on as a guest. I had some sense of what I might find—tracing my father's family back through parents and stepparents, following the path out of Philadelphia back into the Deep South. But I couldn't have anticipated the big reveal. On the show, I discovered that my ancestors, particularly a young man named Charlie Lewis, had arrived in Mobile, Alabama, in 1860 on the *Clotilda*, the last slave ship known to have come to the United States. Charlie Lewis and another hundred-plus human beings had been loaded like cargo onto the ship in Ouidah, in present-day Benin, and brought over to the Land of the Free. This was the first time anyone was able to locate a single specific ancestor aboard the *Clotilda* (which was itself discovered about a year after the show, amazingly).

I can relate the history dispassionately. That's something to practice. It's important. If you let all your emotions in all the time when you're giving historical accounts, you may find yourself too often overcome by sorrow, rage, and wonder. But during the show, and after it, it hit me hard. In 1860, the international slave trade had been banned for more than a half-century, which didn't stop slavers from making the trip. But the *Clotilda* passengers both suffered from and benefitted from timing. They came right on the cusp of the Civil War, and five years later, after slavery was abolished not only by virtue of the Emancipation Proclamation but because of the Union's victory in the war, the *Clotilda*'s (middle) passengers decided that going back to West Africa was untenable and instead established a settlement, Africatown, in northern Mobile. Given how difficult African-American genealogy can be—for starters, many records of slave ownership list people only by their first names—I was amazed to get such a clean line to my past. My past? I was born in 1971, as I've said, many years after the *Clotilda* docked. And yet, without that docking, without Charlie Lewis, eventually no me. It's a mind-bender, and many people feel a version of it, not only every Black person, but every immigrant, every adopted person, every curious person, everyone?

• • •

The *Clotilda* episode, and the story behind it, is so complex that someone should write a book about it. Oh, look, someone has. *Dreams of Africa in Alabama: The Slave Ship Clotilda and the Story of the Last Africans Brought to America*, by Sylviane A. Diouf. The book was published back in 2009, before I discovered my connection with the story. I plead guilty: I become more interested in a subject when I know that I am somehow connected. That's not a huge source of guilt, but it does get me thinking about the way that personal investment distorts history. Events, even the largest and most consequential ones, can feel like closed boxes until we find our way in. And certainly this is true of smaller closed boxes, like the cassette case around *Reggatta de Blanc*. And that's why I decided to put "Does Everyone Stare" not in 1979, the year it came out, but in 1981, the year it came out to me.

At the same time that it's worth being honest about the importance of personalizing history, it's vital not to limit ourselves to personal points of entry. As I've said, I was interested in the African-American episodes of *Finding Your Roots* even before my episode came around, because those stories seemed relevantly similar, but I was also interested in stories that were completely different: Larry David and Bernie Sanders discovering they were related.

Understanding history begins with learning history, and learning history begins with being able to see both inside yourself and outside yourself. Back in 1981, I saw mostly inside myself, which I think I can forgive, since I was just moving out of single digits. Things mattered to me only when they mattered to me, and that wasn't a tautology so much as a survival strategy.

The ten-year-old me wasn't the only one who practiced that strategy. Recently, I watched the Radha Blank movie *The Forty-Year-Old Version*. Blank is a former up-and-coming playwright who, after years of feeling like she had stopped up-and-coming, made an amazing movie about being a woman passing out of youth, an artist passing out of the deadly Zone of Early Promise, a playwright who had fallen into skepticism about the form and was tentatively exploring a move into another form (hip-hop, in fact). In the movie, she writes a play about Harlem and gentrification, and it centers on a corner store.

The play-within-the-movie is held up as an example of what can happen when people compromise their art and themselves too much, when they take things personally in the wrong ways and don't personally engage in the right ways. The movie reminded me of many things (early, down-to-earth hip-hop, early Spike Lee), but one thing that I didn't expect it to remind me of was *West Side Store*. I don't know if the movie was ever finished (I think it was), or if it was preserved, or whether it exists anywhere in the present. If it does, it's valuable, because it relates a history of a time and a place, of a business and the community around it. That movie mattered to me at the time because I was in it, but if that's the guiding principle, history should matter to all of us at all times, because we're all in it.

1982

Argentina invades the Falkland Islands ○ Seven people in the Chicago area die after ingesting cyanide-laced Tylenol capsules ○ An Air Florida plane crashes into the Fourteenth Street Bridge in Washington, D.C., minutes after takeoff ○ Bryant Gumbel becomes the first Black network news anchor when he joins the *Today* show ○ Reverend Benjamin Chavis and his North Carolina congregation block a toxic waste site in one of the first nationally visible campaigns against environmental racism ○ AT&T agrees to be broken into more than twenty regional companies ○ Winter is especially harsh in the northeastern U.S., from January's "Cold Sunday" to a record-breaking April blizzard ○ *E.T.: The Extra-Terrestrial* is released ○ EPCOT Center opens

HISTORY BY THE NUMBERS

Just because everyone sees the same things doesn't mean that everyone sees things the same.

For the most part, in this book, there are rules. Chapters can speak to other chapters, but chapter titles don't respond to (or object to) the titles before or after them. A song discussed at length in a year was released in that year, for the most part. A playlist that follows an essay generally flows out of the ideas set forth in that essay. And the chronologies that head up each year aren't generally in dialogue with the chapters that follow.

This last one has exceptions. We're in the middle of one now. The chronology for 1982 sets forth some of the major events of that year: the breakup of AT&T, the Tylenol murders in Chicago, the opening of the EPCOT Center. But I purposefully left something off the list. On Tuesday, November 30, an earthshaking, culture-changing piece of artwork was released to the public. No, I'm not talking about *Gandhi*, the three-hour biopic of the Indian leader and peace activist Mahatma Gandhi, which premiered that Tuesday at a theater in New Delhi and would go on to win eight Oscars. No, the work of art I'm talking about was only forty-two minutes long, and it premiered all over the world at the same time. I'm talking about *Thriller*.

When major records came out in the 1970s, as I have explained, I was there, but I was very much under the influence of older people, parents, guardians, the lady in my father's band who played *Songs in the Key of Life* in the wrong order, forever scarring me. But *Thriller* was the '80s. I was older. And because I was older, I was present in a different way. I was there. My finger was on the pulse of the culture as that record quickened it, as it climbed the chart rapidly, reached the top, stayed there through the release of seven Top Ten singles, and permanently changed the face of pop music, music videos, and even Michael Jackson.

Being there for history means that you can claim it as your own. But should you? When history intersects with your own experience, when your own experience can start to bend history to its will, how should you respond?

The short answer? I don't know. I can report that even after the huge commercial success of *Off the Wall* in 1979, Michael Jackson grew frustrated that his music was not receiving the critical acclaim he thought it deserved. *Off the Wall* was nominated for only two Grammys, and won only one: best Male R&B Vocal Performance for "Don't Stop 'Til You Get Enough." Jackson was certain that it had deserved Record of the Year, though it wasn't even nominated, and he then set out to make an album that could not be denied. Pairing again with Quincy Jones, who had produced *Off the Wall*, Jackson went to Westlake Studios in West Hollywood. The first song recorded, on April 14, 1982, was "The Girl Is Mine," a duet with Paul McCartney. But just recording those facts seems . . . insufficient. How do you summarize a moment that large?

Maybe there are facts from even earlier. Jackson had been a performer since he was a child, when he and his brothers formed a singing group/soul band in Gary, Indiana. The Jackson family band won a talent show in 1966 with dual vocalists: eleven-year-old Jermaine performed "My Girl," supposedly, and eight-year-old Michael performed Robert Parker's "Barefootin'."

Nope. No better.

• • •

After singing his duet with McCartney, Michael kept singing, too, and writing songs—well, he didn't actually write them down, but sang them into a recorder and then practiced against those tapes until he had the songs committed to memory. By the fall of 1982, enough songs for the new record had been recorded, but neither Jackson nor Jones was happy with the results. It didn't sound like the dominant cultural juggernaut, the chart-seeking missile, that Jackson had imagined. He and Jones ducked their heads and remixed every song. The album was finally completed on November 8, three weeks before it appeared in stores.

Jackson and Jones may have been happy with the record, finally, but histories of the recording process suggest that they weren't necessarily happy with each other. During the months of work, the two of them got along less and less well. For starters, Quincy thought that Michael was spending too much time off on his own, practicing dance moves. Who cared about choreography? An album is not a visual medium!

But Jackson was looking at the bigger picture. That's one way to build yourself into history. Because Jackson was determined to conquer the music world, he knew that the music world wasn't only about the songs on the record anymore. It was also about the videos on TV, and specifically the videos on MTV, the channel that had debuted in August 1981. Michael had released video clips for *Off the Wall*, but they were performance videos, mostly straightforward. "Don't Stop 'Til You Get Enough" had trippy backgrounds, and at one point a triplicated Michael. "She's Out of My Life" had a split-screen that showed Michael from two angles at once. "Rock with You" was the sharpest, because of the clothes (super-sparkly!) and the lights (green lasers!). But all three of those songs had predated MTV.

For the first video of his new album, in light of the advances in the medium, Jackson wanted to go in a new direction, not just performance but narrative. He pursued Steve Barron, an Irish director not yet out of his twenties. The song was the lead single, "Billie Jean," which was a personal favorite of Jackson's, a smooth funk song about an obsessed fan and a paternity claim.

Barron wasn't sure at first if he could take the assignment, though the title of his memoir, *Egg n Chips & Billie Jean*, gives it away. I'm going to quote from it a bit, because when you're revisiting a period of history that you experienced, it's a good idea to give up ground to other primary sources.

> By this stage, I had done 15–20 music videos, including the one that was number one in the UK at the time: The Human League's "Don't You Want Me." Michael Jackson's name wasn't on everyone's lips. Remember that this is a few months before *Thriller* came out. There was, of course, a magic in Michael Jackson ringing you up, but in a way I was more excited about Human League. My wife was really pregnant with my first child at the time and my initial reaction was, "Oh, I don't think I'm going to be able to do that." It wasn't a case of, "we've got to do that." It was my wife who persuaded me.

At the time, MTV faced criticism for being an exclusively white channel. Historically speaking—and why not!—this isn't quite true. It's not true that there were no Black faces on the network, of course. J. J. Jackson, one of the original VJs, was Black. The Specials, the two-tone band from England that combined ska and New Wave, had a Black percussionist, Neville Staple, and a black guitarist, Lynval Golding. Both were in the video for "Rat Race," which had aired on MTV from the very start. And there were even some popular artists on the channel before Jackson even made "Billie Jean." Prince is probably the most prominent: his video for "1999," a performance clip directed by Bruce Gowers (who had also directed Jackson's "Rock with You"), was in reasonably heavy rotation by December 1982. At that time, Prince was an up-and-coming star with plenty of commercial power. But he wasn't Michael Jackson. MTV, overall, was white enough that it started drawing fire from white artists who had always respected Black music and integrated it into their work. The most famous was David Bowie, who confronted the channel in 1983 about its playlist, its responsibilities, and the larger questions of cultural segregation. (A video of that conversation started to circulate again on social media in January 2021, after I had finished this book but in time for me to add this immensely fascinating parenthetical.)

The "Billie Jean" video debuted in March 1983, partly as a result of bullying by CBS Records' president, Walter Yetnikoff, who threatened to pull all the label's artists from MTV unless they put Jackson in heavy rotation. It was an instant sensation and a significant accelerant. "The Girl Is Mine," not only the first song recorded for *Thriller* but the first one released as a single, had come out the previous fall, roughly a month before the album, and done quite well: number one on the R&B chart, number two on the pop chart. But "Billie Jean" was a monster, a big deal when it was released in January and even bigger once the video appeared. It went right to number one, Jackson's fastest-selling single since 1970, and was beaten for bestselling single of the year, by a hair, by the Police's "Every Breath You Take."

The video was so successful that Jackson's following videos had bigger names and bigger budgets. Barron's budget for "Billie Jean" was $50,000, twice what he had ever had for any other artist. Six weeks later, "Beat It," directed by Bob Giraldi, got a budget of $300,000, and by the end of 1983 it had been joined by "Thriller," a $2 million mini-movie directed by John Landis.

I have watched the "Billie Jean" video approximately one billion, four hundred and nine million, seven hundred and twelve thousand, three hundred and forty-six times. I may have counted wrong, but not by much. And to be honest, I'm still not sure exactly what it's about. There's a cloth, a detective, a hobo, some clothes that change color, a woman, an urban landscape, and lots of stuff that glows. I guess it's surrealism, unless it's not. Is it a metaphor for stardom? Is it a profoundly humanistic argument about how we are all connected? Is it an advertisement for pressure-sensitive light-up sidewalks? For that matter, what about the song? Like many of Jackson's songs, it's deeply misogynistic—nearly every female character he sings about is somehow betraying him, leaving him, deceiving him, double-dealing, backstabbing. This sense of victimization, which starts with Billie Jean and Dirty Diana and others, will grow and grow until it's the entire planet that's victimizing him. That'll take a little while.

But whatever the song was about, it was about sales. *Thriller* sold like hotcakes, and then like whatever's much hotter than hotcakes. "Billie Jean" and the videos that followed weren't *Thriller*'s only fuel. They weren't even the biggest booster to sales. (Is that a mixed metaphor? It takes a rocket scientist to know.) For that, look to *Motown 25: Yesterday, Today, Forever*, in May 1983. That event can't be underestimated, so let's not. It was an expansive, two-hour-plus television special celebrating the silver anniversary of one of America's most important pop-music labels (and cultural institutions in general), a Black-owned and Black-operated company that appealed to listeners of all races. But really, that two hours plus was about four minutes, specifically the four minutes when Jackson premiered the moonwalk. The audience of about thirty-five million was changed in an instant. Was it the Beatles on Ed Sullivan, or at least its generation's version? Hard to say, but what's easy to say is that it kicked *Thriller*'s sales into the stratosphere. Post-moonwalk, the record started selling about a million copies a week. And then, as a cherry on the sundae that needed no cherry, there was the Grammy Awards ceremony in February 1984, where *Thriller* took home eight awards, including Album of the Year and the Record of the Year (for "Beat It") that he thought he had been denied the last time out. Best R&B Performance, Male, the award he thought was faint praise to the point of insult back when "Don't Stop 'Til You Get Enough" won it, went to "Billie Jean."

● ● ●

Thirty million copies sold in 1983. Many millions more the next year. Seven singles. Eight Grammys. A $50,000 budget. A $300,000 budget. And 1,409,712,346 viewings of the "Billie Jean" video. Any sketch of *Thriller* reads like an explosion at a calculator warehouse. Even though the album is great, undeniably so, when people talk about it they mostly just talk about the numbers. Its commercial domination was so striking that it came to eclipse everything else about it.

It also kicked off a new period in cultural history. Its outsized sales ushered in an era when many artists, buoyed by videos and a suddenly emboldened record industry, promptly went out and released records that delivered a string of Top Ten singles on their way to topping twenty million album sales. They followed right on Michael's moonwalking heels: Lionel Richie's *Can't Slow Down* in 1983; Bruce Springsteen's *Born in the USA*, Madonna's *Like a Virgin*, and Prince's *Purple Rain* in 1984; Dire Straits's *Brothers in Arms*, Phil Collins's *No Jacket Required*, and Whitney Houston's *Whitney Houston* in 1985. Sales of that magnitude had happened only occasionally before (AC/DC's *Back in Black*, Fleetwood Mac's *Rumours*, or the slow-and-steady-wins-the-twenty-million-sales *Dark Side of the Moon*).

As much as it pains me to write such a statistical analysis of an album I love as much as any other—and that I've taught in class as a musical masterpiece—*Thriller* seems to demand it. Its main quality is its quantity. I've been thinking about it often over the last few years, when the United States has had a leader whose principal concern at (too many) times seemed to be numbers, about crowd size and ratings, about stock market indexes and personal wealth. Those kinds of numbers seem silly and superficial, fake medals pinned on a fake general (and by himself, no less). But it would be equally foolish to turn away from numbers entirely. We live in such a large, complex world that drawing conclusions without them seems blinkered. I've been thinking about that often over the last few months, when we've needed to collect data, to look at it, and to understand it before we're able to make any smart choices about what to do next. This has happened medically and electorally. If we didn't have statistics, we would descend into anecdote—which is, of course, what has been happening when people won't or can't accept overwhelming numbers, a quantity of quantities. This isn't directly related to *Thriller*, but it's worth keeping in mind as we struggle with the fact that its statistical achievement sometimes seems to overwhelm its creative achievement.

There is sometimes a bloodlessness to numbers, but there can also be a blood.

• • •

How to reckon with the sales, with the popularity? How to make sense of it, and if not exactly keep it in perspective, at least explore the relationship between celebrities and their fans? Michael had moments of what I guess you'd call inquiry. Take the video for "Say Say Say," a duet with McCartney that was recorded about a year before "The Girl Is Mine" but released only on McCartney's *Pipes of Peace* album, which came out in October 1983, near the end of *Thriller*'s string of singles. Clearly, "Say Say Say" was meant to capitalize on *Thriller*'s momentum, which of course it did, giving Jackson his seventh Top Ten single of the year, breaking the previous record of six (held by both Elvis Presley and the band that McCartney was in before Wings).

The track itself is a sprightly, slightly bruised song that's not as good as anything on *Thriller* (don't @ me), even though it was a commercial monster, remaining at number one for six weeks, the longest of any of Michael's singles. But the video—directed by Bob Giraldi, of "Beat It" fame—supplies a plot. In a Western town, a woman with a megaphone convenes a crowd. A salesman, played by McCartney, comes out and promises that the "Mac and Jack" wonder potion will give you the strength of a raging bull. Michael, looking slight and weak, volunteers to try it. (The crowd clearly doesn't know that he's the "Jack" in the product's name). He does, and he's able to best a big Black guy at arm-wrestling. They sell out their entire wagon's worth of the potion. But it turns out the big guy was in on it! So was the megaphone lady (that's Linda McCartney). Ill-gotten gains for everyone! Then they shave and put on clown makeup and Michael ogles a girl in a saloon.

But forget about the shaving and the clown makeup. I'm sorry I mentioned them. At its heart, "Say Say Say" is a video about sales. (See the 1:15 mark, where McCartney cracks a smile as he counts the money he's taken from all those poor suckers.) It's also, maybe, a commentary on it. Are those gullible

American pioneers the people who, after watching this video, are more likely to go out and buy the single or one of the two albums they think it comes from, despite the fact that it's a confection at best?

It's about sales in other ways, too, larger and more historical ways. While the two were recording the song back in 1982, Michael stayed at the McCartney home. One night, McCartney disappeared into another room and came back with a . . . gun! Just kidding: he came back with something more powerful—a book that listed all the songs he owned the publishing rights to, both his own and those of other artists. Michael was immediately fascinated. He began to pepper Paul with questions, finally declaring that one day he would buy the Beatles catalog. Paul laughed. Michael last-laughed, buying it in 1985. (The same thing happened, writ smaller, during the filming of the video. Paul and Linda were staying at a California place called Sycamore Valley Ranch. Michael liked the ranch, and said he would buy it, too. This time, Paul probably didn't laugh. Goodbye, Sycamore Valley Ranch. Hello, Neverland Ranch.)

A few years after Jackson's death in 2009, McCartney remembered that there were "Say Say Say" vocal tracks of both him and Michael singing the entire song. He had producers craft a version that flipped the ticket, politically speaking, giving each singer the vocals originally sung by the other. Jackson opens the song, and McCartney follows. McCartney also released a new video where the stars are not Mac and Jack but rather some young dancers showing off a wide range of jookin/buckin moves. It's not a major song, any more than the original, but it's a nice historical gesture, both a compliment and a complement, a story retold that gives new meaning to the story first told.

1983

The United States invades Grenada ○ President Ronald Reagan proposes the Strategic Defense Initiative (SDI), nicknamed "Star Wars" by its critics ○ Alice Walker's *The Color Purple* wins the Pulitzer Prize for fiction ○ Vanessa Williams becomes the first Black Miss America ○ The Brink's-Mat Robbery results in the theft of more than $38 million in gold, diamonds, and cash from a warehouse near Heathrow Airport in London ○ The Internet begins, in some form, when ARPANET is migrated to TCP/IP ○ Guion Bluford becomes the first African-American in space ○ The Australian Dick Smith completes his solo circumnavigation of the globe by helicopter ○ Klaus Barnie, the "Butcher of Lyon," is arrested in Bolivia and charged with war crimes ○ The final episode of *M*A*S*H* airs ○ *Annie* closes on Broadway after six years and nearly 2,400 performances

WHY DOES EVERYBODY HAVE A BOMB?

How do we think about the end of the story when we're still in the middle of it?

Once upon a time, there was a man named Herman Poole Blount. Born in Birmingham, Alabama, Blount, nicknamed "Sonny," grew up as a shy child with a great musical talent and an interest in absorbing as much intellectual history as possible. He spent many afternoons at the lodge of the Prince Hall Freemasons, where the large library afforded him the opportunity to read about everything from religion to magic (he had been named, in fact, after the famous Black magician Black Herman) to ancient civilizations.

After a stint as a bandleader—his group, the Sonny Blount Orchestra, toured around the Southeast—Blount attended the Alabama Agricultural and Mechanical University on a scholarship, left after a year, rededicated himself to music, refused induction into the army, was briefly jailed, and made his way to Chicago, where he became active in the city's jazz-and-blues scene. Somewhere along the way (accounts vary, even Blount's own accounts), he experienced a conversion. Conversion? Maybe better to say recognition, or realization. He came to see that he was not and perhaps had never been ordinary Sonny Blount, but that he was and perhaps had always been Le Sony'r Ra, an alien come from the planet Saturn to preach peace to Earthlings. He soon shortened his name to Sun Ra and started releasing records with his band, which he was now calling the Arkestra.

I mention Sun Ra not only because he's one of the most interesting thinkers in Black music history, a pioneer of Afrofuturism who would affect, directly or indirectly, everyone from George Clinton to Earth, Wind & Fire to Outkast to Janelle Monae, but because when I was a kid he was a regular presence in Philadelphia. The Arkestra had moved there by then, to a house in Germantown where they would live off and on for a decade, and Sun Ra appeared often on WXPN, the radio station of the University of Pennsylvania.

He also kept releasing music at a heroic clip: studio dates, live sets, official bootlegs. It's a messy discography, since Sun Ra worked with multiple labels, often because his work could not find a soft place to land. In 1982, he cut an album called *Nuclear War* for Columbia. The label rejected it, and he subsequently put it out in Italy on the UK label Y Records, and then resurfaced the title song again the next year on the *Fireside Chat with Lucifer* LP.

Sun Ra apparently thought the title song of that record, "Nuclear War," could be a hit, and though I'm not sure what chart he was thinking of (astrological?), I can also hear why he thought so. The song ambles along, not exactly aimless but confidently casual, picking up a little steam, then blowing off that steam. It's a groove song, with Sun Ra on electric piano joined by Samarai Celestial on drums (his real name was Eric Walker, but when you're dealing with the Arkestra, there's always the chance of getting renamed in the deepest reaches of outer space). For a long stretch, it's just the two of them playing, and a repeated chant that both grew out of the kind of communal jazz he had been practicing since the 1950s and anticipated the hip-hop that was starting to emerge.

> Nuclear war (yeaaaaah)
> They're talking about nuclear war (yeaaaaah)
> It's a motherfucker, don't you know

I've seen it described as X-rated, but is it as X-rated as the destruction of the world with weapons that have no regard for human life? In this, it echoes/predicts the argument of Marvin Gaye's "The World Is Rated X," recorded in the early '70s but not released in any form until 1986. Gaye's song, which argues that sex cannot be as profane as death, would reemerge in the twenty-first century on various expanded Gaye reissues, so I won't get back to it until then. But I will get back to it.

● ● ●

"Nuclear War" has many cousins. One of them requires reaching back to Charles Mingus's "Oh Lord, Don't Let Them Drop That Atomic Bomb on Me," recorded back in 1961, around the time of the Cuban Missile Crisis. That song, a drowsy, almost drunken blues, was remade years later by the genius mash-up mind of the late visionary (and my pal) Hal Willner, who put it in the hands of a band that was kind of the Rolling Stones: Keith Richards on guitar and vocals, Charlie Watts on drums, and sidemen like Bobby Keys, Chuck Leavell, and Bernard Fowler. But that was in 1992, after the fall of the Berlin Wall. Back in 1983, Sun Ra and the Arkestra were living in a world with Cold War tensions heating up all around them. Lots of artists were worrying about the Big Flash, and the wreckage it would leave in its wake.

Think about a song as superficially trivial as the Gap Band's "You Dropped a Bomb on Me." Or one as strident as Time Zone's "World Destruction." Time Zone was a band concept headed up by the rap and electronic music pioneer Afrika Bambaataa. For each release, Bambaataa assembled different personnel; for "World Destruction," he worked with John Lydon, formerly the front man of the Sex Pistols, then of Public Image Ltd. Backed by musicians that included Bill Laswell on bass and Bernie Worrell on keyboards, Bambaataa and Lydon open with a chant, "Speak about destruction." The song has nuclear annihilation high on its mind ("We are Time Zone. We've come to drop a bomb on you. / World destruction, kaboom, kaboom, kaboom!"), but Time Zone wants to track the specific process by which it might arrive. Lydon sneers about the rich getting richer while the poor get poorer, while Bambaataa has worked it out in greater detail with a verse about Nostradamus, the Antichrist, the "Democratic-Communist Relationship," and various intelligence agencies and media delivery systems.

All of these songs, though, sit in the shadow of the most popular and most important song about impending annihilation. To get there, let's go back to 1981, to Prince's fourth album, *Controversy*. I didn't buy it right away. I was only ten, my parents were Born Again by that point, and there was a song on the album called "Jack U Off." But I heard about the record, and I eventually heard it, and while it was plenty filthy, like its predecessor, *Dirty Mind*, it was also consumed with current events. The cover image invented a newspaper, the *Controversy Daily*, and showed a series of headlines dealing with religion and gun control. A song like "Annie Christian" dealt with blaming the Antichrist for both the death of John Lennon and the attempted assassination of Ronald Reagan. And "Ronnie, Talk to Russia" had even bigger issues on its mind—it's Prince's plea to the president to set his pride aside and deal with Russia and the threat of nuclear war ("Ronnie, talk to Russia, before it's too late / Before they blow up the world").

The anxiety of "Ronnie, Talk to Russia" carried into Prince's next album, and specifically into its title track. On *1999*, the title song extended the idea. Still nervous about political extremism, rampant faithlessness, and philosophical limits, Prince worried that the world was hurtling toward its demise. But when would that occur? The date he picked was a ways off, at that point, the dawn of the new century: "Two thousand zero zero, party over, oops, out of time," he said. So what was the remedy? "Tonight we're going to party like it's nineteen ninety-nine." Leaving aside the total brilliance in the phrasing of those three *n*'s, syllables tumbling down like dominoes, he's recommending the same thing he had recommended in earlier songs like "Party Up," which advised people to whoop it up rather than go to war. Here, the idea is to dance to keep from crying, specifically in the face of apocalypse.

There's a historical phrase: dancing on the edge of a volcano. Research by my research team, researching, suggests that it comes from a letter by the Austrian composer Alban Berg in 1933, worrying about Berlin as it began a flirtation with fascism he knew it wouldn't be able to control.

> The whole town and all its inhabitants are quite drowned in carnival din, masks and confetti. And on top of that the news of the Reichstag fire. Dancing on a volcano.

Later on, other historians evolved the phrase, adding the idea of the edge, and the idea of "dancing on the edge of the volcano" came to be associated with societies on the brink of political upheaval or coming darkness. The principles seem similar on their faces, but they're actually opposite. The edge-of-the-volcano camp worries that the crowd is entertaining itself without any sense of what's beneath their feet, what's about to blow. They proceed in blissful ignorance, speeding their own demise. The oops-out-of-time camp knows that people are aware of what's going to happen, because they've just been told. They're partying despite that crushing knowledge.

This is a bright line, really, between two ways of thinking about history, and specifically the history that's happening all around you. Should you shut your eyes to the most painful parts? Should you narrow your gaze only to what concerns you and those close to you? Or should you open your eyes wide, take it all in, and then seek out pleasure, comfort, and joy despite what you have just taken in? Should you decide that things don't matter or should you practice mind over matter? Prince counsels the latter, and then some:

> War is all around us, my mind says prepare to fight
> So if I gotta die I'm gonna listen to my body tonight

Again, the lyrics have a nearly perfect feel, with a parallelism that's as good as the trio of tumbling *n*'s in the chorus. If I gotta die, I'm gonna listen.

History may be inevitable, but within that inevitability there are still clear choices that can be made.

Reagan wasn't listening to Prince records—I feel safe making that assumption. After "Ronnie, Talk to Russia," even after "1999," he continued to characterize the Russians as enemies, and to hold up nuclear might as part of the equation. In August 1984, before a national radio address, Reagan was joking with the engineers in the booth. The microphone was on, though, and his comments were famously recorded: "My fellow Americans, I'm pleased to announce that I have signed legislation that will outlaw Russia forever. We begin bombing in five minutes."

Later that year, a single called "Five Minutes" sampled the speech as its only lyrics; the group, Bonzo Goes to Washington, was in fact Jerry Harrison from Talking Heads and the famous James Brown and P-Funk bassist Bootsy Collins. That was not the end of Reagan and talking heads. The following year saw the debut of Max Headroom, a satirical media personality who was considered the first computer-generated character (though he was portrayed by an actor, Matt Frewer, in makeup). Headroom was everywhere in media in the mid-'80s: on TV, in ads, in music—the Art of Noise sampled his voice, complete with its trademark glitch-stammer, for a remix of their 1986 single "Paranoimia." He was also appropriated by the cartoonist Garry Trudeau for his popular political strip *Doonesbury*. Trudeau mashed Headroom together with Reagan to create "Ron Headrest," a virtual version of the president intended as a commentary on Reagan's superficial sloganeering and manipulation of the media.

• • •

In the time it has taken to detour through Bambaataa, the Gap Band, Prince, Berg, and Reagan, Sun Ra and his Arkestra have kept on with "Nuclear War," and the song is still playing, insistent, almost a mantra. Their persistence defeats the horror. Nuclear annihilation happens in a flash. A bright light creases the sky and then there is no more. What better way to prove that's not happening than to groove on through a jazz-funk landscape, casually tossing off profanities as a way of protecting and preserving the sacred fact of the world's existence? Ease on down that road.

In November 1983, ABC aired *The Day After*, a prime-time program that dramatized the events of nuclear war. It was meant to treat the event with minimal melodrama and maximum realism, and ABC handled it more like a news event than a TV movie: printing viewers' guides that were like miniature curriculums, opening up a hotline to handle questions during the movie, and airing a panel discussion afterward that featured, among others, Carl Sagan, Henry Kissinger, and William F. Buckley. The movie reached more than 100 million viewers and scared the hell out of at least one child. I remember catching a piece of it and, before I could fully process what I was seeing, wondering if we had really gone to war. I'm not ashamed to say that I switched over to *The Jeffersons* for a second, which was an episode where George worries that he hasn't done everything on his bucket list (special guest: Rosey Grier). If I gotta think about Armageddon I'm gonna also see a sitcom tonight.

Even without *The Day After*, nuclear war was on the minds of lots of kids. A year before the movie, the same month that *Thriller* came out, Samantha Smith, a ten-year-old in Manchester, Maine, wrote a letter to the Soviet leader Yuri Andropov.

> Dear Mr. Andropov,
>
> My name is Samantha Smith. I am 10 years old. Congratulations on your new job. I have been worrying about Russia and the United States getting into a nuclear war. Are you going to vote to have a war or not? If you aren't please tell me how you are going to help to not have a war. This question you do not have to answer, but I would like it if you would. Why do you want to conquer the world or at least our country? God made the world for us to share and take care of. Not to fight over or have one group of people own it all. Please lets do what he wanted and have everybody be happy too.
>
> Samantha Smith

It's an impressive letter, in the sense that it isn't afraid to ask the hard questions. It also isn't afraid to ask the naive ones. The letter was published in *Pravda*, but when Smith didn't receive an answer from the Soviet government, she wrote a follow-up. That one got a response from Andropov himself. It's too long to reprint in full, so I'll summarize. Andropov reminisced about when the United States and the Soviet Union teamed up to defeat the Nazis. He shared her concern about nuclear proliferation and expressed a desire to disarm. It ended on a personal note.

> We want peace—there is something that we are occupied with: growing wheat, building and inventing, writing books and flying into space. We want peace for ourselves and for all peoples of the planet. For our children and for you, Samantha.
>
> I invite you, if your parents will let you, to come to our country, the best time being this summer. You will find out about our country, meet with your contemporaries, visit an international children's camp—Artek—on the sea. And see for yourself: in the Soviet Union, everyone is for peace and friendship among peoples.
>
> Thank you for your letter. I wish you all the best in your young life.

Smith immediately became a media celebrity. Ted Koppel interviewed her. She went on Johnny Carson. Andropov's letter came in April, and by July, Smith and her parents were in Moscow for a two-week trip. She got along well with the Russian people, though Andropov was unable to meet with her as a result of declining health that would end his life early in 1984. Smith's return to the United States was controversial: Some hailed her as an ambassador of peace while others felt that she and her parents had been useful idiots for Soviet propaganda. Smith became a tween news star, a political correspondent for the 1984 election, and then a television actress. On August 25, 1985, she and her father were flying from Boston back to Maine when their plane crashed, killing everyone aboard. Conspiracy theories, of course, were everywhere, though the official investigation determined that the cause was a combination of pilot error and ground radar failure.

Ronald Reagan wrote a letter to Smith's mother offering his deepest condolences.

Unit Measurements

"Nuclear War" runs out to seven minutes or more. It's not the longest song in this book, by any means. There are three or four longer ones on James Brown's *The Payback* alone. But how short can a song go before it's a sketch? It's like thinking about units of history. What is the smallest moment that can truly count as history? How long did it take for the *Titanic* to go down? How long did it take for Little Boy to fall? Can history happen in a minute? A second? These short songs help me think about stories and how quickly they can be told.

"JAMES JOINT"
Rihanna

Anti, 2009 [Roc Nation], 1:12

When I first heard this, I was sure that the James of the title was James Poyser, one of the Roots, and I was all bent out of shape. How could he have worked on it without me? Turned out not to be him. I'll hold that story until later. But the song stuck with me. It's a masterpiece at a short length. Rihanna packed a whole narrative into two minutes or less. It's not easy to do. For me, the king of that kind of thing is Prince's "Sister," which fits an entire movie's worth of plot into a minute and a half.

"SO MUCH 2 SAY"
Take 6

So Much 2 Say, 1990 [Reprise], 1:09

This track stopped me dead. It's a rapid-fire exercise, like the Animaniacs were humanized. The whole song is about how there's not time to go through it all ("So much to say / So little time"), so it's an exercise in itself. Can you play that again?

"SIDEWAYS"
Rufus

Rags to Rufus, 1974 [ABC], 1:45

Right in the middle of the record is this song. And when you start you're already right in the middle of the song. The groove is going. As it goes, as you walk through it or are walked through it, it becomes clear that you're the food delivery guy bringing food to their rehearsal space. I imagine it as Chinese food. I don't know if pizza culture was a thing yet.

“WORKIN’ ON IT”
Dwele

Sketches of a Man, 2008 [Koch], 1:18

Of all the tribute songs that came after Dilla’s death, all of mine were overdramatic. All the interludes that I put on records based on Dilla songs were airy but ominous, like there was an angel coming down. This track is a cleverer clever way to pay tribute to him without doing karaoke.

“ONOMATOPOEIA”
Todd Rundgren

Hermit of Mink Hollow, 1978 [Bearsville], 1:39

Black people covered Rundgren’s songs. Sometimes when I heard him, I thought that I was hearing a Black artist. I knew I was hearing a Philly artist. His song “Breathless” was on local TV as an interstitial. I got back to him later, when J*DaVey and the Sa-Ra guys put me up to revisiting his work.

“HAVE YOU EVER BEEN (TO ELECTRIC LADYLAND)?”
Jimi Hendrix

Electric Ladyland, 1968 [Reprise], 2:11

We’ve just been through the soundscape of “. . . And the Gods Made Love,” and then we’re at the title track, which is there and gone quickly, but perfectly. It doesn’t require a second verse.

“MAKE ME HOT”
Little Brother

The Listening, 2003 [ABB], 1:37

This was part of their demo before they made an album. It’s Phonte singing, comically, about an encounter in a club, cracking on 9th Wonder, leaning into his Percy Miracles alter ego.

“HEY GIRL (INTERLUDE)—STUDIO OUTTAKE”
Earth, Wind & Fire

The Eternal Dance, 1992 [Columbia], 0:37

When I heard this on the EWF box set, I fell so in love with it that I begged for the master tapes. They sent me the whole song, and it turned out to be boring. When songs aren’t popping off the ground Maurice White has the insight to break them down to their barest bottom. In this case, either he or someone at Columbia was smart enough to spot a perfect thirty seconds in a jam session.

1984

Indira Gandhi is assassinated in New Delhi ○ Ron ald Reagan is elected to a second term, defeat ing Walter Mondale in one of the most one-side elections in modern history ○ Michael Jackson i burned badly during the filming of a Pepsi com mercial ○ The Soviet Union boycotts the Summe Olympics in Los Angeles, where the America Carl Lewis wins four gold medals to equal the achievement of Jesse Owens in Berlin in 1936 ○ The Black physicist and inventor George Edwar Alcorn, Jr., wins the NASA–Goddard Space Fligh Center Inventor of the Year award for his X-ray spectrometer ○ Bernhard Goetz shoots four Black teenagers during a robbery attempt on the New York City subway ○ W. Wilson Goode becomes the first Black mayor of Philadelphia ○ Russell Sim- mons forms Def Jam Records ○ *The Cosby Show*

FILE UNDER

History can be studied intentionally or experienced accidentally.

Though some people have passed into history, they remain here with us. I will return again here to Richard Nichols. Though he's gone, I think about him all the time, and one of the things I think about when I think about him is the time he hung up on me.

I should rephrase that. It didn't happen just once. It happened repeatedly, and over the years I came to see that the hang-ups could be divided into separate categories. There were the hang-ups when another call was coming in on another line and he didn't have the time to warn me that he needed to take it. Click. There were the hang-ups when he made a great joke and wanted to let it hang in the air. Click. And then there were the hang-ups when he was irritated, where he felt that I wasn't quite getting what he was saying, or what he had said. The hang-up I am thinking about belongs to that final category. I don't remember all the specifics, but on the day before he had read something: maybe some lyrics Tariq had written, maybe an article in a magazine. Whatever it was, it had put a bee in his bonnet, and he had sent me an email in which he said something like "I'm picking up a strong scent of Gaetano Mosca." I sent him an email back that said "What???" And then the phone rang. I picked up.

"What what?" he said. I explained that I had gotten his email, and had no idea who his email meant and, as a result, had nothing to say in return. There was a long pause. Finally he spoke. "Do you have the Internet?" he said.

"Yes," I said. "Why . . ."

But he had already hung up.

What he meant, I'm assuming, was that it was ridiculous for me to ask him what he meant by saying "I'm picking up a strong scent of Gaetano Mosca," when I could, with the Internet I had just admitted I had, look up Mosca and learn that he was an Italian philosopher of the late nineteenth and early twentieth century who wrote about the way that all societies are controlled by a political class.

Learning about Mosca was mildly interesting. Then, a few years later, I was reading about the surge, in the mid-'90s, of Mafia-themed names and lyrics in hip-hop. It's a long list, and parts of it may surface later, when we end up talking about the history of hip-hop, and especially the way it moved from an art form that described ordinary life to one that prized conspicuous consumption. At the time, I was working through my thoughts on the matter, but mostly I was making a list: Kool G Rap, of course, Junior M.A.F.I.A., Capone-N-Noreaga, "Wu-Gambinos," Nas's Escobar phase, etc.

Somewhere in my research, I ran across a mention of a lecture given in Milan in 1900, "What Is Mafia," and then a summary. It was supposedly one of the first attempts to make sense of the Mafia as an organized set of principles, no pun intended—it talked about the way that local relationships built a broader power base and the importance of the Mafia's code of silence, which kept it out of the reach of traditional law enforcement. At the bottom of the summary, in italics, was the name of the man who had given the lecture: *Gaetano Mosca.*

The name had stuck in my head, and the second time stuck to the first time. If Rich hadn't hung up on me years before, I probably would have gone right by the italics, ignored them as part of the noise, just two words at the end of a million other words. But instead of filtering them out, I fished them out, like I was Gerald White or Harold Foster (see 1976).

• • •

Back in 1983 and 1984, I did only a few things regularly. I went to school. I played music. And I went to my uncle Preston's house and watched TV with my cousin Marky and three of his neighborhood friends. I should clarify: It wasn't TV—it was MTV. Everyone was doing it, all of a sudden, all the time. Who knows why those kinds of media shifts occur, beyond simple availability and novelty? I was ten, eleven, twelve. I didn't have an elaborate explanation worked out. Now I see it had to do with cable and the exhaustion of programming ideas in the networks, but I'm not a media historian exactly. I have in my stack of articles a piece on how BBC Radio experienced an upsurge during the UK General Strike of 1926, when people couldn't get news from the newspapers and had to turn to other sources. Just joking. I don't have a stack of articles. It's digital. Media shifted.

So there we were, watching MTV. I should clarify again: I wasn't just watching—I was watching and waiting for Michael Jackson's latest video.

Depending on when exactly we're talking about, the video I was waiting for varied. At first, of course, it was "Billie Jean," but then it was "Beat It," or "Thriller" or "Say Say Say" or even "We Are the World." Watching and waiting meant exactly that, though. While I waited, I watched, and that meant that I saw lots of white rock and pop acts before I saw Michael Jackson: Eurythmics' "Sweet Dreams (Are Made of This)," Culture Club's "Do You Really Want to Hurt Me?," Journey's "Separate Ways," Bonnie Tyler's "Total Eclipse of the Heart."

One sticks in my mind. It opened with a shot of a room furnished with only a couch and a chair. Then an older man appeared sitting in the chair. Then a younger man appeared lying down on the couch. Back then on MTV, it usually took about five seconds for the name of the artist and the song to appear in the lower left of the screen. Before that could happen, one of the other guys in the room—the room I was in, not the one in the video—yelled out "Hyperactive!" I was annoyed. I was the one who collected music, who made it a point to know as much as I could. How could they know the video when I didn't? Maybe they were wrong.

When the credit appeared in the corner of the screen, I saw the name of the song—they weren't wrong—and the artist, Thomas Dolby. Now I was doubly (no pun intended) annoyed. I knew of Dolby. I had been a big fan of his 1982 hit "She Blinded Me with Science." I liked it because it was in E minor (see 1979) and also because Dolby had done something Prince also did, which was to design a song with a surprising structure. It had two choruses! I went around the room and asked the rest of them if they knew "She Blinded Me with Science." They weren't sure. One guy said he did, but the way he said it seemed like maybe he was lying.

I calmed down and watched. The video was sort of a sequel to the "Blinded Me with Science" video, with Dolby still cast as a bespectacled nerd who had problems controlling his id. But it was even wackier. It had puppets. It had lots of cubes. At one point, Dolby even played the trombone with his nose! We finished watching the video. We went roller-skating. We caught an episode of *Soul Train* with the Pointer Sisters and Bobby Nunn.

• • •

Back when I saw the video, *hyperactive* was a catchall term for kids who wouldn't sit down when the teacher said to, who seemed to have a hard time listening in class, who broadcast their thoughts at unexpected times. It's the portrait that Dolby paints of himself in the song's lyrics. "Tell me about your childhood," says the therapist (the older man in the chair), and Dolby responds with a story of how he was connected to a machine to control his impulses and then kicked out of school because he "had the funk."

Since then, society has changed the way it addresses this type of thing. There's not as much chucking out of school. There are more diagnoses and more medications, and much more sophisticated thinking around what is considered neurotypical. But plenty of people still suffer from the most common version of the phenomenon: an overactive mind. If that's what Dolby meant, I plead guilty. There's so much more to keep track of, more people, more places, more faces, more connections to make, more mistaken connections to break, both in the life I'm living and in the material I'm learning, whether it's musical or historical or other. Some nights I try to sleep and find my head swimming with names and dates. It's like a playlist that's in no particular order. And it's all encircled by the knowledge that the next day, I have to get up and do it all over again, take in a million more names, places, faces, both from what's around me now and from everything that came before. Those days add up. They add up to history.

Lots of people have lots of (different) advice: 4-7-8 breathing, Piko Piko breathing, standing up out of bed and balancing on one leg, meditation (that last one works). The one suggestion that I haven't seen in enough places is the one I got years ago, at the tail end of the Gaetano Mosca incident.

As helpful as Rich's hang-up had been in motivating me to look up Mosca's name, what was even more helpful was something that somebody else said when I was telling them the story: "You opened a file."

I laughed, and then I stopped laughing. It was exactly the right way to put it. When you're sorting through the chaos of the world, of your own life, of current events, of history (cultural, political, whatever), your main aim is to separate things that matter (or might matter) from things that do not (or probably do not). To that end, you need a guiding principle and a survival strategy. That principle is the file, and the strategy is opening it. When you open a file for a name, for a concept, for a country, then you have a place to put the things you're learning. Not being able to relax and truly see "Hyperactive!" until I had context in the form of "She Blinded Me with Science" was an early illustration of the principle, and I must have done it a million times over the years, but I couldn't understand it fully until I had a name for it.

I didn't think about the "Hyperactive!" video for probably thirty-five years, but I started thinking about it again when I started writing this book and encountered it in a list of videos that ran on MTV at the same time as "Billie Jean." Or maybe it's more accurate to say that I reopened the file.

Two notes have been added to that file during the time I have been writing the book. I learned that Dolby shared vocals with Adele Bertei, whose name rang a bell—I tracked it down, and it turns out that she served as a backup vocalist for Tears for Fears on their "Sowing the Seeds of Love" tour (see 1989). And then the other day I happened to stumble across an interview that Dolby gave in 2011. It included a surprising fact about "Hyperactive!":

> I wrote it for Michael Jackson because I met with him right about the time that I was doing the video for "She Blinded Me with Science" and he was down the hall doing the video for "Billie Jean." He was already a superstar, but this was before *Thriller* took off and went multi-platinum and so on. We became friendly and we talked a lot about grooves and about new techniques, and we were both started by hip-hop and things like that. He told me that, yeah, he was putting new material together, if I had anything to suggest to put his way, then to make him a demo. So, in fact, on the plane back from L.A. to London I put on my headphones and I came up with this groove and bass line for "Hyperactive!" and a melody, which I did send to him. And he said in the end it wasn't appropriate for the new album that he was doing. So that didn't work out. But by that time I was in love with the song so I did it myself.

I couldn't believe it. While I was waiting for a Michael Jackson video, I was watching a Michael Jackson demo! That quote went right into the front of the file, which was full enough that it seemed like it might make for a short chapter. Which it has.

1985

USA for Africa records "We Are the World" ○ Live Aid, a pair of concerts in Philadelphia and London, raises money for famine relief in Ethiopia ○ Mikhail Gorbachev replaces Konstantin Chernenko as leader of the Soviet Union ○ Dian Fossey is murdered in Rwanda ○ Coca-Cola introduces New Coke ○ Nintendo releases the NES ○ George H. W. Bush is acting president for eight hours while Ronald Reagan undergoes colon surgery ○ Gwendolyn Brooks becomes the first Black Poet Laureate of the United States ○ WrestleMania debuts ○ *Calvin and Hobbes* debuts ○ The University of Indiana basketball coach Bobby Knight throws a chair onto the court during a game against Purdue ○ Philadelphia's African American mayor, Wilson Goode, orders the Philadelphia police to bomb the headquarters of the local Black nationalist organization MOVE—eleven people are killed and 250 left homeless

LONG FOR YESTERDAY

How do we handle the past when it resurfaces?

By the mid-1980s, Prince had been with me for a while. I remember buying Prince cassettes and listening to them secretly in my headphones when I was supposed to be hearing instructional drum records. My born-again parents weren't on board with his flamboyant persona or his explicit lyrics. He was a dividing line between us, and I was thrilled to be on my side. This was an issue, especially, after the release of *1999* in October 1982 (it was the same month that John DeLorean was indicted for drug trafficking—*Back to the Future* callback, though the movie came out in 1985, which happens to be the year I'm writing about—double callback!). I had to buy it four times, each time overcoming a parental discarding of the album. If you throw out my record, I'll buy another one. Don't you ever learn? (They were probably thinking the same thing at me: If you buy another one, we'll just throw it out. Don't you ever learn? History is built on the backs of those kinds of cycles.)

The album after that was *Purple Rain*, and at that point even my parents couldn't deny him. He was on the radio, on television, in the movie theater, on magazine covers, atop the charts, and yes, even in our house. He went out on tour, and ended up at the Orange Bowl in Miami, which was temporarily dubbed the "Purple Bowl." At the conclusion of the concert, after a twenty-minute version of "Purple Rain," he made an announcement: "I'm going away for a while. I'm going to look for the ladder."

We didn't know what it meant, but it sounded ominous. There was no social media back then to circulate wacky fan theories ("He actually needs a ladder—he's not a tall person, and he needs to change a lightbulb"), so we worried that he was retiring, or devoting himself to some obscure religious order. What he was really doing was previewing. He reappeared two weeks later with his next album, *Around the World in a Day*.

From the cover art, it looked like a different world. *Purple Rain* had been dark, a mostly black-and-purple photograph of Prince on his motorcycle, and then a column of yellow light (smoke at the bottom, Apollonia at the top), the whole scene pillarboxed with floral wallpaper. *Around the World in a Day* was a painting. Prince had conceived of it himself and written up a list of elements that needed to be in the image, including one old woman (crying), one clown (juggling), and, of course, a ladder. As the painting took shape, more elements were added, including doves, an airplane, a patriotic baby, and portraits of Prince and the band.

When I bought the album on April 22, 1985, that album cover was all I had to go on. Most of the time, Prince's albums were preceded by singles. The song "1999" came out in September 1982, about a month before the album *1999*. "When Doves Cry" was released in May 1984, about a month before *Purple Rain*. But *Around the World in a Day* spun backwards in that respect. The first single, "Raspberry Beret," wouldn't come out until May. And Prince hadn't debuted any material from the new record on tour, either. So between the record store and the record player—actually, the cassette department of the record store and my trusty Walkman—I studied the cover. It was mysterious and trippy. But where the trip was taking us was no mystery at all: the 1960s.

At the time, I hadn't yet immersed myself in the music of the '60s. Or maybe it's more accurate to say that I hadn't immersed myself in the rock music of the '60s. I knew plenty about '60s soul, from Aretha to Sam Cooke to Motown to Stax. I knew the towering hits of James Brown. But when it came to rock, my grasp on history was weaker, especially when it came to the bands from across the pond. A handful of Beatles and Stones songs, a few by the Who, maybe one Kinks komposition. But I wouldn't have known the difference between a Zombie and an Animal, a Yardbird and a Hollie, a Small Face and an Easybeat.

But I knew what the '60s felt like, at least according to the memory of the '80s, and this was it: bright colors, altered consciousness, unexpected sonic flourishes, the desire to both emphasize and question higher forces like god and country, and lots of love. And when I put the album on, there it was. It was there in the title track, which had finger cymbals and an Eastern feel that echoed the Indian music that George Harrison had brought into the Beatles ("Within You Without You" must have been one of the songs I had heard). It was there in "Paisley Park," an idealized portrait of a magical locale ("love is the color this place imparts"). And "Raspberry Beret" had plenty of easygoing sunniness, plus an overall message of free love over soul-killing work. If it's warm, you don't have to wear much more than that beret. Let it all hang out.

So the sound of the record was new, for Prince, and new to me. But what if the new thing you encounter is in fact an old thing? On the one hand, this phenomenon seems related to the idea of sampling I sketched out earlier. When you hear a piece of music from the past, even if it's buried in another piece of music, follow it back to its source. But this was different. Prince wasn't simply sampling *Magical Mystery Tour*. He was absorbing it into his ongoing project, speeding forward while looking in his rearview mirror.

Part of the reason it was difficult to hear the record as a straightforward Beatles homage was because Prince denied it. In an interview he gave to *Rolling Stone* about the record, he insisted it had more to do with his own image.

> The influence wasn't the Beatles. They were great for what they did, but I don't know how that would hang today. The cover art came about because I thought people were tired of looking at me. Who wants another picture of him? I would only want so many pictures of my woman, then I would want the real thing.

He said that he didn't mind the album being called psychedelic, since it was "the only period in recent history that delivered songs and colors," although the band he mentioned by name was Led Zeppelin. But the heart of this answer is at the start: the Beatles "were great for what they did," though it's not clear "how that would hang today." Other artists surfaced '60s-style sounds as shorthand, as a way of importing certain aspects of that decade—peace and love, heightened consciousness—into their own work. Again, there are elements of that on *Around the World in a Day*, especially "Paisley Park" ("Admission is easy / Just say you believe / And come to this place in your heart."). But Prince had a harder edge, an approach that was more rivalrous than reverent. After *1999*, when he went out on the road to tour, he frequently crossed paths with white rock groups, and when he heard their material and saw the crowds they were drawing, it put a bee in his bonnet. *Purple Rain* was written, in part, with that bee stinging him, which is why a song like "Let's Go Crazy" has more than a whiff of a song like the J. Geils Band's "Freeze-Frame." If Prince was competitive with the people around him, he was equally competitive with artists down through history. And he thought the situation was asymmetrical: he could master the music that other artists had created, but they could never do "Kiss."

As a result of all of this—knowing in what spirit Prince had incorporated other sounds before this, reading his interview—I read the record less as homage and more as anything-you-can-do-I-can-do-better, with an implicit question attached at the end of that: Now that I have done better (or at the very least as well), will you bestow upon me the same credit that you gave to those other, whiter bands?

I also read it less as an homage, because it became less of one as it went on, both in sound and in theme. These days, when I think about the album, my mind pushes through those initial scene-setters to the third song, the moody and masterful ballad "Condition of the Heart," which reaches much further back—it has a silent-movie feel that predicts his next film, *Under the Cherry Moon*, and even name-checks Clara Bow. That's where the record starts, temperamentally and thematically. (It's because of records like this that on my own records I don't consider the album started until the third song. Anything before that is previews. But of course it would have been too risky to open a record with a slow song. I once spoke at length to Jimmy Jam about his years producing the S.O.S. Band, and how an album like *On the Rise* opened with the slow-burning "Tell Me If You Still Care." I have a real curiosity about, and admiration for, any artist that dares open up a record with a song like that.) The rest of *Around the World in a Day* isn't in debt to the Beatles or anyone else. It's Prince paying it forward. "Pop Life" bounces along so genially that you might not notice that it's taking on materialism, dropouts, and drugs. "America" starts, stops, and then tears through a critical portrait of the country in the '80s, guitar blazing. And the last two songs, "Temptation" and "The Ladder," set up the tension between sex and spirit that would obsess Prince for the remainder of the decade. It's true, too, that the second side of *Around the World in a Day*, once the album's past the scorching, minimalist "Tambourine," is fairly conservative for such a rebellious artist. The older Prince, later, would become more that way, but he was there all along, in "Controversy" (from *Controversy*), "Free," (from 1999), and the generally knowing tameness of *Purple Rain* ("Darling Nikki" be damned). Still, side two of *Around the World in a Day* was an accurate predictor. As sexual as he was, he also had a conservative point of view—which if you look at history is a part of the right (and the Right) narrative. Behind every politician on the Right is a tree that, if shaken, has forbidden fruit falling.

When the "Raspberry Beret" video came out, it complicated the issue, or maybe resolved it. On the one hand, it showed a new style (both in his fashion and in the style of the piece) that seemed to point to a flower-power uniform: cloud jacket, boots, and a shirt that looked like something from the Young Rascals. But the video also used a different version of the song, an edit of the extended remix, and it represented a pretty overt code-switch away from '60s signifiers.

No matter what I thought about the record, it gave me plenty to think about. Creatively, Prince was evolving. In fact, one of the clearest signs that he was on the move again was the other artists who stepped into his spot. Take a record like "Oh Sheila," by Ready for the World, a Flint, Michigan, band that sounded so much like the earlier Prince that many people assumed it was him, and the people who knew it wasn't him dismissed it outright. I was too young to take the full get-the-fuck-out-of-here position regarding the song. If I was seventeen I would have thrown it away. What was up with this kind of fake English? You gotta be fourteen to fall for that shit. But I was. Later, I realized that Ready for the World was doing more than just imitating Prince. They were responding to the way that history was changing. In the early '80s, Prince had created the Time to shore up the Black side of his audience. That band had played a central role in *Purple Rain* as the Revolution's foil, and scored a monster hit with "Jungle Love." But then they broke up. Morris Day went solo. Jesse Johnson went solo. With no Time left, the balance was thrown off. Ready for the World would not have had a chance if the Time was still healthy. The world turns. History churns.

Around the World in a Day stuck with Prince in some unexpected ways. "Paisley Park" was not only a track on the record, but the name of the label he set up as a Warner Bros. imprint, not to mention his recording complex and home in Chanhassen, Minnesota. The label lasted until 1993, allowing Prince to work with some of his inspirations (George Clinton, Mavis Staples) and to break some young artists (Tony LeMans, the Philly-based Good Question), though he mostly used it to release his own records and those of offshoot acts. Even after the label shuttered, Prince continued to use Paisley Park Studios. As he aged, his relationship to the past changed somewhat. He became less insistent on competition and more open to tribute. On *Emancipation,* the triple album he recorded after breaking free of Warner Bros., he covered a pair of soul anthems, "La La Means I Love You," originally recorded by the Delfonics in 1968, and "Betcha by Golly Wow," recorded by the Stylistics in 1971. (Eh. They're too clean. I don't like my Prince with so much sheen.) He wrote a love letter to the music of others on "Musicology" in 2001, which name-checked everyone from Earth, Wind & Fire to James Brown to Sly Stone. After insisting that history take note of him, he was comfortable enough to take note of history. And then, sadly—at Paisley Park, almost exactly thirty-one years after the release of *Around the World in a Day*—history took him.

• • •

Passing into history. It's a strange idea. You move from existence to . . . to what? The afterlife? Nonexistence? The memory of others? Or are you only a collection of the traces and artifacts that you have left behind? When Prince died, a number of people I knew set out to memorialize him, in a number of ways. Some recorded covers of his songs. Some worked with his estate to manage the release of previously unheard material. Some of them wrote articles about him.

All of those projects included some degree of research, some reconstruction of the facts of Prince's life. And as a result, all of those projects had to contend with the difficulty of retrieving and organizing the past. Prince himself insisted on mystery, sometimes clouding the facts around his birth, or his rise to fame, or the question of who did what on his albums.

Locating and verifying facts about the past isn't easy. Those facts can be slippery. I know this from my own writing, and from the writing of the people I know. It happens all the time: a writer will get his or her hands around a fact, and then, a certain amount of time later, realize that the fact was wrong. Maybe that wasn't the original title of that song. Maybe that tour didn't stop in that city. Maybe a name was incorrect, or a date. Each time this happened—to them, to me—it was painful. No historian (academic, popular, cultural, whatever) wants to get the past wrong. But if you spend any significant amount of time in the past, you realize that it never passes into the present in an unproblematic way. Error is, to some degree, inevitable, and much of history—meaning the recording and transmitting of history—is about how error is handled when it's discovered. Do you admit it immediately? Dig in stubbornly? Explore the process that brought you to the error and try to understand it better? Ask others to understand it better? Maybe there's no wrong answer.

1986

The space shuttle *Challenger* breaks up just over a minute after launch, killing the entire crew, which includes Christa McAuliffe, an English teacher from Concord, New Hampshire ○ Chernobyl explodes ○ Martin Luther King, Jr., Day is observed for the first time as a federal holiday ○ Mike Tyson becomes heavyweight champion, defeating Trevor Berbick ○ Halley's Comet passes close by Earth, the first time since 1910 and the last until 2061 ○ Hands Across America, which links 6.5 million people in a human chain to fight hunger and homelessness, stretches from New York to Los Angeles ○ Len Bias dies of a cocaine overdose two days after being selected as the second pick overall in the NBA draft by the Boston Celtics ○ Oprah Winfrey becomes the first African-American woman to host a national TV show ○ The Statue of Liberty celebrates its centennial ○ Spike Lee's debut feature, *She's Gotta Have It,* releases, kicking off a new wave of Black films

AND YOU DON'T STOP

A historical picture's worth a thousand historical words.

For years, there was only one music cover I had to worry about: *Rolling Stone.* From the time I was young, I paid attention to *Rolling Stone* covers, because I figured they were a timeline of what was important in the music world. I remember Labelle in silver spacewear on the cover in 1975, Muhammad Ali with his head on his hands in 1978, a shirtless (and very hairy) Robin Williams in 1979. There's Steve Martin in front of a giant painting in 1982, Michael Jackson in red and white stripes in 1983, Prince (with Vanity) later that same year (shot by Richard Avedon—see 1973), Eddie Murphy dressed like an old-time movie detective in 1984 (Avedon again), David Letterman in a *Late Night* baseball jersey in 1985.

Taken all together, those '80s covers are like a museum. It's a magazine about records, but culturally it was the magazine of record. When you made the cover of *Rolling Stone*, you were doing more than taking your place on a newsstand. You were taking your place in history's newsstand.

That's why December 1986 was such an important month. The covers that year had mostly amplified stories they had already covered, stars they had already made. There was a Stevie Wonder portrait, Prince with Wendy and Lisa, maybe more than one Michael J. Fox cover. And then the December 4 issue arrived on newsstands, with a first—the editors had decided to put a hip-hop act on the front of the magazine. It was Run-D.M.C., an obvious choice after their huge crossover duet with Aerosmith on "Walk This Way" earlier that year. Taken by the Israeli-born photographer Moshe Brakha, who worked mostly in Los Angeles (that's where the story is set, during a West Coast trip by the group), it's a triple portrait in totem-pole style, Run on the bottom, D.M.C. on the top, Jam Master Jay in the middle. All of them are wearing black hats and gold jewelry. It's a calm photo, no exaggerated grimaces or angry eyes, no hint of threat. Run has an especially sweet expression on his face.

What catches your eye almost as much as the photo, almost as much as the group's name in big purple letters, is the subhead: "Sets the Record Straight on Rap Music and Violence."

The article is framed around an invitation the group has received to hang out with Michael Jackson while they're in L.A. There's lots of hand-wringing on the group's part as to whether or not they fit in Michael's world, or Michael in their world, along with insults about Michael's germophobic ways (Darryl talks about ripping off Michael's surgical mask, which seemed juvenile and cruel then and has a whole different feel now, in the midst of the COVID pandemic), and casual homophobia that probably wouldn't be printed now (not about Michael—Run takes a swipe at Boy George). When I read it back then, I laughed or cringed at comments like this, felt my heart rate speed up a little bit when I read about the rivalry with Kurtis Blow, tried to hear the rhythm in the impromptu raps that were printed along the way. But I read it like a kid, and a fan.

Now, more than thirty years later, my read is quite a bit different. What's almost embarrassingly clear is what I probably sensed back then but couldn't have put into words—the whole thing was designed to introduce hip-hop to a mainstream audience. *Rolling Stone* was mindful of its place in history, the way it served as a gatekeeper, and giving Run-D.M.C. the cover admitted them into at least the lower levels of the pantheon, which also meant having to justify that decision. Here, the justification seems to be about assuring white teens and their white parents that this Black, chain-having, hat-wearing trio isn't about to jump off the cover and grab your car radio. Having established that Run-D.M.C. comes from "Hollis—a middle-class neighborhood in Queens," the article returns to that point several times. They are "hardly products of Watts or Harlem." "All three grew up in Hollis, a neighborhood of one-family homes and well-tended gardens." And then later, a nostalgic flashback to when "Little Joey"—that's Run, Joseph Simmons—"played basketball, listening to his Stevie Wonder and Barry White records, and otherwise led a genteel life."

At times, the approach would be insulting if it wasn't so strange. Run reflects on his father, who worked for the Board of Education: "'My father is a great person,' says Run, sounding like a true product of the middle class."

Maybe the 2020 me is being too hard on 1986. But I don't think so.

Partly this is because of the other main goal of the article, the one laid out on the cover—to let Run-D.M.C. "[set] the record straight on rap music and violence." The approach is to let them have their say about why they shouldn't be associated with violence, but that means associating them with violence first. "For many, Run-D.M.C.'s name is now synonymous with rioting crowds, wailing ambulances and wholesale arrests. Newspaper editorials have blamed the group's driving lyrics for drawing crowds 'bent on havoc.'" It's easy to look at it from across the years and find it ridiculous, but even then it didn't hold water. The incidents the article discusses are about gang beef, and they just happen to occur at a Run-D.M.C. show. As one (white?) cop says, the same thing would have happened even if Ronald Reagan was speaking.

The most interesting parts of the article find the group struggling with the material aspects of their success.

It was, at least in 1986, a complicated issue. Run talks often about how he doesn't care about fancy cars, but then there's a scene of them going to McDonald's in a gold Mercedes. Run doesn't wear fancy jewelry, but the other two "stud their fingers with diamond rings." There's talk of the T-shirts and hats they're selling, of sponsorship deals they're being offered, of European vacations they've taken.

The song that matters here, of course, is not "Walk This Way" but another track from *Raising Hell*, "My Adidas," a shining example of how rap stars back in the '80s celebrated what they owned. Run-D.M.C. spotlights not the price of the shoes, but the fact that they brought the group to concerts, including Live Aid, where "all the people gave and the poor got paid."

It doesn't take much scrutiny to see that this is an especially benign form of consumerism. For starters, it's not about the shoes themselves, in the main. It's about the group's experiences on the way to stardom: the audiences that came to see them, the shows they headlined. And fairly quickly, it's not about them at all—it's about Live Aid, where any arrogance about them being there (as the only hip-hop act?) gives way immediately to the result of the concert, where "the poor got paid."

Soul music was about connection and community. This is sole music. Little of that nuance is communicated in the piece, except for one moment where Run expresses his desire to open drug rehabilitation centers without taking credit ("I'm not going to call them the Run-D.M.C. House. I'll just open them").

For all the violence described or denounced, the greatest threat of the group seems to be that they are extending the dominance of Black music in America. Run says as much: "The reason why they are listening to us is because we are the Michael Jackson of now. Prince was it when *Purple Rain* came out. But we are what's going on right now. We are the music. We are what's hot."

● ● ●

Run-D.M.C. wouldn't remain at that level. The upcoming movie they discuss in the piece, *Tougher Than Leather*, made it famously to movie theaters that summer of 1988 with incident after incident of shootings reported throughout its run. If anything, the infamous Long Beach incident (the concert *Rolling Stone* focused on in the issue) started to haunt them.. Hip-hop may have been moving in that direction—N.W.A's debut came out that same year—but Run-D.M.C. couldn't. The accompanying album was more diverse and ambitious but, without the clear market focus of its predecessor, read as kind of a muddle. The group would refocus for *Down with the King* in 1993, more powerful, more menacing. The trademark Run-D.M.C. outfits were gone for the first time: instead they had bare heads and stocking caps.

I want to skip ahead and look at a picture that doesn't come packaged with a thousand words.

Art Kane was born Arthur Kanofsky in the Bronx in 1925 and grew up with an interest in the way that images represented or redefined history—first through the movies, then through photography. During World War II, Kane enlisted in the army and was assigned to a special unit that put creatively talented young men to work designing military illusions: specifically, fake tanks and trucks (made from rubber, outfitted with real radio equipment) that could be put in position in a way that would trick the Germans into thinking that Allied forces were nearby. The unit, called the Ghost Army, included future famous painters (Ellsworth Kelly), future famous designers (Bill Blass), and Kane, himself a future famous photographer.

When he got out of the army, Kane became art director at *Seventeen* magazine. And then, in 1958, on assignment for *Esquire*, he set out to create the definitive group portrait of jazz. He brought together dozens of singers and players, fifty-seven people in all, on the steps of a Harlem brownstone. Everyone came: Dizzy Gillespie, Count Basie, Thelonious Monk. Kane's photograph became the basis for an Oscar-nominated documentary in 1994, *A Great Day in Harlem*. Pictures, making history.

Forty years after Kane's photo, four years after the documentary, *XXL* magazine decided that it wanted to create a new group portrait for the hip-hop generation. It enlisted the photographer and director Gordon Parks (remember him? *Shaft*?), who had, in 1995, photographed a sequel to Kane's original where he rounded up ten of the twelve surviving musicians from the *Esquire* shoot and brought them back to the same Harlem brownstone on East 126th Street. That's where the hip-hop group portrait would happen as well. The day of the shoot, September 29, 1998, I had to rush-finish sequencing and mastering on the Roots' *Things Fall Apart*. The hip-hop artists waiting to be photographed had assembled at the Metropolitan Community Methodist Church, down the street. EPMD was there. The Wu-Tang Clan was there. Rakim was there. Fat Joe was there. Da Brat was there. E-40 was there. We were there.

But Run-D.M.C. wasn't there—at least, not all of them. D.M.C. and Jam Master Jay were in the group as we walked from the church to the brownstone, as Parks arranged us, checked the light, made sure that every face was visible. But where was Run? He showed up just in time, sprinting down the block toward us as someone imitated the electronic drums from the *Chariots of Fire* soundtrack.

The final photo, with more than 170 hip-hop artists, has become a historical document, just like the one before it. The *Esquire* image hadn't been a cover photo, but rather a spread inside the January 1959 issue (the cover was a cardboard box loaded up with musical instruments). *XXL*'s was going on the cover (a Collector's Issue, no less). One of my first calls after the shoot was to the designer, to ask how the photo, a long horizontal, would be formatted. How many folds? Would it be cropped? I was gunning for the front and not the inner fold. Back then, it still mattered.

Hip-Hop Deep Cuts

All historians have specialties. No one can be an expert on everything. But expertise works in a funny way—specific knowledge about one particular area of a field allows you to walk more confidently through the entire field. I think about that often when I consider my own training in music history, which starts with the soul music that my parents exposed me to, then passed into a period of late-'70s and early '80s rock (soft rock, yacht rock) overseen by my sister, and then moved me into the '80s pop-funk of Prince and Michael Jackson. As a result, I arrived at hip-hop with a certain kind of historical thinking already in place—from the start of the genre, I was able to see it as a historical structure, with top-line hits, middle-line also-rans, and deep cuts that would need to be excavated. Dig?

"MURDERGRAM"
LL Cool J

Mama Said Knock You Out, 1990 [Def Jam]

I loved the album before this one, *Walking with a Panther*, though I can understand why people believed that it wasn't up to his standards. When he came back, he came back hungry. For some reason, it sends me back to "You Can't Dance," from his debut album in 1985. That's my favorite corny LL joint, and maybe my favorite all-time LL joint. Sue me: I loved it when it came out. In fact, I loved it so much that it's the source of a forthcoming humblebrag. (Warning: Humblebrag approaching.) Before Chung King Studios in New York shut down—that was the studio where those early Def Jam records happened—I bought the drum machine that made this song.

"I'M LARGE"
DJ Chuck Chillout and Kool Chip

Masters of the Rhythm, 1989 [Mercury]

Any list of hip-hop deep cuts needs to include a shout-out to Salaam Remi, who produced this when he was still a teenager. Like me, Salaam was a second-generation music-business kid—his father was Van Gibbs, who had started as a musician, worked at various record labels, and produced artists like the Fat Boys and Kurtis Blow—in fact, years before Salaam produced this record, he was playing keyboards on Kurtis's *Kingdom Blow* album. If you're old enough, like me, to remember when cable was still a new concept, you'll remember *Video Jukebox*, which aired on HBO from 1981 to 1986 or so. It was a half-hour showcase of videos that was more eclectic and interesting than the standard MTV rotation. They always played this video, which was in two parts, though we never got to see part two.

“THE ‘MICSTRO’ ”
Radiänce featuring RC

“This Is a Party”/“The Micstro” 12-inch, 1980 [Ware Records]

Even though the MC RC La Rock (not to be confused with T LaRock or Scott LaRock) came from Brooklyn, this song is a Philly classic. In my opinion, it’s one of the greatest of the first wave of old school rhymes that came out between 1979 and 1982. This was before hip-hop songs were treated as pop songs. At first hip-hop was filled with these long songs, six or seven minutes at least, and as long as fifteen. There were no breaks. You had to keep the party going. Full Force then moved toward the “Hip-Pop” format with the UTFO (“Roxanne, Roxanne,” which was also the first time we heard a breakbeat sampled in hip-hop (Billy Squier’s “The Big Beat”). Compact, catchy rap songs? That was unthinkable just a few years earlier. If you look on the credits of LL Cool J’s debut album, *Radio*, back in 1985, it says that it was “reduced by Rick Rubin.” That’s on purpose, not just for his minimalist sound but for the fact that he was distilling the tradition of a sprawling endless rhyme into a series of singles. Before he reduced, there were lots of records like “The Micstro,” but few as good.

“NO OMEGA”
Eric B and Rakim

Let the Rhythm Hit ’Em, 1990 [MCA]

This is my favorite Rakim joint. This is why you know that every hip-hop head subscribes to the Rakim-as-god-MC theory. He bobs and weaves through all the verses, has little iambic pentameter moves, gets into lines and out of them with speed and elegance. “Next episode be smooth as a Persian”? It already is.

“SMALL TIME HUSTLER”
The Dismasters

And Then Some, 1989 [Sure Delight]

Here’s another hidden gem that should have made it. Shortly after “Rebel Without a Pause” by Public Enemy came out, there was a slew of records with these shrill noises. This was the second one I ever heard. When I DJed it live online, Dante Ross told me that people used to get their chains snatched to this joint in the Latin Quarter. “Small Time Hustler” has a section where the Dismasters rhyme triple-style, like they’re Migos’ fathers or something.

"MY PART OF TOWN"
Tuff Crew

Danger Zone, 1988 [Warlock]

Another Philly classic: respect to Ice Dog, L. A. Kid, Tone Love, and DJ Too Tuff. The sample in the song is by the Blackbyrds: "Street Life," from their 1980 album *Action*. When Ray Parker, Jr., was on *Questlove Supreme*, he told me that he played the guitar on that entire record. He also told me that Stevie Wonder could drive. (Though to be fair, he didn't say that Stevie could drive well. "He didn't care about hitting the cars," Ray said.)

"DO THE DO"
Kurtis Blow

Deuce, 1981 [Mercury]

Kurtis had a big hit with "The Breaks" on his first album. The follow-up didn't get as much love commercially, but it's a strong record with lots of the five-minute-plus rap songs that were the going rate in 1981 and a few shorter tracks, including this one. I want to make a plea for Universal to remaster all these records. I've heard a version straight from iTunes that sounds like it's 72-bit: so much digital distortion.

"WHIRLWIND PYRAMID"
The D.O.C.

No One Can Do It Better, 1989 [Ruthless]

Dr. Dre's most traditional hip-hop production. "Whirlwind Pyramid" was the B side to "The Formula," which was released as the third single from the album. And then after "The Formula" comes "Portrait of a Masterpiece," which also deserves a round of applause. Toward the end, the D.O.C. pulls Dre up short. "Hold on, Dre," he says. "Stop the beat. Let me catch my breath." Dre's nonplussed: "Ai-yo, man, why ya stopping? That was funky." The D.O.C. reiterates: "To catch my breath." Now Dre gets it: "All right, you got it. Kick it." When we heard that shit, we were in the lunchroom, and we couldn't believe it.

"GET PEPPED"
Skinny Boys

Skinny (They Can't Get Enough), 1988 [Jive]

Another underrated 1988 track that demonstrates the influence of Public Enemy from 1987: the shrill noises, sirens of various types. The Skinny Boys modeled themselves after the Fat Boys, especially in early beatbox songs like "Get Funky" and "Jock Box" (which was later used as the theme song of the Comedy Central series *Workaholics*).

1987

On Black Monday, world stock markets crash, including a more than 20 percent drop for the Dow Jones Industrial Average ○ Ronald Reagan acknowledges the Iran-Contra affair in a national address ○ The Simpsons debut on *The Tracey Ullman Show* ○ Michael Jackson releases *Bad* ○ James Baldwin dies ○ Reginald Lewis orchestrates the buyout of Beatrice Foods and becomes the first Black CEO of a billion-dollar corporation ○ An unknown man breaks into the signal of two Chicago stations while wearing a Max Headroom mask ○ A few months after Black Monday, a squirrel chews through a cable and temporarily closes the New York Stock Exchange ○ Aretha Franklin becomes the first woman inducted into the Rock and Roll Hall of Fame ○ Rita Dove wins the Pulitzer Prize for Poetry ○ August Wilson's play *Fences* wins both the Pulitzer Prize for drama and four Tony Awards

GREATNESS EXPECTATION

Do great figures drive history forward, or is everyone carpooling?

One of the classic versions of the Great Man theory of history comes from Thomas Carlyle, and specifically from his book *On Heroes, Hero-Worship, and the Heroic in History*. It's from 1841. I wasn't alive then, but I guess my cowriter Ben Greenman was, because he brought it to the table. Carlyle saw history as a chaotic mess given shape and direction by "heroes." His examples were people like Shakespeare and Napoleon, though we have our own, more modern examples: Einstein, Picasso, Edison, FDR, Henry Ford.

Carlyle didn't think that Great Men were the only factor in history, only that they appeared at key moments to affect it. He wanted the Greats to be used as inspiration, to show how certain choices are made and why certain decisions are consequential. Carlyle proposed six types of heroes: gods, prophets, poets, priests, philosophers, and kings. At various times, Prince was all of these. I thought about how he had mastered numerous instruments, how he could seemingly keep four or five bands supplied with material simultaneously. I knew how hard he practiced—as with Michael Jordan, the idea was that the most talented person also worked the hardest—which made the greatness simultaneously even more unattainable and more worth attempting.

For years, Prince never gave me a single reason to question his greatness, and even when the quality of his material slipped slightly, I stayed convinced. I'm thinking back to the two albums that followed *Purple Rain*, *Around the World in a Day* (see 1985) and *Parade*. Both of those records were brilliant, but they found him moving away slightly from the stripped-down, risqué funk-rock of his earlier work. There were more textures, different kinds of risks. But the best funk album of 1986 didn't come from Prince, but from a Jackson. And not Michael. Janet, Michael's youngest sister, released her third solo album, *Control*, a few months before she turned twenty (almost exactly the same age Prince had been when he had released his first record, *For You*, back in 1978). With *Control*, Janet arrived. I don't mean that she arrived at the party. I mean that she arrived and that she was the party. The record had eight bona fide classics, at least, and a shockingly strong opening stretch ("Control," "Nasty," and "What Have You Done for Me Lately") that ensured it will never fade as an all-time stone classic. Even the down moments were up moments. Many people would say that the weakest vocal performance on that record is "He Doesn't Know I'm Alive." But recently—and partly because I have struck up a phone friendship with Janet a little bit—I have started to reassess. Maybe it's the best vocal performance. And maybe it's the best because it lets the album have its peaks and valleys. If it was removed from the album and another undeniable hit was put in its place—like Herb Alpert's "Diamonds," which she sang on the following year—the album would be too dense with hits. You need a respite from wall-to-wall perfection or else you get numb to the achievement you're hearing. Her next album, *Rhythm Nation 1814*, is like that. It's almost a greatest hits record, almost hard to hear, almost exhausting. *Control* had perfect . . . control. In 2020 I was watching *The Morning Show*, the Apple TV series about . . . a morning show . . . and one character whose last name happened to be Jackson said something, and another character said, "Miss Jackson if you're nasty." The character who said it was Black, but she was also thirty, tops, which means that she wouldn't have been born until a half-decade after Janet's album came out, but there was the lyric, still directing conversational traffic decades after the fact. That's control. Miss Jackson if you're dynasty.

The album's greatness was beyond dispute. But was it Greatness? Janet had achieved her breakthrough with the help of the production team of Jimmy Jam and Terry Lewis, who had come from the Prince camp—they were original members of the Time, remember, banished to Prince's bad side after a snowstorm grounded their flight and they couldn't make it back from a production job in Atlanta to rejoin the band? Prince had liberated them, and this was one of the fruits of their freedom. Their presence didn't diminish Janet's achievement, but at the same time it was unthinkable without them.

The situation was complicated further by the fact that Prince, between late 1985 and late 1986, entered perhaps the most fertile period of his entire career. He was writing songs at a breakneck rate, as if nothing could stop him. With his backing band, the Revolution, he put together a double album named *Dream Factory*, but he remained uncertain about the sequence of tracks. He expanded it to a triple album called *Crystal Ball*, along the way deciding to get rid of input from his band—not only from the *Dream Factory* tracks, but in general. In October 1986, he fired the Revolution.

They went their separate ways. Two of them went the same way. Wendy Melvoin and Lisa Coleman had been with Prince since the early '80s, but they had been connected for most of their lives. Lisa, who had come into the band as a replacement keyboardist, was the daughter of Gary L. Coleman, a percussionist for the Wrecking Crew and a friend of the prominent studio pianist Mike Melvoin. Melvoin also had a daughter, Wendy, who was also a musician—a guitarist—and coincidentally Lisa's girlfriend. In Prince's band, they acted as the perfect counterweight, further complicating his already complex ideas of masculinity and femininity and sexual orientation.

On March 30, 1987, Prince finally released the album that had emerged from the swirl of *Dream Factory/Crystal Ball*. It was called *Sign o' the Times*. I listened to the album night and day, amazed by its kaleidoscopic richness, by its pop songs, its rock songs, its funk songs. Whatever sidesteps he had taken, he was now stepping forward again into history. The fact that he was now without the Revolution only seemed to confirm his greatness. Carlyle would have been proud. I was.

• • •

Prince's albums had always been magical. Think about a really good cup of tea, and all the things that make it so good. There's the pot. There's the cup. There's the spoon. There's the water. There's the lemon. And then there's the actual tea. For me, there's something else, too, a bit of extra magic in the form of the honey that I add to it when the rest of the process is done. Prince records always had plenty of that honey: strange chord changes, unexpected shifts in meter. When those moments came, and they came often, I got goose bumps.

Tracking those goose bumps on *Sign o' the Times* was a slightly trickier process. I knew the record had been worked on substantially while the Revolution was still around, but it had emerged when Prince was alone again, and I didn't feel any need to untangle the strands: what came entirely from his own mind, what came from the minds of others.

By August, though, the tapestry was unraveling a little bit. Wendy and Lisa, off on their own, released their eponymous debut record. When I heard it, I had to redo the math. Here was an album that had nothing to do with Prince at all and yet retained some of that honey-in-the-tea magic. And if he had nothing to do with this and it still sounded as brilliant as the music he had come up with, then maybe . . . just maybe . . . he hadn't been the sole source of that brilliance. Or that Genius.

I kept that theory in my pocket until Prince released his next album, *Lovesexy*, in 1988. *Lovesexy* wasn't a slouch by other people's standards, but I definitely remember getting to the third song, "Glam Slam," and experiencing an unfamiliar emotion: indifference. I had never had a let-me-skip-that-song moment before with Prince—"Mountains," from *Parade*, was close, but then he did a trick at the end, code-switched into horn funk. Had that been his idea? Wendy's? Lisa's? Over the years, as I had more access to Prince's rehearsal tapes, I have located a number of moments where he played something straight and told Lisa to dance around what he's playing, to maneuver it into an unfamiliar space. It seems clear that their job was to investigate the stew and figure out how much oregano and paprika it needed to move away from something good, often something very good, into something uniquely great.

• • •

This isn't to say that Prince wasn't a genius. Of course he was, as that carefully worded sentence attests. But the idea itself isn't necessarily real. Or rather, it's as real as we need it to be to keep believing that our art—or our society, or the founding of our nation—was the result of inspired choices by inspirational Geniuses. Those Geniuses are beacons. Think of Picasso. Think of Einstein. Think of Prince. But they are triumphs of marketing as much as anything else. The year before Wendy and Lisa's debut, the year before *Sign o' the Times*, Eurythmics was nominated for a Grammy for Best R&B Performance by a Duo or Group for "Sisters Are Doin' It for Themselves," a collaboration with Aretha Franklin. The song was a feminist anthem, a call to arms that told women it was time to emerge from men's shadows: "There was a time when they used to say / That behind every great man there had to be a great woman." But that, too, ends up being a bit of a dodge. The fact was that behind every great individual, male or female, there was a supporting cast that was instrumental in the creation, communication, and execution of ideas, and that the very notion of solitary greatness had to be reassessed even as it was accepted as a motivational fiction. That's a little unwieldy for a lyric, but not everything has to be a song.

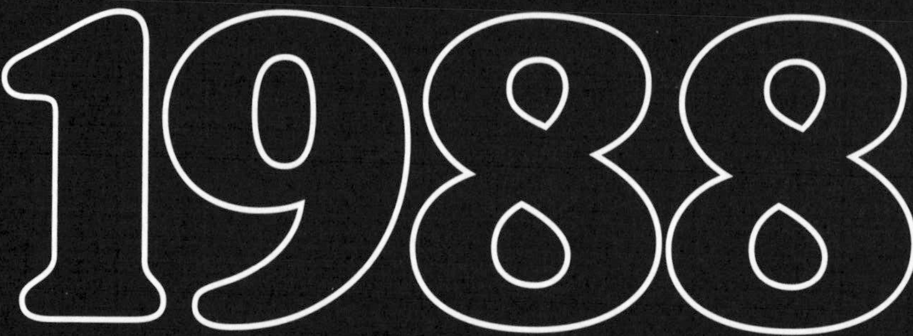

George H. W. Bush defeats Michael Dukakis in the presidential election ○ Crack begins to make its way through American cities ○ An Iran Air jet is shot down by the U.S. Navy, killing all 290 people aboard ○ In the vice-presidential debate, Lloyd Bentsen tells Dan Quayle that he is no Jack Kennedy ○ The Summer Olympics are held in Seoul, South Korea ○ Wrigley Field hosts its first night game in its seventy-four-year history ○ Temple University in Philadelphia offers the nation's first PhD in African-American Studies ○ Police attempt to enforce a new curfew in Tompkins Square Park in New York City, touching off a riot ○ The figure skater Debi Thomas becomes the first African-American to win a medal in the Winter Olympics ○ *Coming to America* comes out

TASTE! HOW LOW CAN YOU GO?

Is there a consensus about the importance of consensus?

Okay. Role-play. It is 2012. You're working at NPR, where you are an intern, which means that you are very young. You spend your weeks talking to the older writers and editors in your office about movies, books, and records. You like hip-hop, in the sense that you spent part of your high school years in the thrall of Drake's "Over," but your frame of reference is limited. You're curious about the great hip-hop records of all time, though. You say so to your editors. "I'm curious," you say. They put their heads together and cook up an experiment. Why not take a classic hip-hop album that you've never heard, one that was in fact released before you were born, and let you listen to it and write a review? "Okay," you say. Your editors are vibrating with excitement. This critical stunt they've cooked up won't just measure how the chosen album has stood the test of time but crack open a bunch of other questions about how canons are constructed and maintained.

The album they pick is Public Enemy's *It Takes a Nation of Millions to Hold Us Back*.

Fade out.

• • •

Fade in. It's 1987, July to be precise. Robert Bork has just been nominated but not yet Borked. Rick Astley has just released "Never Gonna Give You Up." Public Enemy's debut album, *Yo! Bum Rush the Show* has been out since February, introducing the group, its aggro-minimalist sound, and Chuck D's booming vocals. But the single that comes out in the summer, "Rebel Without a Pause," is different. It's both stronger and quicker, with a production that is, in its own way, symphonic. Plus, the lyrics have stepped up their game and then some. They're political, polemical, cuttingly analytical. The first few lines are like an X-ray inside the process of hearing the first few lines:

> Yes, the rhythm, the rebel
> Without a pause, I'm lowering my level

I can't wait for the album. But the rebels without a pause take a pause. There's a second single that comes out on the *Less Than Zero* soundtrack in November, "Bring the Noise," and it's even better, with everything that the first one had, plus a killer chorus ("Turn it up . . . bring the noise!"). A third single, "Don't Believe the Hype," arrives in June 1988, and then, before I can catch my breath, the entire record, sixteen tracks, a master class in the use of hip-hop as a socially relevant art form. Entire books have been written about its genius, so there's no need to gild the lily here. I'll just say that entire lives have been born in the fifty-seven minutes and fifty-one seconds it took to listen to the album.

I had my first real high school job that summer, working in a '50s-themed fast-food place called Big Al's. My responsibilities ran toward French fries and milkshakes. When the Public Enemy record came out, I bought it one morning before work, on cassette of course, and popped it in my Walkman. The transformation was instant. I was transfixed by the first track, "Countdown to Armageddon," which was basically a band introduction from a show in London. I stood still for that. But I started walking just as the second track, "Bring the Noise" started, and within about thirty seconds my walk had completely changed. This record put a rod in my spine and a hop in my step that eventually became a kind of march. Insistent sirens, snippets of political speeches, vocals layered over music layered over vocals—it was all pushing me forward. I mostly got through the first side by the time I got to work, maybe made it to "Caught, Can I Get a Witness." There wasn't any Al, Big or otherwise, but my manager wouldn't let us listen to music while we worked, so I had to put it back in my pocket while I cooked fries. But I kept making excuses to get away for a second—we need more fries?—and sneak to the freezer to hear the beginning of side two, "Show 'Em Whatcha Got," "She Watch Channel Zero?!," "Night of the Living Baseheads." One, two, three, four, five, six, "Kick it!" "Years ago" I put this together. What I was hearing made me larger, more powerful, more capable of seeing what was around me, and also seeing what I needed to do to see more. I understood the title. Being held back was a choice. When I took my lunch break, that was that. No more Big Al. I bought batteries at the drugstore down the street, sat in the park, and listened to the record until it was time to go home. And the next day, after I told my father that I was going to work, I walked around and listened to the album some more. The die had been cast.

I'd say fade out, but there wasn't one.

● ● ●

Back to 2012. Now it can be told that this critical experiment is not a fiction of my own invention. It really happened. I won't name the NPR intern—you can find out online, obviously—but I will say that his experience with the record was somewhat different from mine. In the piece he wrote after hearing it, he reiterates that he didn't know much about hip-hop in general, or Public Enemy in particular, but insists that he approached with an open mind.

It soon closed.

> But when "Don't Believe the Hype" comes on, I'm disoriented—I know I'm listening to one of the most acclaimed rap records of all

> time, but nothing grabs me and sucks me in. Chuck D.'s unvarnished vocals sit front and center in the mix, accompanied only by percussion that, to me, sounds thin and funk guitar samples that, frankly, I find cartoonish.
>
> To me, Chuck D.'s legendary flow also comes across like a caricature. His syncopation strikes me as strange, foreign—and when he does reach for melody, like in the opening verses of "Night of the Living Baseheads," it ascends harshly like the bark of a drill sergeant. It's rough, rugged, built like a tank—and I'm coming at it expecting a Bentley.

Not much is said about side one, apart from the fact that Chuck D's style strikes the intern as "strange, foreign." He briefly gets on board for "Show 'Em Whatcha Got," which he correctly describes as a "short interlude with few lyrics." But then he's back to not-quite-getting-it with "She Watch Channel Zero?!" which he dismisses as "alarmingly dated." And then the review is over.

> As a whole, *It Takes a Nation* leaves me similarly perplexed. But what Public Enemy does offer me is the context to understand how much hip-hop—and I—have changed since our childhoods. Two years ago, I wouldn't have even thought to give *It Takes a Nation* a listen, much less spend weeks processing and writing about my reaction to it. Ten years ago, very few would have pointed to Toronto as a hub of hip-hop creativity.

● ● ●

The intern had ridicule heaped upon him—for bad writing, for bad taste. He took a bad beat in comments sections. I'm not here for that. I'm going to try to handle the situation a little differently. I think he's wrong, of course. But I also think he's a victim.

The intern came to the album in an era of information overload and fragmentation, when damage had been done to traditional content-delivery systems like magazines and newspapers, not to mention record albums and broadcast television. In some cases, that damage was irreparable. On the face of it, that's just historical change. I had LPs, then 8-tracks, then cassettes, then CDs. But if you dig a little deeper, you'll see that the evolution to a whole new way of taking information broke the chain between generations and eliminated the easy transmission of culture and history.

Let's go back to "Rebel Without a Pause." Did I understand the title? Did I know that it was a parody of *Rebel Without a Cause*? I did. But I had grown up in a culture that was more or less continuous from my grandparents' generation to my parents' to mine. The talk shows that aired around the time I was born were famous for mashing up the eras: you could turn on *The Dick Cavett Show* and see Debbie Reynolds and Sly Stone (July 13, 1970). Or Jimmy Stewart and James Taylor (March 9, 1970). Or Frank Capra and Mel Brooks (January 21, 1972). There may have been tensions between one generation and the next, between Black culture and white culture, between rock and roll and pre-rock pop (or, later, between punk and classic rock, between funk and soul, between hip-hop and everything). But those tensions were productive ones, and what they produced were more productive tensions. History existed beside itself.

This was true in Public Enemy's work, as well. Let's go back to "Rebel Without a Pause." When I first heard it, there was a lyric that I didn't understand: "Supporter of Chesimard." Was it some obscure religion? A martial art? That kind of thing sent a fan to the library.

I found one article that gave me basic information, and another that filled in around the edges. It turned out that "Chesimard" was Joanne Chesimard, born JoAnne Deborah Byron, a political activist and Black Panther Party member who, in the early '70s, was arrested on everything from bank robbery to kidnapping to murder charges. She was never convicted until a retrial in 1977 for acting as an accomplice in the shooting death of a New Jersey state trooper named Werner Foerster. She was convicted for that one and given a life sentence at the Clinton Correctional Facility in New Jersey. Two years later she escaped and turned up in Cuba, where she has been ever since. It was a fascinating story. At the time I researched it, her presence in Cuba had been widely known only for a year or so, because of an interview she gave to *Newsday*. The *Newsday* headline also gave the name that she went by, which wasn't her birth name: Assata Shakur.

So I knew what *Chesimard* meant, and that was something. A decade later, it would be something more, when a young rapper with the last name Shakur started appearing on the scene, first with a guest feature on Digital Underground's "Same Song" (as 2Pac) and then as a solo artist. Assata—Chesimard—wasn't related to him, though there were plenty of connections. Her friend Mutulu was Tupac's stepfather, and Assata was friendly with Tupac's mother, Afeni Shakur, born Alice Faye Williams. When Afeni died in 2017, the Internet, seeing only the last name, not thinking further than that, blew up with all kinds of misinformation.

But it had all been sorted out already in "Words of Wisdom," a track from Tupac's debut, *2Pacalypse Now*, that had been produced by Shock G. The song ends with a list of figures who represent a challenge to the currently construed version of America, and they range from Tupac himself to Above the Law to Public Enemy to Assata to Geronimo Pratt to Mutulu.

It's a list that conflates art and life to some degree. At that point, Assata was in Cuba; Mutulu was in jail for his role in a 1981 robbery in which a security guard and two police officers were killed; and Pratt, a former Black Panther and decorated Vietnam vet, was in jail for the 1968 murder of Caroline Olsen, an elementary school teacher in Santa Monica, California. Now, it's true that these convictions may well have been the result of the government trying to muzzle or silence revolutionaries. It's certainly the case for Pratt, whose conviction was vacated in 1997 when it was revealed that the original prosecutor had concealed evidence of his innocence. The information was pretty conclusive. It showed that he had been at a Black Panther meeting in Oakland, four hundred miles away, at the time of the murder. (Additional historical irony? His original lawyer, Johnnie Cochran, had argued the same thing back in 1972, to no avail.)

Regardless, the bulk of the names Tupac mentions, artists, were generally guilty of nothing but rapping.

This is lots of history, along with some lyrics. But it points to what bothered me about the intern. It wasn't the fact that he was ignorant about Public Enemy. Times change and tastes change along with it. If I liked the exact same music as my father, I never would have come around to Prince. And I didn't even mind that the intern thought that *It Takes a Nation of Millions* didn't have a good beat and you can't dance to it (that's an *American Bandstand* reference, but it's not really—it's one of those phrases that people think happened that didn't, like Ed Sullivan saying "Really big shew." History can be deceiving).

But I can't quite get behind his ignorance of everything that Public Enemy's about—everything they refer to, everything they draw together. Their lyrics contained multitudes. This is true culturally: "Bring the Noise" mentions Sonny Bono and Yoko Ono, LL Cool J and Anthrax, inclusively. It's also true historically. "Prophets of Rage" mentions Marcus Garvey, Nelson Mandela, Margaret Thatcher, along with Gabriel Prosser (a blacksmith and slave who planned a slave rebellion in Virginia in 1800, was ratted out by two other slaves, escaped, was apprehended, and was hanged) and Denmark Vesey (who planned a similar rebellion in Charleston in 1822, was also caught, and was also hanged). The music is such a rich repository of history that turning away from it is a form of turning away from what it contains. Just reviewing it for its ability to inspire dancing is unforgivable, not because you're rejecting *It Takes a Nation of Millions to Hold Us Back*'s place in history, but because you're rejecting all the other places in history illuminated by the record. That may be another difference. I felt young coming into the record, untested, uneducated. I didn't feel that Public Enemy was serving me. I felt that I was serving them.

The one track that briefly intrigues the intern, "Show 'Em Whatcha Got," has what he says are "chopped chants" by Chuck D and Flavor Flav that remind us that "freedom is a road seldom traveled by the multitudes." That's a Frederick Douglass quote. That shoots me forward to 2017, when President Trump opened up Black History Month by meeting with Black leaders and running quickly through some names: Martin Luther King, Jr., Harriet Tubman,

Rosa Parks. It's Black history at an elementary school level, the kinds of figures you learn about in second grade. But when he got to Douglass, he was seemingly stumped, and offered up this immortal quote: "Frederick Douglass is an example of somebody who's done an amazing job and is being recognized more and more, I notice."

If history doesn't pass through to the people who occupy the highest offices, there's bound to be trouble. A nation of ignorance holds us all back.

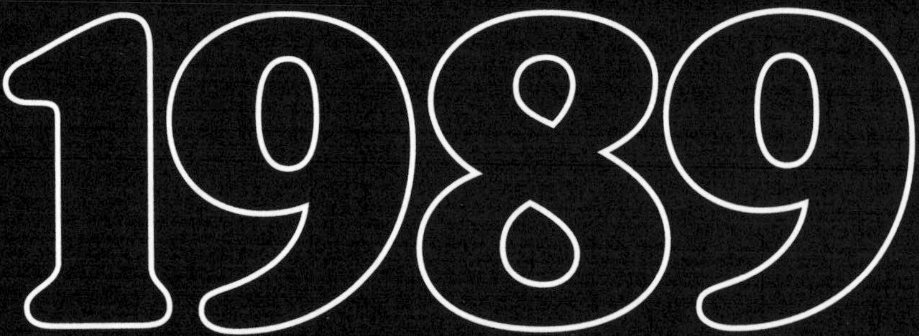

The Berlin Wall falls ○ George H. W. Bush becomes the forty-first president of the United States ○ Roughly 100,000 students gather in Beijing's Tiananmen Square to protest the Chinese Communist Party's authoritarian practices ○ The *Exxon Valdez* oil spill occurs in Prince William Sound, Alaska ○ In the "Velvet Revolution," more than 200,000 Czech students demand the end of the country's Communist government ○ The Ayatollah Khomeini dies ○ Ted Bundy is executed by electric chair in Florida ○ Lyle and Eric Menendez murder their parents ○ David Dinkins is elected the first Black mayor of New York City ○ Barbara C. Harris becomes the first Black female bishop in the Anglican Episcopal Church ○ Time, Inc., and Warner Communications merge, forming Time Warner ○ *Batman* opens, with Michael Keaton in the title role ○ *Seinfeld* premieres ○ Pete Rose agrees to a lifetime ban from baseball for gambling ○ Tim Berners-Lee outlines his plan for the World Wide Web

SEEDS OF CHANGE

Mining ideas from history, and minding history's ideas.

Spike Lee's first feature, *She's Gotta Have It*, came out in 1986. Lee had done a film before, the student short *Joe's Bed-Stuy Barbershop: We Cut Heads*, which wasn't so short (an hour), and those two movies established the formula for much of his early work—talkative characters, strong sense of community, a backdrop of social issues.

By 1989 Spike was on to *Do the Right Thing*. Everyone knows that story except those who don't. I'll do the write thing (sorry, sorry) and retell it. The setting is Bed-Stuy, again, on one of the hottest days of the summer. A pizza delivery boy, Mookie (played by Lee), makes his rounds. He tangles, somewhat good-naturedly, with the owner of the pizza place, Sal (Danny Aiello). It's not that Sal's not a nice guy—he is—but he's also a racist to some degree, in the sense that everyone his age is. He has ideas about the races, ideas about the Black race. The symbol for all this is the wall of the pizza shop, which is filled with celebrity photos Sal has collected over the years. As Mookie's friend Buggin' Out (Giancarlo Esposito) notices when he stops in for a slice, all the celebrities are white: Joe DiMaggio, Frank Sinatra, Al Pacino, Robert De Niro, Liza Minnelli. As Buggin' Out puts it, "How come you got no brothers up on the wall, here?"

If you want better representation, Sal says, get your own pizza place. "This is my pizzeria. American Italians on the wall only." In fact, Pavarotti's up there, too. Not American. But Sal's point is taken.

Sal has two sons, Vito and Pino, played by Richard Edson (who had appeared in *Tougher Than Leather*—see 1986) and John Turturro. They divide neatly into nice and mean—Vito accepts people for their character rather than for their race, while Pino most certainly does not. Also on the scene is Radio Raheem, played by Bill Nunn, a hulking Black man who carries around a boombox wherever he goes. And the tension between the races isn't simply a Black-and-white issue. There's a brutally funny (but also brutal) skirmish between Radio Raheem and Korean shop owners when he goes in to gas up his boombox with new batteries.

Dissipation, race relations, as Stevie Wonder says in "Pastime Paradise" (*Songs in the Key of Life*, side two, track three).

The movie tracks the minutiae of Brooklyn life: kids opening hydrants, Mookie visiting his girl. And then one fateful day, as the summer refuses to relent, temperatures boil over. Buggin' Out and Radio Raheem go to Sal to demand that he put some brothers on the wall. Sal pushes back angrily and bashes Radio Raheem's boombox with a bat. The conflict moves into the street. The police come. One of the cops puts Radio Raheem in a chokehold and kills him. The crowd blames Sal for Radio Raheem's death, and Mookie throws a trash can through the front window of the shop, which is then set on fire.

Exploitation, mutilation, as Stevie Wonder also sings in "Pastime Paradise." And escalation. And violation. And desecration. There's a tentative reconciliation, where Mookie visits Sal. Over the course of the movie, these two characters have been near the center of the spectrum, farthest from the hate that burns at the extremes. They've used humor and a shared work ethic and a respect for each other's intelligence to build a bridge away from the conflict. But here, they can't quite make it. They're both too bruised and hurt. Mookie keeps asking for his money. What happened doesn't take away the value of his work. Eventually they come to a tentative peace. Sal pays Mookie.

And then, dedication. The movie—dedicated at the top to Yusef

Hawkins, a sixteen-year-old from East New York who was attacked by a mob of white teens and then shot to death—ends with a list of a half-dozen African-Americans who died as the result of police brutality or racial violence. I'll name them, because time shouldn't be an engine of forgetting.

Eleanor Bumpurs, a woman in her late sixties who was shot by New York City police in 1984 during an eviction. Michael Griffith, a man in his early twenties who was, in 1986, beaten by a white mob, chased onto a highway, and hit by a car, killing him. Arthur Miller, a prominent Black businessman and community leader in Brooklyn who was killed by a police chokehold in 1978. Edmund Perry, a teenager shot by a plainclothes police officer in Harlem in 1985. Yvonne Smallwood, a twenty-eight-year-old Bronx woman who died in police custody in 1987 while awaiting arraignment. Michael Stewart, a twenty-five-year-old graffiti artist who was arrested for tagging the First Avenue station in 1983 and then hogtied and beaten to death while in police custody.

Those are the shortest versions of the stories because going on longer strains the heart. Lee lists them in that order. At first it seemed to me a chaotic order, hopscotching from year to year and proving that history both repeats and predicts itself. It was only much later that I realized it was alphabetical. When you're reading through hurt, you see some things very clearly and other things not at all.

But those six names were a constellation clustered in the years before the film. Now, with many nights in between, there are others in the sky next to it. There is a constellation from 2012 to 2014: Tamir Rice, Trayvon Martin, Eric Garner, Michael Brown. And then, during the time I was starting this book, more names appeared: George Floyd, Breonna Taylor, Ahmaud Arbery, and Rayshard Brooks. The most recent at the time of writing, Jacob Blake, was walking back to his car in Kenosha, Wisconsin, after trying to break up a fight, when he was shot in the back seven times. Brooks was also shot in the back by police. Arbery was shot by non-police, apparently for sport.

We're in 2021 now. I've left the movie behind for a little while. And in 2020, it felt like every death of this sort had higher stakes, partly because it did. Floyd's murder, caused by the knee of a Minneapolis cop, happened early in the coronavirus pandemic, but people still came out en masse to protest. Blake's death touched off a temporary work stoppage (or wildcat strike or boycott—pick your term) by NBA players and led to a league playoff (held in Orlando, Florida, in a bubble, to prevent the spread of coronavirus) laced with an explicit Black Lives Matter theme. Players could wear the names of victims or general social justice slogans on their jerseys. And within days, Blake's death was partly papered over by the shooting of two white men by an armed seventeen-year-old vigilante, also in Kenosha, in the midst of urban unrest that stemmed from protests over Floyd's death. In the present, in this cauldron of protestors and counterprotestors, activists and agitators and alleged anarchists, there's a surplus of what will eventually become history.

• • •

Back in 1985, I got on board with Tears for Fears, an English pop band that had a huge record that year with *Songs from the Big Chair*, which sent two songs to the top of the chart ("Shout," "Everybody Wants to Rule the World") and a third to number three ("Head Over Heels"). It was what I guess you'd call proto-emo, with intensely personal lyrics, soulful singing, and catchy melodies. But it was also DJ music. Back in that summer, in every block party, most DJs wouldn't be caught dead without two copies of the "Shout" 12-inch, with its tough-as-nails drum programing. It was the go-to backdrop of most freestyles. And it was also rap music. As emo as "Head Over Heels" was, you'd be hard-pressed to find a rap group that didn't use that anthemic, superhero-sounding piano intro for their walkout music. That intro was almost like hip-hop's "Hail to the Chief" that year.

The group labored over the follow-up, like many groups, and in August 1989, about a month after *Do the Right Thing*, they released the lead single from their third album, which was called *The Seeds of Love*. By then, I was working a normal day job at a record store. I would get paid on a Friday, cash my check on a Saturday, and then use my employee discount to buy a bunch of records on Sunday. As I have explained, much of the music I bought, and much of what I believed about what I bought, was directed by *Rolling Stone* back then. *The Seeds of Love* got a four-star review. Michael Azerrad wrote it.

> The first single and the album's centerpiece, "Sowing the Seeds of Love," is a joyous call to activism carried by an over-the-top production that hauls out every last bell and whistle from the Beatles' *Magical Mystery Tour* era.

That's what he wrote, that's what I read—once before I listened to the record, once after—and that's what I believed. I saw the single as a funkier version of the "I Am the Walrus" chord progressions. My Beatles vocabulary was just starting to open up at the time. Back when Prince released *Around the World in a Day* in 1985, I was a rank novice. Now I knew a little. The spur, weirdly enough, was a *Jet* article—in 1987, Paul McCartney had given an interview about the twentieth anniversary of *Sgt. Pepper's Lonely Hearts Club Band*, and that had sent me back to all the albums. So by 1989, when Azerrad mentioned the Beatles, I was perfectly positioned to hear them. And that's mostly all I heard. The fact that "Sowing the Seeds of Love" was an explicitly political song that chided the prime minister, Margaret Thatcher—"Politician granny with your high ideals, have you no idea how the majority feels"—escaped me entirely.

The Seeds of Love wasn't the only time that I let *Rolling Stone* lead me by the nose. It wasn't even the only time that month. The review of Terence Trent D'Arby's second record, *Neither Fish nor Flesh*, was a lead review, complete with a Robert Risko illustration. I hadn't really liked D'Arby's debut, *Introducing the Hardline*, that much. His TV performances were better. But that second album intrigued me, partly because of the Risko, partly because *Rolling Stone* had printed out the entire subtitle, "A Soundtrack of Love, Faith, Hope & Destruction." The people around me always had a penchant for those kinds of lavish, pretentious subtitles. Years later, Tariq wanted to call our first album something like *Brothers and Sisters Hanging on a String of Positivity While Dangling over a Sea of Negativity*. Rich vetoed that and quick.

Those two albums, the Tears for Fears and the Terence Trent D'Arby, were part of a new kind of record buying. That fall, I was no longer in high school, but I still went back to my high school. I got there in September to talk to the kids who were still enrolled. I don't know what I said to them—probably that I was on my way to work or something. Then they would go inside and I would stand outside and think about what I was doing. Maybe I was doing nothing. Maybe I had to find something to do. When I went to the record store under those new conditions, I was buying albums as an adult for the first time. It wasn't like getting albums when I was a little kid, or even a big kid. I was making choices, making decisions. I had to ponder my new status.

Sometimes the music helped. I went into *Neither Fish nor Flesh* with a generous spirit, and I wasn't disappointed. Like *The Seeds of Love*, it reinforced the benefits of maximalist production. Again, his first album had been stripped down, which to me made it sound thin and forgettable. This was more than produced. On "Roly Poly," he credited himself with playing "Keyboards, Marimba, Electric Piano [Fender Rhodes], Organ [Cathedral Organ], Piano [Piano & 'Jazzesque' Piano Fills], Percussion [Special Light Tan Sainsbury's Cardboard Box #382a], Cuica [Quica], Percussion, Sounds [And Other Sound Manipulations]," credited the drums to Ecneret Tnert Ybra'd (get it? because they're backwards?), and even included a line for "Other [Cardboard Box Roadie]" that he credited to his alter ego, the Incredible E. G. O'Reilly (get it? EGO?). Critics liked to point to these kinds of things as proof that he was a victim of his own out-of-control self-concept, but he was clearly in on the joke. I always thought that Lenny Kravitz had to pay for the sins of Terence Trent D'Arby—another arty Black singer-songwriter who had to justify his presence against mainstream suspicion. Back in 1987, D'Arby had declared that his debut was better than *Sgt. Pepper*. Now he seemed determined to prove it on wax.

Back in the sampling chapter, I wrote about the nostalgia cycle, and how it directed the use of certain eras of soul and funk as the foundation for certain later eras of hip-hop. *The Seeds of Love* highlighted another version of the cycle, which was what happened when pop singers experienced a certain burnout: again, as a result of the huge success of a record, or the exhausting touring schedule that followed, or the endless interviews, or the pressure to come back with an album that was just as strong. They tended to turn inward, to regress slightly to the music that had inspired them, partly for comfort, partly for strategy. It seems likely that something such as that was behind the evolution of Tears for Fears, whose two songwriters, Roland Orzabal and Curt Smith, had both been born in 1961, which meant that they grew up in an England besotted by the Beatles. They were responding to their cultural dominance, letting it guide them through their dizzying ascent. In light of that, in light of the light they made (the artwork for the album and its singles were filled with suns, sunflowers, and similar symbols), "Sowing the Seeds of Love" remains for me a completely successful late-'80s pop single, retro without being entirely derivative, perfectly balancing inspiration and recycling, with a message that's rooted in two distinct time periods but is also universal.

And yet every time I hear that song, I think about another of 1989's best singles, one that came out about six weeks before "Sowing the Seeds of Love." It was Public Enemy's "Fight the Power," and while it was technically the lead single from the group's third album, *Fear of a Black Planet*, the album wouldn't be released until April 1990. In 1989, it was, to me, to everyone, a song of the summer—it came out on the Fourth of July—and the theme song of *Do the Right Thing*. The "Fight the Power" video was filmed by Lee in the streets of Brooklyn in late April and plays like a cross between a block party and a Black Power rally. The video's great. But it's the song that will last forever. It begins with a sample of a speech from the civil rights leader Thomas "TNT" Todd, and specifically from a speech about Black Americans and Vietnam: "Yet our best-trained, best-educated, best-equipped, best-prepared troops refuse to fight! Matter of fact, it's safe to say that they would rather switch than fight!" In its day, it was a recognizable parody of the Tareyton cigarette slogan ("Tareyton smokers would rather fight than switch"). But it's also hard proof that not all '60s callbacks are equal. Tears for Fears's 1967 was the summer of love. TNT Todd's 1967 was the summer of the Algiers Motel incident (see this book's introduction). Sometimes the light you're seeing is coming from a sun or a sunflower. Sometimes it's coming from something burning.

Singles I Actually Dig

Singles can be rough going, especially very popular ones. It's often hard to admit that you were one of the eight billion people who streamed "Gangnam Style" at its hottest. That's how irony culture works. My biggest records in DJ sets now are "Ice Ice Baby" and "U Can't Touch This," and I wouldn't have dared play them at any hip-hop cred party twenty years ago. All the songs I spin for ironic purposes are now legit parts of people's enjoyment.

"EVERYBODY WANTS TO RULE THE WORLD"
Tears for Fears

Songs from the Big Chair, 1985 [Mercury]

My family took a trip out to California via Trailways in 1985, in the summer. This was in the final era of the ghetto blaster (see Radio Raheem, this chapter). It was widely accepted that your music could invade the personal space of others. We had one of those kinds of guys on the bus, or really a group of them: a small guy, a bigger guy, and a woman, and they were playing "Juicy Fruit" over and over again. My dad didn't like it. He asked them to quiet down. He was six-foot-four, and he could be intimidating. At one point some casting directors saw him at some event and asked him if he had considered acting. They sent him a script. It was *Witness*. They wanted him for the Danny Glover role. My dad's insecurity about his reading skills caused him to sabotage that moment. Anyway, on the bus, not acting, he stood up and he threatened the guy. This was before Wesley Snipes in *New Jack City* made dark sexy. Back then anyone dark was more threatening. These two guys with the boom box looked just like Turbo and Ozone from *Breaking*. The little one of the pair turned the volume down. The big guy called my dad's bluff. "Man, you ain't gonna do shit. I'll fuck you up." My dad took a step toward them. My mom was screaming, "Lee, don't do it." The driver pulled the bus over. They kicked the boom box crew off the bus. That's stuck in my mind as a near-miss, a situation that could have been bad. When we got out to L.A., one of the first days we went driving up the Pacific Coast Highway to a seafood place, and while we were eating "Everybody Wants to Rule the World" came on over the PA system. It just gave this entire trip more light and a feeling of hope.

"SEPTEMBER WHEN I FIRST MET YOU"
Barry White

The Man, 1978 [20th Century Fox]

This is one of my last romantic memories of the 8-track. We were driving all across America in my dad's van during the late '70s, 1976 to 1979. This 8-track was blue, the actual casing, which was a rarity. Only some labels had different-colored 8-tracks, and only 20th Century Fox had blue.

"STILL SOUND"
Toro y Moi

Underneath the Pine, 2011 [Carpark]

I don't know how many songs my mind can really absorb, though I have thought about it. Seven thousand? What I know is that it's absorbed that many, which means that I can only rotate in a few new ones each year. This song holds the same space as Herb Alpert's "Route 101." It's one of those songs that would wind up on the audience mix on a Friday Fallon—they are loose, fun, with people thinking of weekend plans. It sounds like a song the Wrecking Crew would have played forty years earlier.

"BRASS IN POCKET"
Pretenders

Pretenders, 1980 [A&M]

When I was in *West Side Store*, a movie, toward the end of elementary school (see 1981), I remember listening to pop albums in the car as I drove up to Northeast to make the movie. Whenever my runner picked me up to take me to the location, it was Squeeze or the Police, or Elvis Costello's *This Year's Model*, which was in a cracked case on the floor. The Pretenders' debut was one of those albums, too, and this was the song that I gravitated toward. It was a pleasant memory at first, but not for long. On set that summer, my castmates had a nickname for me, *moulinyan*. Back at school in the fall, I remember calling someone that, and instantly the adults swooped down. "Ahmir, to the principal's office." A teacher, Mrs. Surles, explained to me that the word was a racial slur. They wanted to call my parents. I remember genuine confusion. I didn't want my parents called. It felt like I was in trouble.

"CLOSE TO ME"
The Cure

The Head on the Door, 1985 [Elektra]

For two years of high school I went to a smaller school, City Center Academy in Philadelphia. It was sort of a Breakfast Club, a magnet school. We would take trips to the art museums, and when we drove, different kids would control the stereo. There was one cool kid, Matt, who would make mix-tapes. When we got to the museum, we had to slide the van seat to let the passengers out. "Close to Me" was playing when the Black kids and white kids were all together, sort of like our version of *Reality Bites*.

"TOO SHY"
Kajagoogoo

White Feathers, 1983 [EMI]

In the summertime, on the video show on our local UHF, WPHL-17, they played Bill Cosby's show—not *The Cosby Show*, but the one from the early '70s where he was a physical education teacher—then *Davey and Goliath*, and then videos. This was on often, and I was drawn immediately to the bass line, which I now realize is actually three or four of them for the different parts of the song.

1990

Saddam Hussein invades Kuwait, leading to Operation Desert Shield ○ Nelson Mandela is released from prison ○ The Baltic States—Lithuania, Latvia, and Estonia—declare their independence from the Soviet Union ○ Douglas Wilder of Virginia becomes the first African-American governor in the history of the United States ○ The Hubble Space Telescope is launched ○ Buster Douglas knocks out Mike Tyson ○ The Motion Picture Association of America introduces the NC-17 rating, which replaces X ○ Leonard Bernstein retires from conducting after forty-seven years, and dies five days later ○ John Gotti is arrested ○ Sharon Pratt Kelly is elected mayor of Washington, D.C., the first African American woman to lead a large American city ○ Carole Ann-Marie Gist of Detroit, Michigan, becomes the first African-American Miss USA

RETURN OF THE IMPRESSED

When you say you study history, what do you mean?

Living Colour, the metal-funk-pop-rock band, formed in New York by Vernon Reid in the early '80s, had a hard time getting signed, for all the reasons you'd imagine. Reid had started off playing with Ronald Shannon Jackson, a towering figure of avant-garde jazz, and his time with Jackson had taught him that categories were fine for historical shorthand, but not necessarily great for artists. But the lack of category, while great for artists, wasn't necessarily great for bands looking to get signed, let along Black rock bands with one toe in funk and a determination to bring real politics into their music.

In 1985, Reid was a backing guitarist on *Primitive Cool*, the second solo album by the Rolling Stones' front man, Mick Jagger. Jagger took notice of Reid and helped bring Living Colour to the attention of record labels. Epic signed the band, and in 1988 they released their debut, *Vivid*, which charted around the world (Top Ten in the United States) and netted them a Grammy (Best Hard Rock Performance, for "Cult of Personality"). Jagger produced two songs, sang backup, and developed a complicated relationship to the band—not personally, but in terms of the history of race and music. Reid, in a 2013 interview, reflected on those early years, and Jagger's role:

> He's literally the embodiment of rock 'n' roll. I wish I had been able to spend more time with him because he had this insight about music. You find in talking to the British rock people connected to the blues that they have a certain perspective on it . . . I remember Mick Jagger made Corey Glover a tape of blues songs from his own collection, which was really fantastic.

Jagger not only helped with the record but took the band out on tour; Living Colour opened some shows for the Stones in the fall of 1989, on the "Steel Wheels" tour. By that point, the biggest thing in American rock and roll was Guns N' Roses, who also opened some Stones shows. In Los Angeles, during a four-night stand at the Coliseum, both bands were opening: Living Colour first, Guns N' Roses second. Guns N' Roses was touring not only behind their debut, *Appetite for Destruction*, which had been released in 1987, but off a stopgap EP, *G N' R Lies*, a mix of fake-live performances and new tracks that had spawned the hit "Patience." The EP closed with "One in a Million," a tale of Rose first arriving in L.A. that used racial slurs for Black people (yes, that n-word), derogatory terms for gay people (yes, that f-word), while also taking swipes at immigrants (they "come to our country" and "talk so many goddamn ways").

The day of the first show, while Living Colour was doing radio promotion, "One in a Million" came up, and Reid denounced it. That night, Rose responded from the stage, insisting that in his mind, the n-word wasn't limited to Black people. "All you people calling me a racist, shove your head up your fucking ass," he added diplomatically. The next night, Reid went right back out and elaborated: if you don't have a problem with certain kinds of people, don't use words that make it seem to every reasonable person that you have a problem with those kinds of people. I'm paraphrasing.

• • •

Living Colour's sophomore album, *Time's Up* (Jagger returned to provide some backing vocals), was released in 1990 to high expectations. The title track opened with chronological sound effects (chimes, ticking) and then launched into a thrashy Bad Brains–style song that warned about environmental destruction.

The second song, "History Lesson," maybe wasn't a song at all. It was a short composition overlaid with vocal samples from an old Black-history record starring the actors Ossie Davis, Ruby Dee, and James Earl Jones:

> In Africa, music is not an art form as much as it is a means of communication.
> A Negro has got no name.
> Quite often, the words of the song are meaningless.
> A Negro has got no name.
> We are wearing the name of our master.

There was plenty else on *Time's Up* that I loved: the jagged lead single, "Type"; the funk strut "Love Rears Its Ugly Head"; the gentle ballad "Solace of You." But "History Lesson" hit me especially hard, for a million reasons. In my mind I was thinking of all my white friends in school. I wondered if they knew that it was the strongest thing that they could walk away with after listening to the album. It changed not only how I felt about *Time's Up*, but the album form. It's where I learned that brief interludes could serve as my narrator to the story. I remember reading a quote in *Rolling Stone* where Ed Stasium, who produced the record, said that his son said listening to it was like "reading a book."

● ● ●

But Living Colour was nothing if not smart, and the more time you spend with "History Lesson," the more slippery it becomes. The song before it, the title song, imagines the end of history as the result of human carelessness and greed. The song after it, "Pride," has a chorus that begins, "History's a lie that they teach you in school."

And what of "History Lesson" itself? In the history of history—in the group of writings that think about how historians operate, what expectations they make, where they clearly disclose the limits of their own personal perspective—there's a concept called *scale*. What it means, roughly (and I mean very roughly), is that historians have to choose the size of the history they're telling. Large-scale history might look at a long time period or a wide geographical span, which might mean that the conclusions drawn are broad and sweeping. Small-scale history might focus on one village or even one family, or it might restrict its scope to a shorter duration. Those conclusions tend to be more precise, but they aren't as easily transferred to other places and times. Historians negotiate scale constantly.

Part of what's at stake in conversations of scale, of course, is the validity of the largest labels. Think of Reid's point about Guns N' Roses. Racial slurs, or derogatory terms for people of a certain sexual orientation, are offensive not only because they're said maliciously, but because they group many different types of people together. If I happen to have the same skin color as you, that doesn't mean that I share the same beliefs, or voting habits, or even the same language. In that light, "History Lesson" comes to feel like a dodge, if a brilliant one. There's no "Africa," just like there's no "China" or "Black people." Every big history is in fact a collection of smaller histories. And just because it's intoned by a famous actor doesn't make it true. Again, Living Colour is entirely aware of this: if you're not on top of the message, you don't assemble a short song where one of only five lines is "Quite often, the words of the song are meaningless."

● ● ●

And yet there are histories, and they can show us what was there, and lead us to understand what is still here. A few years back, I wrote a series of magazine articles on the rise and fall of hip-hop, or at least the way that hip-hop moved from a genre of great social promise to one concerned largely with commercial success. One of Rich Nichols's abiding concerns was the birth of Black culture in America—how it really started. "Think about Sunday." I'm putting the quotes on because I'm quoting from conversations back then that Rich and I had in and around the creation of that magazine series. "Think about Sunday. Start with Duke Ellington's 'Come Sunday' if you want. Then go back in time a hundred years, and a hundred years before that."

Think about Sunday in the United States back then, whenever then was, when the country was a largely religious nation that set aside a day for worship. That day, that Sunday, meant being devout, meant church, which meant an absence of work, for the most part, which also meant a day off for slaves. I can't say that this is true in every case, but it stands to reason that if the white masters had their eyes oriented heavenward, they were less likely to check in on the slaves. That created a kind of freedom within enslavement, and that in turn created culture—dances, amateur theatricals, speeches, cooking, songs. Often, the tools they used were cast-offs from white society, or things they made themselves. "We know how Black cuisine, or soul food, used ingredients from around the edges of the food that was prepared for the masters and mistresses: ends of vegetables, parts of animals, etc. They didn't want 'em. The slaves got 'em." (Those early Rich notes, again, resurfacing.) The same is true for music, where instruments included makeshift drums, old guitars, the guts of old fortepianos.

Slaves managed to make art for themselves, but they weren't the only audience. The white masters might have been preoccupied with church, but their job was still to monitor the (free) labor, so they no doubt watched some of these performances and tried to fit what they were seeing into what they already knew, or rather what they already thought they knew. Let's assume that many white people truly did believe that their Black slaves were inferior, or even that they were not quite human. Well, what to make of these theatricals, these declamations, these songs? "Most likely, some white observers tried to untangle the meaning of what they were watching and hearing, and while it's a stretch to compare this to a modern audience that has extended respect to a performer, it is a form of spectatorship."

How could an absence of humanity be explained in the face of singing, dancing, playing music, often with great sophistication? Over the years, over the generations, these various complex acts of creativity were absorbed into a larger category: Black art. Again, that's a strange way to think about it, especially when you think in terms of scale. When you order Mexican food, do you ever think about what that really means, how you're conflating various regions and time periods, how you're distilling centuries of cultural thought about food and dining, how you're overlooking a million questions about the agriculture and technology and economy and medicine? Of course not. But let's suffer with the generalities for a moment. White eyes looked at Black art. Sometimes they saw something that caught their interest: a phrase, a gesture, a way of looking at the world. And when they did, they tried to control it.

"What does that mean? I'm asking a rhetorical question and a real one at the same time. Remember, control is complicated. If you're going to control something, the one thing you don't do is eliminate it completely. Then you have nothing to control." Add to that that eliminating it might have felt like an aesthetic crime, strange as that may seem. It might have affronted beauty. "Right, because white slavers, even though they were horrible humans, were still humans, and they probably laughed at funny skits and were moved by eloquence and felt tears welling up when they heard a sad song. So these engines of white power didn't roll right over Black art. They didn't kill it. They just took it away and exaggerated it, burlesqued it. 'Black' became exaggerated to the point where it was mostly comic, sometimes melodramatic, dignity gone again. And the biggest piece of that, of course, was blackface. White performers in mid-nineteenth-century America had a great way of showing everyone that they were playing Black—they actually took burnt cork and rubbed it on their face. They weren't themselves now. They were Othered. And this reminded people what they were when they weren't corking themselves like the Other. Their whiteness became, specifically, non-Blackness. And blackface had its own carbonation. It reduced the sophisticated artistic achievements of Black Americans to more flat and more insulting (but oddly still as complex) imitations by white Americans. No one thinks that blackface performances gave an accurate portrait of American Blacks. But did they accurately collect white ideas about Blacks?"

• • •

Let's go back to rock and roll—or rather, one specific moment in rock and roll. (Scale!) In the early 1950s, there was a heavyset R&B singer named Big Mama Thornton who worked out of Houston sometimes, Los Angeles other times. In 1952, at Radio Recorders Annex, a studio on Santa Monica Boulevard, she recorded a song called "Hound Dog." The great bandleader Johnny Otis, one of her mentors, played drums on the record, which became a big R&B hit.

Four years later, a young white southerner named Elvis Presley, who had recorded mostly slower songs like "Heartbreak Hotel" and "I Want You, I Need You, I Love You," covered "Hound Dog," and the thing blew up. It got to the top of both the country and R&B charts, and to number two pop. And it amplified a narrative about Elvis that he was a white pirate, a hijacker, who had built his career on the backs of Black artists. It had happened before, with "Good Rocking Tonight" (originally recorded by Roy Brown) and "Mystery Train" (originally recorded by Junior Parker). Neither was a big hit, but that wasn't the point. The point was that they weren't Elvis's to take. He had created his sound—and in fact built his entire aesthetic identity—on the backs of Black artists. Elvis was denounced as the latest (and greatest?) example of inappropriate appropriation. Public Enemy was still seething about it in 1989, in "Fight the Power," when Chuck D scoffed at the idea of an Elvis stamp: "Elvis was a hero to most but he never meant shit to me."

Living Colour picked up that thread on *Time's Up*, on "Elvis Is Dead," a rollicking satire that starts with a fake Elvis sighting ("Tabloids scream / Elvis seen at a shopping mall") and includes a rewrite of Public Enemy's verse:

> Elvis was a hero to most
> But that's beside the point

But behind this story there's an ever-shifting backdrop. The supposed Blackness of the original song is complicated by the fact that "Hound Dog" was written by Jerry Leiber and Mike Stoller, two Jewish kids from Los Angeles. And while there's no question that Elvis took a hayride on Black R&B, how different is it from the Mick Jagger who had such a special connection to the blues? I'm not saying it isn't different. I'm asking how different it is.

And maybe Living Colour—a what-goes-around-comes-around Black rock band of the highest order, complete with British spelling—is asking, too. "Elvis Is Dead" includes a rap from none other than Little Richard, a contemporary of Elvis who also had a ringside seat for the early rounds of rock and roll. Little Richard's verse is sympathetic toward Elvis and critical of those who are hijacking his legacy:

> Presley was a good performer, on stage he was electrifying
> When he was ill, his fans got sick and moaned when he had died
> To all you pimps making money on his name
> How do you sleep, don't you feel the shame?
> He went through the test, he's out of this mess
> Be my guest and let him rest

The song saves its most brilliant stroke for just after that, when it shifts into a parody of Paul Simon's "Graceland," the title song of an album that had plenty of its own issues with white performers absorbing/appropriating Black (in this case, African rather than African-American) music: "I've got a reason to believe we all won't be received at Graceland."

So in the end, whose face exactly is black? Whose is white? And whose should be red with embarrassment? Who is visible? Who is overlooked? Who sees others? Who sees themselves clearly? I go to the last song of *Time's Up*, "This Is the Life," to the last line: "In this real life / Try to be less blind."

The Gulf War begins ○ A cyclone in Bangladesh kills 140,000 people ○ Terry Anderson is released after seven years as a hostage in Beirut ○ A Michigan physician, Dr. Jack Kevorkian, is banned from assisting in suicides ○ Clarence Thomas is confirmed to the U.S. Supreme Court despite allegations of sexual harassment from a former aide, Anita Hill ○ Magic Johnson announces that he has HIV ○ Julie Dash releases *Daughters of the Dust*, the first feature-length film written and directed by a Black woman ○ John Singleton becomes the first Black filmmaker to be nominated for an Academy Award for Best Director, for *Boyz n the Hood* ○ Freddie Mercury dies of AIDS ○ Time publishes a sweeping critique of Scientology ○ Twenty-seven-year-old William Fadell of Spring Park, Minnesota, dies after being struck by lightning at the U.S. Open at Hazeltine National ○ The body of President Zachary Taylor, who died in 1850, is exhumed to see if his death was the result of arsenic poisoning; no poison is found ○ Super Nintendo is released

FURIOUS STYLES

When styles change, what else around them has to change?

Before the next decade, a declaration:

Life has stages, and each of those stages requires a different way of absorbing or communicating history. When I sketch out the periods of my own life, I find that they corresponded (very roughly) to decades. The first decade of my life was when the seeds of knowledge were planted by others—parents, teachers, sometimes other kids. The second decade was when I first saw the roots and shoots poking up, the beginnings of whatever was growing from the knowledge that had been planted by those others. The beginnings of understanding, you might say. That was the period when I started to explore on my own, to learn to collect information, to test it against what I had been told. We've been there already. I call it the '80s.

Then came my third decade, when I first went out into the world and tried to sell (or even give away) the fruit that I had harvested from those roots and shoots. For me, that meant the beginnings of my career as a musician. I wasn't a professional yet, and I certainly had no sense of whether or not I would actually make it, but that question had been asked and was in the process of being answered. I had been a child. I had been a student. And though I was still both of those in some ways, I was also, for the first time, an adult. A young one, certainly, but a person with a vision of what kind of world I might want to live in and what I thought it might be able to give me (and, less important at first, what I might be able to give it). The world was changing—it is always changing—but my place in it had changed, too, and my position, which meant that I was looking differently, from a different spot. In a sense, I was less analytical, because suddenly there was more life to live. In terms of this book, that will mean shorter chapters, a quickening of pace, an acceleration through history motivated by a desire to become part of it. (Whether that also means more narrative momentum, a rush toward a climactic conclusion, is a trickier question. Real history has plots, but it doesn't always have Plot.)

• • •

On to 1991. It's the twentieth century's only palindromic year, but it's also proof that history moves in only one direction. A paradox? A paradigm!

• • •

I had always studied musical styles. I studied them as a kid, watching my parents in their bands. I studied them at my performing arts high school. I studied them being a band leader and a musical director, a producer and a DJ. But over the span of my own life, I came to understand more and more clearly that they had lifespans. In the late '80s, the most radical production in hip-hop came from the Bomb Squad: Hank Shocklee at first, then Keith Shocklee, Eric "Vietnam" Sadler, Gary G-Wiz, Paul Shabazz, and Bill Stephney, depending on when in the collective's evolution you happen to request a group photo. The Shocklees were actually Boxleys, and brothers, Hank the younger (born in 1967), Keith the older (1962), and they came out of the same scene as Chuck D: at first, a sound system called Spectrum City, then the circle of aspiring rappers in and around Adelphi University on their native Long Island. Stephney was a program director at WBAU, Adelphi's radio station, and Spectrum City got a spot on-air in 1982 or so (another local rapper, Flavor Flav, showed up at BAU around the same time).

There's one Spectrum City single, "Lies" backed with "Check Out the Radio." "Lies" opens with a version of "La Marseillaise," and "Check Out the Radio" has some of those tiptoeing horns that would later become a Bomb Squad trademark, and a catchier chorus (which would resurface almost two decades later, in altered form, on "The W," a bonus track on the Wu-Tang Clan's *Iron Flag*). On both, Chuck D, who goes by "Chucky D," shares vocals with Aaron Allen, who goes by "Butch Cassidy." The single went nowhere, and the group went with it for a little while, retreating for a while, retrenching, and reemerging in 1987 as Public Enemy.

When I heard their records and started to get a handle on their aesthetic—and this would have been those first two Public Enemy records, *Yo! Bum Rush the Show* in 1987 and *It Takes a Nation of Millions to Hold Us Back* the following year—I was attracted to them immediately. What I heard, what I felt, was my dad's entire record collection thrown into a blender. I was accustomed to sampling in hip-hop, but up until then it had been one at a time, two or three at most. Those Bomb Squad productions made me feel like I was hearing fifty samples at a time. I know that's an exaggeration. It might have been a dozen. It might have even been a baker's dozen. But it sounded like fifty. That was the point. It was four soldiers making enough of a commotion that the enemy army over the hill thought they were about to face a force of a hundred. It was a precise mess, organized chaos, weaponized noise. It was also a high-wire act.

In those early days, the Bomb Squad had a meticulous blueprint of the masonry of sound they were building, but it didn't always extend to the business side. That level of renegade production, where samples were piled on top of samples, couldn't last long. Companies start getting litigious: That's my track in your track, and I don't feel Reese's Peanut Butter Cups about it as much as I feel District Court. So it was a short-lived glory period: I'd add the third Public Enemy album, *Fear of a Black Planet*, Ice Cube's *AmeriKKKa's Most Wanted*, and Bell Biv Devoe's *Poison*—the Bomb Squad didn't do the title track, which was Dr. Freeze, straight-up canonical New Jack, but the majority of that record was theirs. On the low, I like the first Terminator X solo album, *Terminator X & the Valley of the Jeep Beats*. Then there's the soundtrack to *Juice*, which they executive-produced.

Most of those records—*Juice*, Cube, BBD, Terminator X—were from 1990–1991. It was an explosive period. The U.S. Congress passed (and then made good on) a resolution authorizing the use of force to liberate Kuwait. That touched off the Gulf War, which began with Operation Desert Storm in January. It was, among other things, a made-for-TV war: General Norman Schwarzkopf was on often, talking about this airstrike or that one, many of which featured the Guided Bomb Unit-28, better known as the "bunker buster." Against that backdrop, the Bomb Squad enjoyed its last golden year. But the best examples of their artistry weren't even the best-known. Within that same twelve-month span, there were two other projects that, despite flopping commercially—not as bad as "Lies," but still—showed them to be at the height of their powers.

One album, out in May of that year, was called *Bazerk, Bazerk, Bazerk*, and was credited, in supremely unwieldy fashion, to Son of Bazerk featuring No Self Control and the Band. Son of Bazerk was a Long Island–based act, and the album that the Bomb Squad made for (and around) them was almost like a novelty record. In the lead single, "Change the Style," every lyric was a reference to an old soul record, and beats would switch in the middle of a rhyme—there might be a slow-jam section followed by an up-tempo funk section followed by a hardcore part. The group never quite got traction, but it got reaction—specifically from Ice Cube, who was working with the Bomb Squad on his debut during the same period they were Bazerking. He heard one of the songs, decided that he wanted it for himself, and refashioned it as the title song of *AmeriKKKa's Most Wanted*. (Over there, with Ice Cube behind it, it hit even harder. The cymbal is so damned violent! Those Bomb Squad beats make even a peaceful dude like me want to mug somebody in the face.)

The other underrated Bomb Squad showpiece was the debut by Young Black Teenagers. The name, which was given to them by Chuck D, was ironic. They weren't Black. (Though they were young, which makes it not as ironic.)

(Though they weren't teenagers—irony restored!) Their members included DJ Skribble, who became an MTV fixture in the early '90s on shows like *The Grind* and *Spring Break*, along with Kamron, Tommy Never, First Born, and ATA. The cover of that first album, which came out on Hank Shocklee's own label, S.O.U.L. (Sound of Urban Listeners), was a straight parody of *Meet the Beatles*. And while they didn't touch off a cultural revolution in the same way—or really, in any way—that first album stuck with me.

Not in all ways. Lyrically, it's extremely of its time, which is a nice thing that people say when they want to say that something is dated. There's a song about Kelly Bundy from *Married . . . with Children* called "Nobody Knows Kelli" (she'd have a surprisingly long life in hip-hop lyrics, turning up fifteen years later in Spank Rock's "Bump"). There's one about Madonna called "To My Donna" (the group was mad at Madonna for using Public Enemy's "Security of the First World" in "Justify My Love"). And there's a song called "Traci" about "this girl around my block" who "gets my [horn sound effect] as hard as a rock." (I didn't put the "[horn sound effect]" there out of prudery. It's actually in the song. Honk!) Those three songs, and more than a few others, are filled with juvenile misogyny. I'm neither judging nor excusing—just describing.

But forget about the lyrics for a second. Focus on the sound. The group was distinctive in that at various points all five of them would rhyme at the same time, so there was a vocal sophistication to the attack (maybe those Beatles comparisons aren't that insane). But the real draw of the record is the production: the sheer nerve of the Bomb Squad going crazy. Producers with a strong hand were one thing. Producers with a dense and undeniable artistry of their own were another.

It sent me back thirty-five years, to that moment at Motown when Otis Williams, the baritone singer in the Temptations, introduced the producer Norman Whitfield to the music of Sly and the Family Stone. Sly was trying something new, and something risky—a mix of shared lead vocals, fuzzed-up guitar, gospel harmonies, and break beats—and Williams wanted his producer to hear it. Whitfield wasn't sure at first, but then he was sure, and for the next six years he built on it to create Motown's own psychedelic soul: the first song in that style, "Cloud Nine," was followed by "Runaway Child, Running Wild," "Ball of Confusion," and "Papa Was a Rolling Stone." But the Temptations got tired of their peerless vocal abilities being pushed into the background as Whitfield's increasingly ornate productions took the spotlight. Songs would stretch to ten, eleven minutes, but the first half would be purely instrumental, and the fact that the compositions were brilliant didn't offset the hurt the group felt when people in the halls at Motown started referring to them as the "Norman Whitfield Choral Singers." One of the worst offenders—or best achievers, depending on who you were—was "Masterpiece" in 1973. The title sounded grandiose and was, especially given that the word never appeared in the lyrics, which were about the hopelessness of ghetto life. The masterpiece in question, clearly, was Whitfield's production. The group itself didn't appear until well into its own song.

Times changed between 1973 and 1992, of course, and the Young Black Teenagers were no Temptations, but a song like "My TV Went Black and White on Me," even though it had lyrics, felt instrumental, because it was such a powerful and peerless demonstration of the Bomb Squad's abilities and ambitions.

After 1991, the Bomb Squad lost its pole position among hip-hop producers. In part, it was the result of the theft of a number of production disks for a new Public Enemy album, more than a year of work at least. Hank Shocklee has said in interviews that the loss of the disks caused more than a work shortfall. It caused a loss of confidence. The momentum that had accumulated since 1989 dissipated, not just for Public Enemy but for the production team. That was part of the story. The other part happened at the far western edge of the continent, in Los Angeles, where Dr. Dre was pioneering a new style, slowing everything down and cleaning everything up. He showed off his new moves on *The Chronic*, which dropped in December 1992. *The Chronic* changed everything sonically, but it wasn't just a record. It was a protest record, the end-cap of a tumultuous stretch in Los Angeles that had started back in March 1991 when an amateur video captured four police officers brutally beating a drunk driver named Rodney King. The video went viral before there was such a thing. It was viewed and reviewed, incorporated into endless political discussions and pop-culture references (see, for example, the video for Public Enemy's "Can't Truss It," the lead single from the first post-theft album, which was rushed together by Shocklee and the rest of the Squad). The four officers were charged with assault and use of excessive force. The trial was moved from Los Angeles County to Ventura County, partly in response to the intense media scrutiny. In April 1992, the largely white jury returned acquittals for three of the officers and failed to reach a decision on the fourth. In Los Angeles's Black neighborhoods, those verdicts lit a fuse that had already been shortened by decades of police brutality, and the whole city quickly detonated. Like a bomb.

1992

George H. W. Bush becomes ill at a state dinner in Tokyo, vomits into the lap of Japan's prime minister, Kiichi Miyazawa, and faints; the dinner is televised ○ Bush is defeated by Bill Clinton in the November presidential election ○ John Gotti is convicted of murder and racketeering and sentenced to life in prison ○ Mike Tyson goes to prison after he is convicted of raping Desiree Washington; he will serve just under three years ○ Arthur Ashe announces he has AIDS; he will die a year later ○ Sinead O'Connor rips up a picture of Pope John Paul II on *Saturday Night Live* ○ The Ruby Ridge raid results in the death of a U.S. marshal ○ Dr. Mae Carol Jemison becomes the first African American woman in space when she travels on board the space shuttle *Endeavor* ○ Carol Moseley Braun is elected the first African American female senator, representing Illinois

ECHO PARK

Reenactments, historical and cultural, and how they frame the past.

In the summer of 1992, America was mired in an economic malaise, with high unemployment that was weakening the presidency of George H. W. Bush. It wasn't the only news, of course. Los Angeles was still reeling: sixty-three dead, more than two thousand injured, and a billion dollars in property damage in the unrest that followed the acquittal of the Rodney King cops. Johnny Carson had just retired from *The Tonight Show*. Manuel Noriega was just about to be sentenced to a forty-year prison term. But much of that summer was about politics, as the country moved toward the presidential election that November. Some of the political events were truly newsworthy, like the arms reduction treaty that Bush signed with Boris Yeltsin. Others were otherwise. In the middle of June, Vice President Dan Quayle appeared at a New Jersey spelling bee, where he took it upon himself to correct a young student who had spelled the word *potato*. Quayle wanted to put an *e* at the end. *Potato* doesn't have an *e* at the end.

But *En Vogue* does. The Oakland vocal group, which consisted of Dawn Robinson, Terry Ellis, Cindy Herron, and Maxine Jones, had released their second album, *Funky Divas*, back in March, and in June, they released their second single, "Giving Him Something He Can Feel." In a year where tempers flared, the song gave off a different kind of heat, sultry and seductive. At the time, I saw the song mostly as a video, and a very alluring and successful one. This clip was directed by Stefan Würnitzer, who had also directed Paula Abdul's "Rush Rush" the previous year (an homage to *Rebel Without a Cause*—see 1988).

"Giving Him Something He Can Feel," the video, found the group in slinky, sultry, and seductive mode, going onstage in a nightclub in front of mysterious high rollers. Still, I don't think I understood its power until they were the musical guests on *Saturday Night Live* and performed "Free Your Mind," which borrowed its title from Funkadelic's 1970 album *Free Your Mind . . . and Your Ass Will Follow* and its sound from the guitar-injected-into-Black-pop formula that had been in place since Janet Jackson's "Black Cat," at least. In watching that performance, I felt myself missing "Giving Him Something He Can Feel."

But what was I missing? Was I missing En Vogue's version only, or the musical lineage it represented? "Giving Him Something He Can Feel" was not a new song, but a cover of a 1976 hit sung by Aretha Franklin, written and produced by Curtis Mayfield, from the album *Sparkle*. Aretha and Curtis had been major figures of the 1960s and early '70s, but the mid-'70s found them both slightly adrift as solo artists. Just slightly. She was still one of the biggest female soul singers in America, maybe even at the top of the heap, but no longer at the top of her game. Her last artistically undeniable record had been *Hey Now Hey (The Other Side of the Sky)* in 1973—a great album with legendarily bad cover art that stiffed a little commercially. Her last truly popular record had been *Let Me in Your Life* the following year. After that, she made a pair of albums—*With Everything I Feel in Me* and *You*—with Jerry Wexler and/or Arif Mardin, the brain trust of Atlantic Records, and then moved on to new producers. It's weird, because those albums (along with the slightly later *Almighty Fire*) are my Aretha. I respected the big hits, but they happened when I was young. They were part of the official story. I got into the albums that people think of as her down period, and I know every song on them. I love "Mr. DJ (5 for the DJ)." Incredible songs. But the market didn't agree. Other singers, like Chaka Khan, were on the rise.

Mayfield, for his part, had cooled as a solo artist as well, instead taking up refuge in a series of soundtracks that followed *Super Fly* (see 1972): he did *Claudine* with Gladys Knight and the Pips in 1974 and *Let's Do It Again* with the Staple Singers in 1975. So the pairing on *Sparkle* made sense, even more so given that it, too, was a soundtrack. Directed by Sam O'Steen, a legendary film editor (*The Graduate*, *Chinatown*) who was maybe a little less legendary as a director—this was his only feature—the movie told the story of a girl group from the late '50s and early '60s riven by personality conflicts and struggling with the fact that their lead singer's obvious star power and future as a solo act was jeopardizing their existence. They were a Supremes manqué, basically, played by Irene Cara (in the Diana Ross spot), Lonette McKee, and Dwan Smith and saddled with the unfortunate name of Sister and the Sisters. (Because they were sisters! Get it?) Philip M. Thomas, back when he was billed that way, played their manager, Stix. Lester Wilson choreographed the movie. His assistant was Michael Peters, who went on to choreograph Michael Jackson's most famous videos, including "Beat It" and "Thriller."

Sparkle has several significant pleasures and several moments that misfire. The music is a massive asset, particularly "Something He Can Feel" (the original carries that slightly shorter title). But it's a strange asset. As a song about the way that love (and sex) overcome "a world of ghetto life," it's inspirational. As a song that claims to be telling part of a historical story, on the other hand, it's disorienting. It's Curtis Mayfield, in 1976, writing a contemporary song whose fictional function is to tell part of a story that stretches from the late '50s to the mid-'60s. It's Aretha, a solo star who was never in a girl group of that sort, performing that song under somewhat sketchy conditions—the soundtrack album uses music performed in the film and strips away Cara's lead vocals so that Franklin can furnish new ones. The song doesn't sound like the era (or the group) it's supposed to represent, which probably accounts for its success (it topped the soul chart and went Top Thirty pop) but definitely accounts for its overall sense of strangeness. It's like seeing your reflection through a pair of funhouse mirrors that offset each other and almost, but not quite, return the image to normal.

And that's only the original. When En Vogue decided to record the song sixteen years later as a standalone piece, they added more mirrors. They were a group in the '90s covering a song from the '70s that pretends to be set in the '60s—the result is both a master class in the differences between those eras and proof of the power of an enduring song—not to mention a legitimate girl group covering a song by a solo star about a girl group struggling with the emergence of a solo star. When you listen to the 1992 version, you're hearing a Rubik's Cube of history, and an unsolved one at that. (Oh, sorry: '80s reference.) Is the original song really a reflection of '60s ideas and styles, or of '70s ideas about '60s ideas and styles? Which are more prominent in the '90s version, if either? Once you've answered those, go on to questions three and four and five. Who is being inspired by who? (I know that's not grammatically correct, but Aretha's "Who's Zoomin' Who?" got into my head, and it won't get out. Oh, sorry: another '80s reference.) Who is interpreting who? In the equation that attempts to calculate the relationships among Sister and the Sisters, Aretha, and En Vogue, who is reaching back to who, and which third term might be skipping a factual middle term to connect more genuinely with a fictional first term?

There's a coda, which is that En Vogue fell victim to the *Sparkle* syndrome themselves. Dawn Robinson, who would have been considered the lead singer, left the group in 1997 for a solo career. Because this story can never be straightforward, Robinson's version of the *Sparkle* syndrome wasn't the traditional one, at least not right away. At the time she left, Raphael Saadiq, late of Tony! Toni! Toné! (the Oakland soul group that had broken up after the album *House of Music* in 1996), and Ali Shaheed Muhammed, late of A Tribe Called Quest (the hip-hop legends who would break up after *The Love Movement* in 1998—more on that later), were in talks to form a new group with the vocalist D'Angelo, who had released his debut, *Brown Sugar*, to massive critical acclaim a few years before. But D'Angelo was tied up recording his second record, so the group was retooled for a female vocalist, who turned out to be Dawn Robinson. The band, Lucy Pearl, put out one record and then disbanded. Robinson did have a solo record of her own in 2002, but it didn't carry her to Diana Ross or *Sparkle* heights. (The album that D'Angelo was laboring over, *Voodoo*, would come out in 2000 and immediately be acclaimed as a timeless classic. Let's say a possibly timeless classic: I have to tread lightly in my praise of it because it's an album I worked on extensively as a copilot, songwriter, drummer, and creative partner. In some footnotes, you can see your own feet.)

There's a coda to the coda, too. In 2012, a group of Black music stars, old, new, and in between, came together to film a new version of *Sparkle*, keeping much of the original movie's structure and many of the names. There's still a Sparkle, this time played by the closely named Jordin Sparks, who had won the sixth season of *American Idol* back in 2007. There are sisters, played by Carmen Ejogo and Tika Sumpter. There's a Stix played by Derek Luke. The mother of the girls, played by Mary Alice in the original movie, is played by Whitney Houston in her last acting role, twenty years after her debut in *The Bodyguard*, which spawned the best-selling soundtrack album of all time. (Houston would die tragically three months later, in the bathtub of her room at the Beverly Hilton, hours before she was scheduled to attend the hotel's pre-Grammy party, and the finished film would be dedicated to her memory.) The story is updated, to some degree. While the first movie took place in late-'50s and early '60s New York, this second movie is set in 1968 Detroit. The difference, of course, is more or less the lifespan of Motown—*Sparkle* 1.0 looks at the period just before Motown took hold of young America, while *Sparkle* 2.0 moves ahead to when Motown was forced to adapt to the new sounds flowing in from rock and roll and psychedelic soul. Both are flawed films with good performances and (just to cover an idea from an earlier paragraph) oddly unfaithful relationships to the eras they claim to be re-creating. The second movie includes a performance of "Something He Can Feel" (back to the original title now—respect for 1976) that is as much a tribute to the En Vogue video as anything (respect for 1992). If *Vertigo* wasn't already taken as a title, this movie should have used it.

• • •

The same year that En Vogue covered "Giving Him Something He Can Feel," there was another soul cover that seemed stranger but was in fact far more straightforward. It was a new version of a 1977 ballad by the Commodores, the funk and soul band fronted by Lionel Richie (their *Sparkle* moment occurred in 1982, when Richie left for a solo career you may have heard about). This time, the song was recorded by the alternative-metal band Faith No More. That year, the group released its fourth album, *Angel Dust*, the first one creatively overseen by the group's lead vocalist, Mike Patton—he had been hired for the previous record, *The Real Thing*, but only after most of the album's music was recorded. That previous album produced a giant MTV hit, "Epic," that I saw all the time. For *Angel Dust*, Patton was on board from the very beginning, and it reflected his influences, which moved away from more traditional hard rock into a dizzying mix of cabaret, funk, and experimental music. The song titles hint at the tone(s) while still not being able to fully capture them: "Jizzlobber," "RV," "Crack Hitler," "Everything's Ruined," "Be Aggressive." I wouldn't have bought that album back in 1992, and if I had, it would have been the final mindbender: it might have broken my brain completely, and I'd still be sitting there in a chair, staring out into space, face blank.

The album proper ended with a gentle instrumental version of John Barry's theme from the 1969 movie *Midnight Cowboy*. It was entirely out of character, which meant that it was entirely in character for the kitchen-sink-and-then-some aesthetic that Patton was practicing. During the same sessions, they had recorded a version of "Easy," and it was released on an EP later that year. When I heard about it and tried to fit it into what I knew about the album—I hadn't heard it yet, but I was hearing wild things—I tried to imagine what it would be. An evil circus-music version? A speed-rapped version with a klezmer backing? My imagination was running away. The truth was even more shocking. It was a straight version, almost entirely faithful to the Commodores, sung by Patton with sensitivity and nuance. It both respected the original and gave it enough new context so that it stood on its own (when Lionel Richie sang that he was "high, so high," there was an electronic sound that peeled up out of the mix; Faith No More went for a more aggressive guitar).

What allows it to move through time so easily? Partly it's the nature of the original song, which isn't designed to reflect a specific historical-cultural moment. No '60s, no '70s, no '90s, no tangle. It's a song by a Black band intended to move seamlessly into the white mainstream, sort of the opposite of what Al Sharpton said about James Brown (see 1974). It's also an elegant description of a familiar emotional response: in the wake of a breakup, the singer insists that he's not doing as badly as people might think. Times have changed, but he hasn't. He's still easy like Sunday morning (again, not any specific Sunday morning in any specific year in any specific place). Universal emotions, handled correctly, can be skeleton keys that unlock doors up and down history's corridor. Know it sounds funny.

History Repeats Itself, but How?

When I would hear songs on the radio, my mind would open to admit them and then harden around them. They became official events. If I learned later that there was an earlier version of the same song, it could come as quite a shock. I might even consider that earlier version an imitator. I know that doesn't make logical sense, but what about life is logical? I think this is a version of what the philosopher says: "Life can only be understood backwards, but it must be lived forward." Whenever I think of that quote, I think of Kriss Kross pants, moving backward and forward through life. But they weren't the philosopher who said it, right? Research! Okay. It's Kierkegaard. Anyway, covers.

"UNO ESTA"
Yesterdays New Quintet

Angles Without Edges, 2001 [Stones Throw]

The song is originally by Bobbi Humphrey, from her 1975 album *Fancy Dancer*. I remember my uncle Junie having that 8-track and also remember that I didn't like anything on Blue Note. I thought it had a really boring logo. I tuned out of Donald Byrd and Marlena Shaw. As hip-hop came in, all those records became favorites. It was written by the Mizell brothers, who also wrote "Boogie Oogie Oogie" (see 1978), and while I didn't mind their disco thing, I didn't like their jazz formula, the way they grouped the vocals. Only when I found this project, which was Madlib's way of teaching himself jazz, did I credit this song.

"K-JEE"
MFSB

Saturday Night Fever, 1979 [RSO]

Because of when I existed, when I grew up, because of when fate located me on the historical timeline, I saw (heard) the MFSB version as the definitive take on the song. It was my original. It wasn't until I did a DJ gig for Gilles Peterson in England, where he played the Nite Liters original, that I realized MFSB's had been a cover. That happens. It's like a version of the Kierkegaard principle from above. Life is lived in one direction but understood in the other.

"ROCKY RACCOON"
Lena Horne

Lena & Gabor, 1970 [Skye]

"Rocky Raccoon" is, like so many Paul McCartney songs, a kids' record that's not a kids' record. That's a big part of his appeal, that his compositions are so conducive to singalongs. This version was made with the Hungarian guitarist Gábor Szabó, and it has the perfect campy tone.

"EVERYDAY PEOPLE"
Billy Paul

Ebony Woman, 1970 [Neptune]

I don't know why it's hard for me to say that I like PB&J. I can see why people gravitate toward the original of this song. It's probably the first song of white guilt America could latch on to that taught that we were all one and the same. And it's more Sly (pun intended) than it seems, more subtle, but there's still that sloganeering aspect, even a little cliché. When I first heard this cover, Billy Paul sounded like an out-of-control Muppet, all unhinged scatting. The prime reason I chose it was that there were two label types for Philadelphia International records. There's a yin-and-yang symbol with white dots in the middle. Some early records, like this and the O'Jays', didn't have the white dots in the middle. In my mind, they deserved more attention—they were like redheaded stepchildren somehow.

"I CAN UNDERSTAND IT"
New Birth

Birth Day, 1972 [RCA]

Bobby Womack had recorded this the year before, in a much softer and bluesier version, with a little country tinge, even. This is way more up-tempo, like a James Brown take almost. Back then you always had to have at least seven to eight covers handy to keep your live show flowing. And they definitely did this live. There's a performance on that Ellis Haizlip show, *Soul!*, which is the most definitive performance of a non-JB James Brown song I've ever seen.

"IF SHE BREAKS YOUR HEART"
The Foreign Exchange

Leave It All Behind, 2008 [Foreign Exchange]

This was the rapper Phonte and the producer Nicolay, and they were pioneers of sending each other tracks and then starting a group. This intersects with the Stevie Wonder argument I've made elsewhere in this book (and more than several in my life), which is that while the songwriting stayed strong, the musical execution was way too dated. There were three frustrations of the *Jungle Fever* soundtrack. The song "Lighting Up the Candles," heard in the movie, coming through a clock radio, almost sounded like an Amy Winehouse–type '60s homage, almost a real '60s song. But when I got the album it was just '90s programming. Excluding "Feeding Off the Love of the Land" from the record was another sin. And then this one, where the drum programming sank him. COTDAMN, if the drums had just been warm this could have been his sequel to "You Got It Bad Girl."

"STARS/FEELINGS"
Nina Simone

Live at Montreux 1976, 2012 [Eagle Music]

I don't know how many people have seen this performance, where she covers Janis Ian's "Stars" and Morris Albert's "Feelings." She has many covers, but this pair—and this approach—gets me every time. It's so devastating, the way she takes the most trite and simple song and just tears into it, or tears into herself with it.

"MOODY'S MOOD"
Aretha Franklin

Hey Now Hey (The Other Side of the Sky), 1973 [Atlantic]

Her version was the first one I loved, when I heard it as a seven-year-old. My mom, I remember, would chime in and object. She'd say that Billy Eckstine's version was much better, that Aretha was much too jumpy. I didn't know the value of "There I go, there I go, there I go," but I liked the way she began, which made the song start like an adventure.

"GIMME SOME MORE (VERY LIVE)"
The JBs

Funky Good Time: The Anthology, 1995 [Polydor]

The studio version is on *Pass the Peas*. And then there's this live cover. Is a live version of a studio song performed by the same band a cover? I think it is. It's a re-presentation of the material under different circumstances. I don't know who's playing bass live, whether it's Fred Thomas or maybe Sweet Charles Sherrell. But whoever is doing it adds extra notes. The opening has seven notes for the bass in the album version. Here it's turned into ten notes that make the whole difference in the song. Where he places them, the rhythm wakes. It's weird, because as a hip-hop producer you want what gives you more space, so you can work with it. The more filled the room is with furniture, the more you're forced to see the original vision. So you wouldn't think this version would get me. But it does.

"CUT THE CAKE"
Average White Band

Live at Montreux, 2005 [Eagle Rock]

This is another live version. There's the original, of course, and then there's the live version on *Person to Person*. Years later, this Montreux Jazz Festival performance was released in full—pieces of it came out on a record called *The Atlantic Family Live at Montreux*. This version has Alan Gorrie's best ad-libs. I think he didn't realize it would be released to the public, so he was working with the live audience. When you don't think something is going to be purchased, there are karaoke references, ways of tipping the hat to inspirations and contemporaries. It's very loose and present.

1993

Bill Clinton becomes the forty-second president of the United States ○ Don Cornelius steps down as the host of *Soul Train* ○ The Branch Davidian compound in Waco, Texas, is raided, beginning a fifty-one-day standoff that results in the death of four ATF agents and five Branch Davidians, including their leader, David Koresh ○ A van parked underneath the North Tower of the World Trade Center explodes; six are killed and more than a thousand injured ○ Joycelyn Elders becomes both the first Black and the first female surgeon general of the United States ○ Toni Morrison becomes the first Black American to win the Nobel Prize in Literature ○ *Jurassic Park* is released ○ Charley Pride is admitted into the Grand Old Opry ○ Brandon Lee is killed during the filming of *The Crow* ○ $7.4 million is stolen from a Brinks depot in Rochester, New York, in the fifth-largest robbery in American history

X MARKS THE SPOT

Big ideas are seductive, but seduction is risky.

Spike Lee's *X*, his Malcolm X biopic, came out just before Thanksgiving of 1992. Malcolm's X was a rejection of his slave name, Little, and a stand-in for the true name he felt he could never know. But an X is also a crossroads. Just ask Lawrence Parker.

Parker had been born in 1965 in the Bronx, a few months after and a few miles north of Malcolm's assassination at the Audubon Ballroom. As a kid, Parker had a strong interest in the spiritual beliefs of others, which earned him the nickname "Krishna." That was shortened over time to Kris, shortened again to KRS, and then lengthened by "One." By the process, Lawrence Parker became KRS-One, among the first and most important socially conscious rappers. Starting in the mid-'80s, KRS-One formed Boogie Down Productions with DJ Scott La Rock, and put out one classic album, *Criminal Minded*, before La Rock was murdered. La Rock had gone with his fellow DJ D-Nice to work things out with a group of men who had beaten up D-Nice after they caught him talking to one of their girlfriends. Or maybe ex-girlfriends. It's somewhat lost to time and why would it matter anyway? It's a story of senseless murder. La Rock, D-Nice, and others drove a Jeep into the Highbridge projects in the

South Bronx to talk to the men. The peacekeeping mission was unsuccessful. As they drove away, shots were fired at the Jeep. One entered though the side and struck La Rock in the back of the head. He was unaware that he had been shot. He thought that he had hit his head on the dashboard. At the hospital, he was wheeled into the operating room and died.

KRS-One soldiered on, keeping the Boogie Down Productions name but evolving his subject matter. *Edutainment*, from 1990, included songs about vegetarianism and skits featuring Kwame Ture, formerly the Black Panther and civil rights activist Stokely Carmichael. After *Sex and Violence* in 1992, KRS-One retired the BDP name and reemerged as a solo act with 1993's *Return of the Boom Bap*.

One of the standout cuts was "The Sound of da Police," a straightforward protest against police harassment that ran through a litany of bad cop behaviors: assuming that any young Black man in the park is dealing drugs, following Black drivers without cause . . . In the middle, there's a moment of verbal gymnastics where KRS-One drills down into history via homophonics. "Take the word *overseer*, like a sample," he says. "Repeat it very quickly in a crew for example." He rapid-fires "overseer" until it's transformed into "officer," and explains how Black people have spent three, four, forty generations dealing with white authority. Why should one group of people, one kind of people, separated by melanin and nothing more, be under the heel, under the knee, under the oversight of another? It's a rhetorical question. They shouldn't.

• • •

Fleet and blunt, curious and confident, KRS-One has always been capable of great things in his lyrics. But he can also descend into conspiracy. I want to shoot ahead to 2009, to the *Austin Chronicle*.

> KRS-One came through Mohawk Saturday and mesmerized the crowd like few other MCs can or ever could, dropping an endless parade of hip-hop classics and righteously preaching at the crowd

> about whatever happens to be on his mind. This night it was Obama ("The new world order just put on a black face") and inciting chants of "9–11 was an inside job." There's a reason it sounds like the Blastmaster has been kicking it with local celebrity conspiracy theorist Alex Jones. The day before the Mohawk performance, KRS phoned in to Jones' show from Dallas.

KRS-One and DJ Alex La Box-of-Rocks? There's a duo. One of KRS-One's main complaints, which he articulated elsewhere, including in a documentary called *The Obama Deception,* was that Obama was the same-old, same-old, just a new mask on the old global control mechanisms. "If they controlled it before, what makes you think they're not controlling it now?" he said in an interview, not getting any more specific about the "they" or the "it."

Vague *they*s and *it*s are generally fodder for conspiracy thinking. As I write this, we're in the midst of an era when Americans seem unusually susceptible to conspiracies, or at least tolerant of a president who seemed very interested in the way that other people's susceptibility to conspiracies increased his control over them. That's not a great trait. I think we can agree. But even on the right side of history (the correct side, I mean, not the political right), there are works that traffic in similar thinking. Less stupid, certainly, less malicious, and less sadistic, but with the same notion that there are hidden forces moving the gears of history, a Wizard (or Wiz) for every Emerald City.

Take Howard Zinn's *A People's History of the United States.* When I read Zinn years ago, I liked the book. The writing was vivid, and it illuminated parts of history I hadn't thought much about. It worked to shine a light. Years after that, when I started thinking about history for this project, I revisited Zinn and some of that illumination fell into shadow. I read about how more traditional historians described and valued Zinn's project, and why they had concerns. Because Zinn was writing a popular text, he didn't source things like an academic would. He also based much of his argument on anecdotes, and sometimes bent a timeline to support a conclusion. Some historians refused to continue on with him under these conditions, while others recognized that he was engaging a wider audience in important historical questions, cut him slack, and moved on. I was somewhere in the middle.

The criticism that bothered me the most was in an article, by a Stanford history professor named Sam Wineburg, called "Undue Certainty." Wineburg looked at Zinn's interpretation of why the United States dropped the atomic bomb on Japan. The traditional narrative taught in schools for generations had to do with bringing the war to a speedy close, and in the process saving the lives of hundreds of thousands of soldiers who would have died had the fighting dragged on. Zinn took a completely different view, arguing that the bomb was dropped quickly so that the Soviet Union could not enter the war. I'm not going to get deeply into the substance of the argument. My main goal in this book isn't to substitute my analysis (which would be far from expert) for existing analyses. But I do want to help teach people to learn history by reminding them to question their reading habits, reassess where they locate authority, retain a healthy skepticism. I was especially interested in what Wineburg says about Zinn's reasoning:

> It seems that once he made up his mind, nothing—not new evidence, not new scholarship, not the discovery of previously unknown documents, not the revelations of historical actors on their deathbeds—could shake it.

All the things that Wineburg lists should shake a mind. In fact, they are exactly what should shake a mind. Holding so tightly to an idea that you will not let new facts sway you doesn't sound like a good idea. In fact, from where I'm standing in 2020, it looks like one of the worst. Over these last few years, everything from Birtherism to claims of election fraud to vaccine paranoia have passed into a zone where made-up minds remain unshaken no matter what. Worse: their made-up minds then grasp the promise of new evidence or documents, no matter if that evidence or those documents are actually delivered. Recently, here in America, we saw a wave of citizens pledging allegiance to the election-fraud theories of people like Lin Wood and Sidney Powell, who promised proof in the form of testimony and documents and high-tech detection over and over and over again while never actually providing it. It was then left to those citizens, the ones with their minds made up, to express a belief in these theories, even as the narrative that supposedly explained them became more and more outlandish and involved a less and less plausible cast of characters (Hugo Chávez, voting machine inventor! Mike Pence, double agent!). Legitimate evidence, scholarship, documents were not only ignored but branded the enemy, because they took people further away from their made-up minds. Conspiracy tightened around the populace like a constrictor.

Months after his appearance in *The Obama Deception*, KRS-One set about elucidating. But rather than distance himself from the conclusions, he just set himself up as a more sophisticated messenger: "I don't disagree with the message of the movie, but KRS is a little deeper than the movie projects." Going deeper is better, unless you are just drilling down into your own already-reached conclusions and your refusal to revise them. That's the problem with conspiracy theories of any stripe—they lead you to the One Big Epiphany, and the endorphin rush of that moment directs you to see everything that follows as following logically, which is in itself illogical. Go out and collect more facts, both those that support your conclusions and those that challenge them. Listen to the other side even as you protect your own side. Don't close yourself off to new information, and don't be afraid if that new information is eroding beliefs that give you comfort.

• • •

After *Return of the Boom Bap*, KRS-One released a self-titled solo album, maybe as a way of reintroducing himself. Just before it, the Roots had an album of our own, *Do You Want More?!!!??!* On that album we had a song called "Silent Treatment." We were high on it. We thought it would take us higher. So it got a very unsilent treatment, with a number of remixes. There was one that leaned into dancehall, one that leaned into jazz, a great one by Tariq that paid homage to a Philly classic, "Kick the Ball," by the Krown Rulers.

We also had a remix produced by Da Beatminerz. They were a production team from Bushwick that consisted of Evil Dee and Mr. Walt, really two brothers named Ewart and Walter Dewgarde. (This is one of the rare cases where even though I'm sure they thought their normal names weren't cool, they may have been just as cool as the cool nicknames they assumed.) Da Beatminerz recorded us at D&D Studios, one of New York's legendary locations, on West Thirty-Seventh between Eighth and Ninth Avenues. That place was quite something. It was like a museum of every person who had ever recorded there: old blunt ashes, old snacks in the machine. Artifacts accumulated. While Tariq was working on the vocal, I had some time on my hands. I went out to play pool on my own. Ding! Ding! I kept hearing this little bell. I went down the hall until I found the door with the ringing behind it. The first face I saw was DJ Premier, and the second was KRS-One. They were working on "MCs Act Like They Don't Know," which would end up being the first single from his second album. I wondered how they were making the bell noise. What had they sampled it from? It had been bedeviling me all afternoon. The answer made me laugh. It was an actual bell. So whatever theory I had cooked up in my mind evaporated immediately. Sometimes a bell is just a bell, or a historical fact. And sometimes MCs should admit that they don't know.

1994

South Africa holds its first truly democratic, multiracial elections; Nelson Mandela wins and becomes president ○ Nicole Brown Simpson and Ron Brown are murdered ○ O. J. Simpson, a prime suspect in the murder of his ex-wife, leads police on a slow-speed chase in a white Ford Bronco driven by Simpson's friend A. C. Cowlings ○ The Northridge Earthquake strikes ○ Jeff Bezos founds Amazon ○ Baseball players strike ○ Aristide returns to Haiti after democracy is restored ○ Ronald Reagan discloses that he has Alzheimer's disease ○ The Chunnel opens, connecting England and France ○ The world's first Internet radio broadcast goes out from WXYC, the student station of the University of North Carolina

IN THE SUN I FEEL AS ONE

When you find yourself at the crossroads of history, look in all directions.

This was in April 1994. I was back at my dad's house, keeping him company after his second heart attack, helping him run errands. And then at night I was sitting up in bed exhausted, flipping channels on the TV to wind down from the day, half awake and then a little less than half. Eventually, out of a fog of something like sleep, I heard the news.

It was important to me. Even though I was starting out in hip-hop and even though much of my musical knowledge backed up into soul, funk, and pop, I was the right age, and I understood his project, specifically the way he turned anger into art. If you were around at that time and your life had been changed by Public Enemy, Nirvana wasn't an impossible stretch. And suddenly, Nirvana was impossible, because Kurt Cobain was no more.

What's strange isn't that I know the exact date—it was April 5, 1994—but that I know the day of the week, which was a Tuesday, and also what was on TV while I was flipping around channels. It was *Roc,* the sitcom starring Charles S. Dutton, and specifically an episode where Andrew and Russell had a feud. Andrew was Roc's father, played by Carl Gordon, and Russell was his brother, played by Richard Roundtree. That's right. Shaft was in *Roc*, playing a gay Black man, which was more than unprecedented for the time. Russell had been on *Roc* earlier in its run, and there was even an episode with a gay wedding back in 1991. (It's probably worth noting that the spring of 1994 was a stretch where TV was engaging even more with gay characters. The same-sex kiss between Roseanne Barr and Mariel Hemingway aired on March 1 of that year and Ellen premiered on March 29. Russell/Roc deserves more credit.) Anyway, I was dozing off, and then coming back, and dozing off, and coming back, through an episode of *Roc* where Russell decided that he was moving to Paris, and Andrew was hurt, and the two of them didn't talk to each other for a while. And then I heard that Kurt Cobain was dead.

A few minutes after the news report, Rich called. "We're fucked," he said. He explained what he meant. Cobain's suicide meant the loss of a major rock act for Geffen, his label, which happened to be our label also. And Geffen had also lost or was in the process of losing its other two major rock bands. Aerosmith had actually signaled its departure back in 1991, when the band had signed a big new contract with Columbia, but they still owed Geffen three of six records, which they were in the process of completing as quickly as they could. Guns N' Roses had released *Appetite for Destruction* back in 1987, *G N' R Lies* in 1990 (see 1990), and then the twin *Use Your Illusion* albums in 1991. But by 1994, the band was mired in a prolonged creative paralysis, and the 1993 LP *The Spaghetti Incident?*, named for the way that one of the band members stored drugs in a common refrigerator, seemed like it might be the last anyone would hear from the band for a while. (They had no idea.)

That made Cobain's death more than personal. It made it professionally consequential. On the phone with Rich that night, I got a master class in how dominoes are set up and how they might fall. That fateful decision, made by another man for his own reasons, or helped along by others, or staged—I don't get much into the conspiracies—had ripple effects to spare, and we were floating on the surface of the pond.

Rich convinced me that we needed to finish the record, quick, and get the hell out of dodge. We finished. We got out. We went to London, where we hid out for the better part of the year, learning more about British DJs, sound engineering, and one another. And then in January 1995, we came back and appeared on *The Daily Show with John Stewart* to perform the album's first single, "Proceed."

People like to say that the rest was history. It was, in a sense—in a narrow and personal sense. We were launched by *Do You Want More?!!!!??!* It was the start of what we're still in. As we went about making the beginning of our history, did we think excessively about the way that it grew from another moment in history? I don't think so, at least not consciously.

A few years ago, I was given a whole new game board in the form of reissues of Roots records. Tariq and I were asked to write an essay about our overall frame of mind at the time we recorded the original record, and I also wrote song-by-song commentaries. That meant listening to the album all over again, and actively rather than passively, which meant not only releasing a flood of memories (like Cobain's death) but trying to tag them before they flew away. What it really meant was becoming a historian—a subjectively compromised one, sure, and one who was in a position of authority that wasn't likely to be challenged from outside, but still a historian. I had to recall events, relate them in a coherent way, and then in some cases interpret them.

I put the historical lens over *Do You Want More?!!!!??!* To me, the album had always resolved into four quarters. The first quarter started in December 1993 and ended in early January 1994. The second quarter went from late January 1994 to February 1994, and the third quarter from late February into March. The fourth was Cobain. In my mind, I went backward through the quarters, extracting memories, trying to build them into something larger. I thought about when Rich first called to tell us that we had booked studio time, and that we had better hurry up and write some songs, didn't we think? That was first quarter. I thought about when we had to rush through a first batch of songs to get them on an EP that was being promoted by the British label owner Gilles Peterson (also first quarter). I thought about "You Ain't Fly," a song where a guy disses a girl but that we rewired so that the guy is actually exposing himself as a clown (that's second quarter). I thought about when I had to play the keyboards on a song called "I Remain Calm" because Scott Storch, who usually played for us, was off working with Billy Joel (that's third quarter).

What started to emerge was a narrative of the album, meaning an account of the events that became more than just a list. For example, the first quarter started up at Nebula Sounds in Northeast Philadelphia, which was between forty-five minutes and an hour away from my house by car. We had done our first album, *Organix*, up there. On those drives, we did lots of talking, telling each other what we had been up to in the wake of *Organix*, worked out our ideas, and worked through our nerves. By the second quarter, we had moved back to City Center to record at Sigma, which meant that each of us found our way to the studio on our own via public transportation or on foot, which meant no long drive, which meant no camaraderie and clubhouse-in-car atmosphere on the way up. That was one small historical observation, a description of the differences between two micro-eras, but a legitimate one. History was planted. History grew. It was a plant, giving off oxygen, letting us breathe.

• • •

The Nirvana song that resonates with me the most, or among the most, is "Pennyroyal Tea," for its melody, for Cobain's vocal, but also for the way it embodies the difficulty of the recording process, and how one song can have many versions that, taken together, tell a larger story than the so-called official release. Cobain originally wrote the song in 1990, I think, and first performed it at the famous OK Hotel show in April 1991, which was also the first show where they played "Smells Like Teen Spirit." "Pennyroyal Tea" was not included in the set of songs for *Nevermind*, but made the band's next record, *In Utero*, which was produced by Steve Albini and came out in September 1993. Cobain didn't like Albini's mix, and in fact had already sent two songs back to be remixed by Scott Litt. "Pennyroyal Tea" was the third, and Litt reworked it on November 22, 1993, the thirtieth anniversary of John F. Kennedy's assassination. "Pennyroyal Tea" was the third single to go out from the record, after "Heart-Shaped Box" and "All Apologies." It was released in

April 1994 and immediately recalled, most likely as a result of the unfortunate title of its B side, "I Hate Myself and Want to Die." It was like the single never happened. Sometimes historical events unfurl in a way that creates excessive discomfort for those observing them, and corrections are required. Think of it as sending history back for a new mix.

1995

Timothy McVeigh and Terry Nichols bomb the Alfred P. Murrah Federal Building in Oklahoma City, killing 168 people ○ O. J. Simpson is found not guilty of the murders of Nicole Brown Simpson and Ronald Goldman ○ The Unabomber Manifesto is published ○ Bernard Harris is the first African-American astronaut to perform a space walk ○ The Million Man March is held in Washington, D.C. ○ Sarin gas attacks in the Toyko subway system kill twelve ○ Michael Jordan returns to the NBA ○ Selena is murdered by the president of her fan club, Yolanda Saldivar ○ Lonnie Bristow is appointed president of the American Medical Association, the first Black president in the organization's history ○ *Toy Story* is released

PRESENT, TENSE

Sometimes you can see history happening right in front of you.

You read about turning points in history—Gutenberg's first printing press, the French Revolution, penicillin, the Bomb, the moon landing—and try to imagine if the people there knew that they were witnessing something so momentous. If you had pulled them aside at the time and asked them about it, would they have told you, definitively, that they were ringside for a crucial moment in cultural history, or military history, or medical history?

I wonder about this all the time, because the one time I was present at a Moment in History, I knew it.

• • •

Hip-hop was too young to have a funeral, and yet there it was, at the Paramount Theater at Madison Square Garden, in August 1995. I was there because the Roots had been nominated for an award, Best Live Act, on the strength of the shows we were putting on in the wake of the release of *Do You Want More?!!!??!*

I say that the event was held at the Paramount Theater, but really the theater had been divided into three subtheaters. What I mean by that is that the seating was thematic. As I entered the theater, I could see that the seats on the far left were occupied by the Bad Boy team. They were the hottest company in hip-hop at that moment, with the hottest producer (Puff Daddy) and the hottest star (Biggie). In the middle of the theater was the Death Row crew, Los Angeles come east in the person of Snoop Dogg, Suge Knight, Dr. Dre, and more. Tupac Shakur was not there: he had been shot the previous November, and then, while still recovering, was sentenced for a sexual assault conviction from the previous year. The shooting escalated the beef between the two coasts and the two campuses; Tupac was sure that Puffy had been in on the shooting, and maybe even ordered the hit, along with Biggie and Jimmy Henchman.

I sat with all the other artists who were neither Hard East nor Hard West: the South, the Midwest, Mobb Deep, Wu-Tang, Busta Rhymes, Outkast. Nas was in that section with us. I remember seeing him come into the theater, with a Tommy Hilfiger shirt that looked at least a size too big for him. The shirt felt like a metaphor, even years before I learned that he had borrowed money from Steve Stoute to buy it.

If the big backstory was the growing tensions between East Coast and West Coast, between Bad Boy and Death Row, the awards battle was looking to be something else. The two biggest records of the year, the two most important and acclaimed, were Nas's *Illmatic* and Biggie's *Ready to Die*. *Illmatic*, released in April (the same month the Roots ran off to Europe), had been given the coveted five-microphone rating by *The Source*, considered a gold standard. Biggie had gotten four and a half mics. *Illmatic* was a throwback, or maybe it wasn't yet a throwback—maybe it was still just an example of what people considered a great hip-hop record, strong from door to door, coherent production, an MC with a vision, and so on. "N.Y. State of Mind" sampled "Mind Rain" by the Philly legend Joe Chambers and painted vibrant urban pictures: "On the corner bettin' Grants with the cee-lo champs / Laughin' at base-heads, tryna sell some broken amps." (Historical footnote: cee-lo was a Chinese dice game long before it was a guy, and it had real currency in '90s rap lyrics: it's also mentioned in Kool

G Rap's "Blowin' Up in the World," A Tribe Called Quest's "Vibes and Stuff," and dozens of other songs. Dozens: also a game. The first and last time I ever played—cee-lo, that is—was on tour with Cypress Hill in Japan. In two minutes I managed to lose two hundred bucks. A fortune to me back then.)

Ready to Die was something else, a blockbuster that was designed as one, with an awareness that it needed to have hit singles and an artist who could deliver them. It was a critical success, but more than that, a commercial monster. (And it even had its own cee-lo lyric, in "Me and My Bitch.") That night, award after award came up, and every one went to Biggie. Nas, already small inside his shirt, got smaller. I watched him shrink. He had a look on his face not just like he was losing awards, but like he was losing himself. I remember telling Tariq that he would never be the same. And he never was. After that night, Nas reconsidered his entire program. He went home and supersized himself. He tried for broader strokes and bigger hits. *It Was Written*, his next record, was his most commercially successful release, but it was slicker and more radio-ready than *Illmatic*, with an overt move toward a street-hustler persona. It didn't sound like Nas so much as it sounded like Nas sounding like Biggie, who, weirdly enough, cited Illmatic as his blueprint for *Ready to Die* (Puff's north's star was *The Chronic*).

The Nas-Biggie battle set the tone for the next generation of hip-hop. Should rappers tell stories that were human-size, that reflected their own personal wisdom and their community, or should they reach toward something abstract and aspirational? Stoops or speedboats? But that was only the tip of the 1995 Source Awards iceberg. The West Coast figures in attendance let it be known that they were none too happy with the East Coast rappers, or even the audience. Snoop and Dre made no secret of their disdain for a marketplace that had suddenly experienced a change of heart after a clearly successful year. The numbers didn't lie: The Chronic was loved all over the world. Especially in NYC. (Why the sudden change of heart was more the challenge. Quiet as it was kept, I suspect there was disdain for *Ready to Die* dominating the night. The clear answer is people love the struggle, just like I love my music, struggling, not too polished. Hip-hop, at least "credible" hip-hop, was now polished. It was like watching Steph Curry. He makes it look too easy. It's no fun cheering someone who doesn't give you peaks and valleys. See *Control*, 1987.) Puff came back in the other direction: "I live in the East, and I'm gonna die in the East," he said, thankfully not prophetically. And Outkast was jeered mercilessly. (André's attempt to hold the negativity at bay—"We just want y'all to know the South's got something to say"—went onto *Aquemini*, at the end of "Chonkyfire.") The most controversial remarks came from Suge Knight, not surprisingly. He already had a reputation for strongarm tactics to collect more artists for his label. That night, he went after the competition, knocking the Bad Boy aesthetic ("Any artist out there that wanna be an artist, stay a star, and won't have to worry about the executive producer trying to be all in the videos, all on the records, dancing—come to Death Row!").

The historical stakes, again, were clear even then, in the moment. Just a few years before, hip-hop artists, whether from West or East or South, had thought that we were all in it together, that even though we might have had our differences here and there—different tastes, different talents—we were first and foremost a community. But here was that community fracturing right before our eyes. When Dr. Dre was announced as a nominee for Producer of the Year, people actually came to their feet, not like they were being powered from below, but like they were being pulled from above. Conflict marionettes. Stood up in challenge, like they couldn't wait for him to win just so they could cause trouble. The tension in the room thickened. John Singleton announced the winner, and I suddenly felt unsafe. I got up to go. Dre won, and the place just erupted in booing. Snoop had a kind of unfunny punch line on that one: "The East Coast ain't got love for Dr. Dre and Snoop Dogg?" I was probably out to the lobby by then, but I had no thought of going back. The previous year, there had been some tension. A Tribe Called Quest won Best Album, and as they were coming up to the stage, Tupac started his performance. Maybe someone started his tape early or gave him the wrong cue. It didn't feel malicious. But it still caused an immense amount of tension, to the point where I wasn't sure I wanted to be there again in 1995. John Singleton made the moment worse with an "oh oh . . . Dr Dre." The five seconds of space after "oh oh" was all I needed. I was out. I ran for my life, date in tow.

I don't want to make too much of it, like I was fleeing from a war zone as the bombs went off all around me. But that's exactly what was happening.

• • •

I have written earlier about En Vogue, and Dawn Robinson, and how when she left the group she ended up in another group, Lucy Pearl, where she basically replaced D'Angelo, who was too busy making his sophomore record. That's the second half of the history whose first half is this. I was running out of those Source Awards, happy that nothing worse than boos had happened, and a man who didn't look familiar to me pressed a cassette into my palm. That kind of thing happened all the time back then. Hey, man, check out this record. Or more often, Hey, man, check out my record. This was one of the former—the guy who was handing out cassettes wasn't the artist, but some kind of independent street-team marketer. I glanced at the cassette and the name I saw rang a bell: D'Angelo. Bob Power, a producer who had worked with A Tribe Called Quest, had been talking him up. To me, based on what I heard, he was smooth R&B. I wasn't tremendously interested. But the moment was so charged from what we were escaping, so explicitly historic, that I held on to the cassette.

That, too, turned out to be history. The first time I played that record, I knew that I had discovered an artist who was capable of synthesizing all the different strands of contemporary Black music—soul and funk and hip-hop and whatever this new thing was that he was creating. I wasn't a fan so much of mid-'90s R&B, which struck me as mostly superficial cliché. But this was something different, something amazing. The rift I had witnessed inside could not be repaired, except that here was music powerful enough to repair it. There was rubble in the room and magic in my hand. (There was an extra irony in that I had missed a chance to play on *Brown Sugar*. Bob had invited me to record in a D'Angelo session with Ron Carter, the bassist. But Ron had backed out because the song on tap was "Shit, Damn, Motherfucker." He didn't like the language. I begged off and never went back. From that moment, I was determined to connect with D'Angelo, and I did, through his second record, *Voodoo*, and beyond.)

That day was nothing but consequence, history in every way.

• • •

Did the mainstream world take notice? When you look up August 3, 1995, on This Day in History sites, there's not much. CNN en Español premiered. But I know better. Back in elementary school, they would occasionally show an old newsreel series from the 1950s called *You Are There*, which was like a sober version of *Drunk History*. Hosted by Walter Cronkite, it used real-life reporters and embedded them back in actual events. Actors would play famous people from the past—James Dean played the outlaw Robert Ford, Paul Newman played Brutus. I have a vague memory of a reporter interviewing Grant and Lee at Appomattox. *The Electric Company* parodied it with a segment called "You Weren't There," whose tag line was "You weren't born yet, you were out of town, or you just weren't paying attention." For that 1995 Source Awards, for the fault line it exposed in the hip-hop world and the great art it led me to discover and then create, I was born, I was in town, and I was paying attention.

Put You in My Mix

I don't know if I thought of mixtapes as history when I first started making them, but that's exactly what they were: anthologies that demonstrated how I both respected the past and understood the present. Some songs worked perfectly on any tape. Did that mean that they communicated some idea that worked in any context, in any time, under any circumstances? Were they cultural skeleton keys?

"NEVER STOP LOVING ME"
Curtis Mayfield

Something to Believe In, 1980 [Curtom]

I first heard this in London, where I stole it from our tour manager Nou back in the early '90s. It became a mixtape staple. Why? Is it the greatest song? No. Is it the most powerful? No. But there's something about it that lets it survive in any environment. Curtis's falsetto, maybe, or the forthright romantic lyric, or the fact that it was on an already-out-of-the-way Curtis album, *Something to Believe In*, in 1980, and was the last song—even the people who made it to the album didn't make it to "Never Stop Loving Me."

"DO YOU KNOW"
Madlib

Beat Konducta, Volume 5: Dil Cosby Suite, 2008 [Stones Throw]

I knew this only because of the original Con Funk Shun track. I never thought to give it a second listen. But sped up and heard through the ears of Madlib, the song has a musicality I hadn't previously realized. I noticed that the bass is really good. He took the right parts of that song and then pieced it together. What he made is a shoo-in for any mixtape.

“OPEN YOUR EYES”
Platinum Pied Pipers

“Riding High”/“Open Your Eyes” 12-inch, 2003 [Ubiquity]

With Bobby Caldwell, in the original, the urgency of the message, “Hey, Doofus, I'm standing right in front of you,” doesn't stand so high. And Common took over the association with “The Light,” which means that there's a generation that thinks of this as a song for Erykah Badu. (I famously didn't like “The Light” and tried to discourage Common from putting it on the album. Dilla was making miracles by the hour and this just never hit my gut like the more experimental stuff. I do respect his ability to make “normal” songs though. This is Dilla's “I Just Called to Say I Love You,” a song I only appreciate some 20 years after the fact.) But for some reason Dwele singing “How could you be so blind” rings more strongly than any of the other versions. I made a song with this without giving Tariq any context. He turned it into a conscious thing about society rather than a love song. It went on the shelf.

“HEY GIRL”
Donny Hathaway

Live, 1972 [Atlantic]

This live album has many classic moments. Some people love—love—“Everything Is Everything.” There's white-music cred in his cover of “Jealous Guy.” But this is musical and beautiful, his best vocal.

“KEEP HIM LIKE HE IS”
Syreeta

Syreeta, 1972 [MoWest]

I have come to make the (huge) assumption that when Syreeta and Stevie collaborated, she wrote the lyrics and he the music. It's based on a *Soul Train* interview when Don Cornelius asked her about her version of “Blame It on the Sun,” which went into an awkward TMI moment. Stevie's version of life is so beautiful and sunny. I wondered if he wanted this song to be so gender-specific. But it works.

“BABY THAT'S BACKATCHA”
Smokey Robinson

A Quiet Storm, 1975 [Tamla]

That to me is probably Smokey's best fast song of the '70s, and it's perfectly located on the original album. It's somehow not strong enough to open the album—especially not when “Quiet Storm” is your opener—but it can hold up the rest of side one.

“SHED”
Macy Gray

The Id, 2001 [Epic]

I am frustrated by this song, because I worked on most of this record, and this is the only song I didn't work on. I hate when my favorite song is somehow outside of the majority I worked on. For her it was a throwaway that she added at the end, after the official last track. But for me, it's the one that lasts.

“HIGH UP ON THE HOOK”
Alice Russell

My Favorite Letters, 2005 [Tru Thoughts]

A nearly perfect longish soul song (six minutes) from the English singer. This is one of the rare songs that's both dreamy and fully feel-good—the dreaminess doesn't have any sense of discomfort or escape, which sometimes happens. There's a Northern Soul throwback feel to it.

“GENEVIEVE”
Cymande

Second Time Round, 1973 [Janus]

I stole this from a mixtape, too, from my Roots bandmate Hub way back in the beginning. In those days Hub was actually kind of the mixtape guru, my unlikely mentor. He would make them for the tour bus. He had about five ninety-minute mixtapes filled with these kinds of songs. I realized that the atmosphere changed depending on which tape he put on. I realized the power of background music wasn't just in making people relaxed. It could change their moods entirely.

“IN MEMORY OF ELIZABETH REED”
The Allman Brothers

Idlewild South, 1970 [Atco/Capricorn Records]

I always put this closer to the end (of a mixtape, not this list, though it's also at the end of this list, which is a kind of mixtape-in-print). I don't think anyone is expecting it to come from me. It's a way to show my range that's not too showy.

1996

Bill Clinton defeats Bob Dole to win a second term ○ Lyle and Erik Menendez are found guilty of first-degree murder in the deaths of their parents ○ Ted Kaczynski is arrested on suspicion of being the Unabomber ○ Tupac Shakur is shot to death in Las Vegas ○ Kofi Annan becomes secretary-general of the United Nations ○ The Khobar Towers bombing kills nineteen U.S. Air Force personnel and one Saudi Arabian national ○ Tiger Woods makes his professional debut as a golfer at the Greater Milwaukee Open ○ George Walker becomes the first Black person to win the Pulitzer Prize for music, for *Lilacs, for voice and orchestra* ○ Ron Brown, the first African American secretary of commerce, is killed in a plane crash ○ Fox News launches ○ California voters pass Proposition 209, which outlaws affirmative action throughout the state

YOU'VE GOT ME FEELING EMOTIONS

Even the most impersonal history is personal.

I want to start with a robbery.

Late in 1995, Mariah Carey released her fifth album, *Daydream*, which earned her some of the best reviews of her career and also contained some of her biggest singles: "Fantasy," "One Sweet Day," and "Always Be My Baby." *Daydream* was nominated for six Grammy Awards, and early handicapping had it as a favorite for at least half of them. David Bauder of the Associated Press was typical with his preview: "At the risk of sounding like a broken record (scratched CD), give it to Carey." (One of the other artists with multiple nominations that year was D'Angelo, with three for *Brown Sugar*.)

Mariah came to the ceremony like a queen waiting to be crowned, opening the telecast with a performance of "One Sweet Day" where she was backed by Boyz II Men. The stage was set. Awards started coming. But none of them were coming Mariah's way. You know how they show the nominees, and then, when the winner is announced, everyone else (the losers?) keeps pleasant smiles on their faces, clapping supportively and sometimes even enthusiastically? It happened the first time. It happened the second time. But it happened less and less as the night went on.

She was stung, to the point where she didn't perform at the ceremony for a decade.

• • •

Here in 2020, I've been reading Mariah's autobiography, *The Meaning of Mariah Carey*, which surprises me a little. The fact that I've been reading it, I mean. She's a major pop-culture figure of the last three decades, sure, but I wasn't sure what a memoir would offer.

Plenty, as it turns out. The depth of the book got to me, and the honesty, and the sense of humor. Some of the writing was excellent, like when she described racism as "a first kiss in reverse." Her account of her childhood was painful, with a minimum of inspirational cliché, and her account of her marriage to Tommy Mottola at times darkly comic (like when Mariah went to Burger King and Mottola supposedly sent a posse of armed men to find her).

But I don't want to give too much away. Read it. Or do what I did for the second half and listen to it on audiobook—in some ways, that was even better, because Mariah read her book herself, and hearing it in her voice showed me which stories she thought were profound and which she thought were faux-profound, which were genuinely dramatic and which were melodramatic, which were ironic and which were straightforwardly comic.

I was most drawn to her account of her songwriting process, and specifically the way that actual events in her life became the basis of her biggest hits. What I learned over and over again is that songs that, at the time, sounded like product (masterful, but still) pumped out by a mid-'90s R&B song machine were in fact rooted in personal experience. "The Roof," a 1998 song about a rooftop assignation from her *Butterfly* album, had always seemed like a kind of fantasy, a *Romeo and Juliet* update, but the book makes it clear that it was about a rooftop kiss with Derek Jeter in the waning year of her marriage to Mottola. It's her first "docu-song," she writes. And in this case, a kiss isn't just a kiss. Her connection with Jeter ran deeper—it wasn't just stepping out, but a way of her exploring her own feelings about being biracial (he, like her, had a white mother and a Black father).

I went back to an earlier song, "Always Be My Baby." At first, it was as I remembered: gentle acoustic guitar in the opening, a bit of a doo-wop feel (with Mariah backing herself, of course). But as the song went on, it started to feel different, largely because of the way the memoir had moved my mindset. It wasn't that she dished on the origins of "Always Be My Baby." She didn't. But even without a specific backstory, I couldn't return to the place where I thought of it as something generic. The book, and my experience with it, anchored her whole body of work, not just specific songs, in autobiographical reality.

● ● ●

For that personal dimension to burst out in full in 2020, and then to wash back over her entire catalog, is especially sweet given how hard various forces worked to keep Mariah's music generic. And by "various forces," I mean Sony Music, which owned Columbia, Mariah's label for the first decade of her career. As Mariah's marriage to Mottola wound down, Sony showed less and less support for her, and specifically less interest in letting the more personal side of her art emerge. The tension between artist and company came to a head with the end of the marriage in 1998. For the album after *Butterfly, Rainbow*, Mariah wanted to release the highly personal "Can't Take That Away (Mariah's Theme)" as a single. Sony resisted, instead suggesting more up-tempo (and less intimate) dance tracks. Frustrated that the label wouldn't respect her wishes, Mariah started posting messages on her webpage that asked fans to request (or even demand) "Can't Take That Away" as her next single. It was a staredown, and eventually Sony blinked, but gave the song only a limited release so that it couldn't chart very high.

Not every artist had to struggle for autobiographical visibility in his or her own work. The same year that Mariah released *Daydream*, another superstar put out a record filled with personal business. I'm talking about Michael

Jackson. The album was a double, called *HIStory*, and it was divided into *HIStory Begins*, which had fifteen of his greatest solo hits up until that point, and *HIStory Continues*, with fifteen new songs.

HIStory not only addressed all these issues—commercial art versus personal expression, the tension between the text of a song and its subtext, how much you had to know about an artist's personal life to properly appreciate his or her work—but put them center stage. The title frames the debate. *History* has become a vexed term because it contains the word *his*, and many women have argued that the word writes them out of events (it's not the right etymology, of course—it comes from the word *histoire*, or story—but it has led to the not completely satisfying coinage *herstory*). But it doesn't have to be about gender, even. When Sun Ra, in the 1980 documentary *A Joyful Noise*, says, "They say that history repeats itself. But history is only his story. You haven't heard my story yet," he is speaking about the general problem of one unique individual being mishandled by the generally accepted account of things, whether that means excluded, papered over, or absorbed.

Jackson takes Sun Ra's point and all-caps it, suggesting (in true hubristic fashion) that history is in fact *his* story. History began when his solo career did, and it's only his new music that is allowing history to continue. In case anyone was at risk of missing his not-very-subtle point, he drove it home with an impressively egomaniacal promotional campaign. When, in the course of designing the *HIStory* package, Epic (his label, also part of Sony Music) asked him if he had any ideas, Michael was ready. He asked them to build a statue of him.

Everyone saw how ridiculous an idea that was. Build a statue? So instead they built nine, each one thirty-two feet tall, showing Jackson decked out in military garb. In the summer of 1995, Sony shipped them to various European cities. One of them floated down the Thames River, forcing Tower Bridge to be raised so it could pass through. One was installed in Alexanderplatz in Berlin. Others found their way to the Champs-Élysées in Paris and the Piazza Scala in Milan. If you weren't lucky enough to see the statue in your local river or plaza, a picture of it was available on the cover of every single copy of the *HIStory* album.

Despite the campaign, the songs were often strikingly personal, especially the new ones. Jackson had always been a master at communicating emotions. Even though his music belonged sonically to disco, or streamlined funk, or pop-soul, many of the songs reached back into earlier traditions like the blues. I'm thinking of two in particular, "Your Ways," from the Jacksons' *Triumph* in 1980 (written by Jackie but sung by Michael) and "Working Day and Night," from *Off the Wall*. Both are songs of jealousy, misunderstanding, and (sometimes barely) contained anger. In "Your Ways," the problem is an unstable woman. "I don't understand your ways," Michael sings. "What have I done to deserve this madness? All I feel is sadness." In "Working Day and Night" the complaint centers around how much Michael has to work, and how much loving those extra hours of labor are costing him. Both songs seem like they were inherited directly from Joe Jackson, the family's patriarch, in the sense that if you take the lyrics at face value they are very much the plight of ordinary men, laborers, lunch-pail types. If you pan up from the white cuffs, you can see the blue collar, and it's fun to imagine stripping away the songs' sonic sheen and reworking them as a Chicago blues, maybe something from Junior Wells, sequels to "You Don't Love Me, Baby" or "You Lied to Me."

By the time of *HIStory*, Jackson was the most famous person in the world, which meant that his concerns had changed. What perplexed him and vexed him weren't matters of love anymore, but matters of celebrity, of privacy, of the way that extreme amounts of attention could both elevate and destroy a man. There's a song called "Tabloid Junkie" where Michael addresses the "hounding media in hysteria," opening with a collage of all the nasty rumors about him propagated by the press and then reminding us all, in the chorus, "Just because you read it in a magazine / Or see it on the TV screen / Don't make it factual." And "They Don't Care About Us" is one in a long line of songs where he identifies with history's victims (or at least his idea of them), momentarily loaning them his power so they can be seen and heard.

But these are philosophical approaches to the idea that there is a real person behind the popcraft. One isn't philosophical at all. "D.S.," a snarling funk-rock song with guitar courtesy of Slash, takes aim at Tom Sneddon, the district attorney of Santa Barbara County, who had presided over the 1993 investigation into Jackson for charges of child sexual abuse. Though that investigation was closed without any criminal charges being brought, Michael felt that the investigation alone was a form of wrongful accusation, and the result was this strange song, in which he avoided slandering Sneddon by printing lyrics that claimed the song was about someone named "Dom Sheldon." That's what the "D.S." of the title is—initials. But that's just a smokescreen. Throughout the song, Michael clearly sings the name "Tom Sneddon," and at one point even "Thomas Sneddon," which is rendered in the slanderproofed lyrics as "Dom S. Sheldon." Let's be perfectly clear. No one Michael Jackson knew was named Dom S. Sheldon. I would be slightly surprised if there has ever been anyone on Earth with that name. But he did know someone named Tom Sneddon, a "cold man" who was trying to "get [his] ass dead or alive," who would "stop at nothing just to get his political say," who was possibly even "brother with the KKK." If Mariah Carey waited more than two decades to almost courteously fill in the autobiographical content of her songs, Jackson put his backstory front and center, punching as he went, using the full weight of his celebrity to attack Sneddon's character. Whether that was a successful strategy or not is in the ear of the beholder, and different beholders may have different levels of tolerance for grievance music deployed by one of the world's most powerful artists.

• • •

These two cases represent opposite ends of the spectrum, but they touch on the same question, which is how well the events of history can be understood without at least a partial understanding of the lives of those who participated in the events. It's not clear that we have to know Thomas Jefferson's exact mood when he signed the Declaration of Independence or how Winston

Churchill felt about his wife, Clementine, during the Blitz. Not everything rises to the level of relevance, and in songwriting, which is what we have been talking about, there's probably a higher threshold. But all too often, these kinds of details are passed over entirely. We often get a version of history where people do things but we don't know how they're doing. There is a movement among some historians that looks to engage more closely with the history of emotions. Peter Stearns, a historian at George Mason University, has written about the changing role of shame—very prominent in some eras of American history, less so in others—and how it might be helpful in investigating everything from wealth to family structure to politics. (From where I'm writing, here in 2020, we could use a little more of it.)

But again, this is a question of scale. Drawing larger conclusions about the way emotions defined an entire country during a specific period is one thing, but that's not quite the same as giving an account of the so-called private events that preceded and motivated the so-called public decisions of individuals. In the end, this is important because history is about the movements of people, and all people have emotions, and often those emotions have hold of those people.

About a week and a half before Mariah got stiffed at the Grammy Awards, there was another competition, this one held not in Los Angeles but in my hometown of Philadelphia. The thirty-two-year-old Russian grandmaster Garry Kasparov, then the world chess champion, beat IBM's Deep Blue in a match, proving that humans could still win in games of strategy and skill. At least for a (very) little while. After extensive reprogramming and retooling, Deep Blue faced Kasparov again in New York the following year and won. Kasparov didn't take the loss lightly. He accused the company of cheating, alleging that human experts had directed the computer's choices during the match. IBM refuted this, insisting that the company had followed the rules, allowing programmers to change the code only between games.

For more than two decades, Kasparov struggled with losing to Deep Blue. More specifically, he struggled with his feelings about losing to Deep Blue. Articles over the years describe him as "angry," "bitter," and (his own phrase) "a sore loser." His willingness to speak freely about his emotions added additional depth to what would otherwise be a relatively flat story about the moment artificial intelligence began to outstrip human intelligence in one narrow area. By filling in the backstory just a little, Kasparov gives us a reminder that the best kind of history is not only the history of events, but of the human struggles behind those events: the anger, the lust, the frustration, the ways in which everything from art to politics offers opportunities to process pain and disappointment. Would an account of the achievements of ten generations of supercomputers with no mention of the people involved even be a history, really?

Deep Blue had no comment on either its loss or its win.

1997

Princess Diana dies in a car crash ○ Madeleine Albright becomes the first female secretary of state in U.S. history ○ Thirty-nine members of the Heaven's Gate cult are found dead in a house in a San Diego suburb, victims of a mass suicide ○ The Notorious B.I.G. is killed in Los Angeles ○ Mother Teresa dies ○ Mike Tyson bites off a piece of Evander Holyfield's ear ○ *Titanic* opens ○ African American women participate in the Million Woman March in Philadelphia, which emphasizes health care, education, and self-help ○ Wynton Marsalis's "Blood on the Fields" becomes the first jazz composition to win a Pulitzer Prize in Music ○ President Bill Clinton issues a formal apology to the Black men exploited in the U.S. Public Health Service Tuskegee Syphilis Study

MOVING LIKE YOU'RE STANDING STILL

Does history carry everyone along at the same rate?

I've been thinking about how personal history intersects with the history around it. Not when people are prime movers of history, necessarily, or when they are moved by larger forces like game pieces on a board, but a third version, which is when people's emotional state affects the way they see what's going on. I am thinking about it because I just wrote about it from one perspective, how singers like Mariah Carey and Michael Jackson manage the use of autobiographical content in their work. Now I'm going to look at it from another perspective: my own.

This story is largely set in 1997, but it has a cold opening that's set back in 1993, on December 5 specifically, which was the night that Geffen Records was throwing a party for the Roots to celebrate our signing to the label. The morning of that day, it felt like good news only, a major achievement to be placed into the annals and hailed for generations to come. The Roots are signed! The Roots are signed! But history works in mysterious ways, sometimes pulling a thread just as you're starting to stitch. Sometime between morning and night, the day of triumph went off the rails when my mother explained to me that she was planning to get a divorce from my father.

I wasn't supposed to pass the news along to my dad. My mom told me that she was going to talk to him. But I had something of my own to tell my dad, which was that I was in a rap group, which was news to him. As I have written this book, I have thought often about how history happens twice: once when an event actually occurs and once when people discover that it has occurred. That second time is the first time for them, because they didn't know about the first time.

When I graduated high school, my dad had a very clear idea of how my life would go. I would work a day job selling life insurance, put some money in the bank, and when I had saved enough I'd go on to Juilliard, where I had been accepted but couldn't for the moment afford to start. Music school would set me up for the career he assumed I'd have, which was becoming the musical director for a popular singer or taking up a similarly stable job that would allow me to enjoy the benefits of music without suffering from its uncertainties. Which he knew all too well himself.

It wasn't a terrible map. But I went into uncharted waters. There Be Monsters. I got fired from my life insurance job on my birthday. I wanted to take off for my twenty-first in 1992, but I compromised and came in for the night shift, thinking I could make up the time. I couldn't. I got fired. I was relieved and the rest is history. The rest, at least immediately: I, and went to work at a local record label, Ruffhouse, where I soaked up information about the music industry while trying to move forward with the hip-hop group I had co-founded, the Roots. We put out one independent album and then got signed to Geffen Records, and at that point I couldn't keep the news from my father any longer. I figured it was a safe time to come clean. Just talk fast: Listen Dad the future you had in mind for me didn't quite happen the way you imagined but you can put that frown away because it's not like things ended up worse they ended up better a major label signed us and there's a party for that tonight. When I told him, he asked me for money. It wasn't the response I had expected. I wasn't prepared emotionally and I wasn't prepared practically, either. I had given some money to my mom to help her get through her suddenly changing circumstances. I did give my dad a little bit of cash.

By now, the day was so far off the rails that I could barely see them. But there was more. Part of going over to Geffen, and possible big-league stardom, was quitting my day job at Ruffhouse. That was sad, because I had loved my time at the label. I spoke to Chris Schwartz, who knew that we had been trying to make it. I gave him one day's notice, and he accepted the news happily. All he asked was that I ease the transition by touring my replacement around the label, showing him or her the best way to do this and that. It was a her, as it turned out, a young woman named Santi White, from the Philadelphia area, also interested in learning the music business so she could steer her own career as an artist. (This was an example of history happening before it ever happened—she would make her mark more than a decade later as Santigold.)

I was standing with Santi and her boss, a woman named Davida Garr, and I mentioned the record-release party. Both of them were happy for me, of course, and both wanted to come, but Davida had an additional request. "There's this new group," she said, "and they're sort of like the Roots. Is there any way they can do a set at your label party?" She mentioned the group. I had heard of them, and I had even heard one of their songs, and she was right to notice some similarities. I told her that I would do what I could, and then I did what I could, which was to get the group onto the bill.

That night, before our show, a van pulled up outside, carrying the group that Davida had asked me to include. People started to pile out. First came a handful of Rasta-looking guys. I typed them immediately, but then had to do a double take when I recognized one of them. It was Abdul Hassan Sharif, an actor I had seen in movies like *Zebrahead*. What was he doing there? And then a few minutes later, the stream of Rasta guys tapered off and a young woman emerged from the van. I recognized her, too, also as an actor. One of my jobs at home was to work the VCR (see 1977), and one of the shows I had to tape was *As the World Turns*, which meant that I ended up seeing a certain number of the episodes myself. Back in 1991, there had been a subplot involving a homeless teenager. And this was her! I started to say her name. Not her real name, which I didn't know yet, but her character's name. "Kira," I said.

She said, "Shhhh."

That turned out to be Lauryn Hill. The group around her turned out to be the Fugees.

• • •

Now we come to the part where actual history actually comes back into the picture. The part where the world turns, you might say.

Within just a few years, the Fugees would be huge. The Roots album we were celebrating that night, *Do You Want More?!!!??!*, would come out in January 1995 and go gold (eventually—meaning some twenty-three years later, after sales peaked around 300,000 at the time of release, nothing to write home about as far as I was concerned). The Fugees would release their debut on Ruffhouse in February 1994, to modest sales, largely overseas, and their second album for the label in February 1996, when we were finishing up our next, *Illadelph Halflife*. Ours went gold again (and again, eventually). Theirs, *The Score*, went number one in nearly every country in the world and ended up moving more than six million copies.

Midway through that meteoric rise, we toured with them, and it was clear which group was capturing the public consciousness at that point. They were getting more ink, more adulation, more radio play. Some articles at the time implied a tension between us, but that's just a media creation. Sells magazines. We got along great, especially offstage, where we could just tell jokes and play pranks on each other. I've talked often about how at some point I was thinking less about playing a certain breakbeat and more about where in the hotel I was going to ambush Lauryn with a water balloon. But one thing was clear. They were, through 1996, occupying a larger slice of history. Many summaries of that year in hip-hop have them as the second-most-important story, behind the death of Tupac. And one or two even have them first.

What I thought about then, again, was mostly breakbeats and water balloons, but I have since thought often about how history leaves out much more than it takes in. Think of all the parts of history, all the people in it, who have been forgotten. I don't think the Roots are among them, of course. But I do think that we didn't burn as brightly as other artists did for short bursts, and the Fugees aren't the only example of that. It happened almost every year, in fact: Digable Planets in 1994, Outkast in 1995, then the Fugees, then Erykah Badu in 1997, then Lauryn Hill herself in 1998. "The Sweetest Thing" was a transitional track, released as she was leaving the Fugees and heading toward her solo career. (It appeared on the soundtrack to the romantic comedy *Love Jones*, which came out in March 1997, the same month that the Notorious B.I.G. was shot to death in his car at the intersection of Fairfax and Wilshire in Los Angeles.)

Some rapid rises felt stranger than others. Take Erykah. The Roots had worked extensively on her debut, *Baduizm*, writing and producing three tracks, "Otherside of the Game," "Sometimes (Mix #9)," and "Sometimes . . ." Erykah and I used to go to movies and restaurants and then instantly I'm spelling my name for some guy with an earpiece so that I can go backstage.

Part of this is a story about moving between decades—going from that tween and teen zone, where you're entirely a spectator to history, to the young-adult and adult zone, where you're on the edge of the stage. That's a strange transition for anyone. If you grow up idolizing sports stars and become one yourself you have to get used to the idea of your name in the box scores. If you grow up obsessed with foreign policy and you find a job in the field yourself, you have to get used to the idea of your name in the conference notes.

But there's another story, too, which has to do with speed, which has to do with distance over time. Each year seems long, but it's also only a year. History has lots of those. And so when a phenomenon, a person or a company or a country, surges into view, we say that it's making history, but really it's only making history at the time. Every year is filled with them: 1997 has Mary Kay Letorneau and Andy Green, Kelly Flinn and Doris Angleton. Do you remember some of them? Any of them? History elevates but also erases. In the end, that's because people play the short game. They have to. They are here on earth only for a limited time, and during that time they do everything they can to make sure that they get theirs, whether that means love or sex or money or creative satisfaction or some other kind of notoriety. But history plays the long game. History is the long game.

For years, when I thought about the Roots' plight, I thought of the story of the tortoise and the hare. There we were, shell-shuffling along, releasing our records and playing our shows, building our audience and registering with critics, as all these rabbits rushed by us. I figured that we'd keep trundling and that eventually we'd see all those rabbits sleeping by the side of the road as we passed them by. But I came to see that even that was the wrong metaphor, the wrong fable.

My epiphany happened later, in 2014 or so, when Rich Nichols was in the hospital, dying of leukemia. We were talking about Dave Chappelle's comeback shows at Radio City Music Hall that summer, and then joking about a show the Roots had done at Radio City some years before, 2006 or so. We were able to sell the place out for two nights, and Nas had come to do the show with us. There was a point in our soundcheck where I was watching Nas as he watched us, taking note of the fact that his mind was blown. He was on the phone telling his people how great we were: "Man, you have to hear this! They sound just like the record, only better!" I was amused at first, then flattered, and then insulted—insulted because I realized that the only reason he was so impressed was that he hadn't heard us before. This was always my biggest fear, that we were Rudolph the Red-Nosed Reindeer, and here was proof. Hip-hop still hadn't listened to us. By the time Rich and I were talking about it in 2014, everything had come full circle: Nas was also a guest at the Chappelle shows, and he had his own live band and everything, Roots-style. I said something about how hip-hop had finally caught up to us, though what I meant was more of the tortoise and the hare, that hip-hop had finally slowed down enough to see that what we were doing was the right kind of trundling all along. Rich shook his head, best as he could. He was sick. "You're missing the whole plot," he said. "My plan all along was never to make sure that you guys were in the winner's circle. But I'll be damned if you're not the last to lose. Everyone's gonna lose, you know. Time's gonna run out the clock." Those were his last words to me.

1998

James Farmer, the former leader of the Congress on Racial Equality (CORE), is awarded the Medal of Freedom by President Bill Clinton ○ Clinton addresses rumors of an affair with Monica Lewinsky ○ A forty-nine-year-old Black man, James Byrd, Jr., is dragged to death by white supremacists in Jasper, Texas ○ Matthew Shepard, a gay college student, is found tied to a fence near Laramie, Wyoming, and later dies ○ Google is founded ○ Jesse Ventura is elected governor of Minnesota ○ Michael Jordan wins his sixth title with the Chicago Bulls in his second three-peat ○ The comedian Phil Hartman is murdered by his wife ○ The National League of Women Voters elects its first Black president, Carolyn Jefferson-Jenkins ○ For the first time, the New York Stock Exchange is closed in honor of the birthday of Dr. Martin Luther King, Jr. ○ Lillian Elaine Fishburne becomes the first Black female rear admiral in the U.S. Navy

FAIR AND UNFAIR USE

How should we understand our responsibility to the figures of the past?

Outkast was one of the groups that came out of nowhere and blew up big, and in 1998, they were about to get bigger. With the release of their third album, *Aquemini*, they not only established themselves as the heart of the southern rap scene, but solidified their personality as a group made up of two almost irreconcilable individuals. It was right there on the cover, Big Boi all pimped out in his throne, André 3000 staring off pensively into the middle distance.

The opening track, "Hold On, Be Strong," is abstract and gentle, with unconventional instrumentation and the title chanted in almost New Age style. That's followed by "Return of the 'G,'" a declaration of purpose where first André and then Big Boi reiterate their different-but-the-same, together-but-apart connection. Maybe the bond is even stronger because it's always pulling itself apart.

The next song was the first single.

It's preceded by a skit at a record store where they're unboxing the new Goodie Mob album. "You ain't got that new Outkast," says one man. A second man is unimpressed. "First they were pimps, then they were aliens talking about their Black rights in space." The song doesn't take place in space. It's fully in the club, a party anthem. Andre's verse makes a push for continued innovation: "Baby boy, you only funky as your last cut / You focus on the past, your ass'll be a 'has-what.'" This is a view of history as a history of innovations. If you stay where you are, you're nowhere.

While the harmonica break midway serves notice that they are part of the southern juke-joint tradition, the song's main hook was what everyone remembered. Spoke-sung in a deep accent, it warned other groups to get out of the way: "Ah hah, hush that fuss / Everybody move to the back of the bus."

The song's title picks up on that idea by referencing a historical figure not mentioned in the lyrics at all: Rosa Parks, who was arrested after refusing to move to the back of a public bus in Montgomery, Alabama, in December 1955. Parks's arrest touched off the Montgomery Bus Boycott and was one of the signal events of the civil rights movement. Parks was not the first to defy the racial segregation on southern buses, of course. There were famous cases from the 1940s, including one involving Bayard Rustin. And Parks was not the first to be arrested in Montgomery: about nine months earlier, a fifteen-year-old Black girl named Claudette Colvin was arrested for refusing to switch seats. But civil rights organizations had decided that Parks, the secretary of the Montgomery chapter of the NAACP, was the perfect candidate for protesting the law and setting up a court challenge. (The case that eventually found its way to the Supreme Court, *Browder v. Gayle*, was named for Aurelia Browder, who had been arrested about a month after Colvin, eight months before Parks.)

Parks was an indisputable civil rights icon, beloved and decorated across the decades. That's why it was more than a little confusing when she sued Outkast and its label, LaFace, over the song. The lawsuit argued that the group had used her name without permission, and in a song she found vulgar, no less. (It's not vulgar, by hip-hop standards or maybe any standards: I think there's one n-word and one incidence of the word *ass*.)

But the broader argument was kind of fascinating. Writers, artists, and so on were protected by the First Amendment when it came to discussing public figures, so on the face of it, the lawsuit would seem to have no merit. However,

Parks's lawyers argued that First Amendment protections didn't apply specifically because the song had nothing to do with her. The lack of artistic connection between the title (which used her name) and the song (which did not) gave her a path to claim that the work damaged her reputation. To prove that the song and its title were not meaningfully connected, Parks submitted to the court a variety of documents, including interviews with Big Boi and André in which they admitted that it wasn't about her at all and a translation of the song from rap-speak to . . . English? That translation is below. I am still waiting for Outkast (or really, anybody) to turn it into a song.

> "Be quiet and stop the commotion. OutKast is coming back out [with new music] so all other MCs [mic checkers, rappers, Master of Ceremonies] step aside. Do you want to ride and hang out with us? OutKast is the type of group to make the clubs get hyped up/excited."

The initial lawsuit was dismissed quickly. Parks attempted an appeal with Johnnie Cochran as her lawyer (see 1988), which also failed, but in 2003 the case was allowed to proceed. Finally, in April 2005, the two parties settled, with Outkast/LaFace agreeing to pay Parks a cash settlement and to develop educational programming about Parks's life in conjunction with the Rosa and Raymond Parks Institute. Parks herself got to enjoy the resolution only for a little while. She died in October of that year.

• • •

I'm no lawyer, but to me the lawsuit was ridiculous, an ambulance-chasing situation plain and simple. It feels like someone in the family who stood to make money off Parks brought it to her estate's attention. That happens in the music world all the time: older singers have a nephew or stepson who is always on high alert when it comes to protecting their name. It looks like heroism except for the part that's greedy and opportunistic. In truth, I think of Outkast's title, whether or not it's on top of a song about Parks, as yet another version of a sample. When you hear a snippet of music that you like but can't place, you go back and find it. The same is true for a name. That's all the song was doing, planting a seed. The name-check worked for her, I'm sure—how many young hip-hop fans were perplexed by the title and cracked an encyclopedia?

Outkast's title illustrates a broader principle, too, which is that figures from the past need to resurface in culture, or else they risk being forgotten. Rich used to tell me that the greatest thing to ever happen to Stevie Wonder was Eddie Murphy's *Delirious*. Eddie had already impersonated Stevie on *SNL*—and this was the early '80s, during a period when Stevie wasn't at his absolute tip-top as an artist. I personally love *Journey Through the Secret Life of Plants*, his 1979 mostly instrumental double album. I make no secret of it. But when I tell other people, they can't believe it. The first time I told Rich, he said, "Get the fuck out of here." I didn't. But I knew what he meant. (*Journey* was the album where Stevie was chasing technology. He was Yamaha and Sony's guinea pig. They would give him new instruments and he would just use them immediately, clearly of the belief that he could make them work without a plan. Sometimes his confidence failed him. Take a song like "Outside My Window." Inside my head, this song is perfect. But outside my head, the drum sound is like a flyswatter. There's no way around it.)

Even his next record, the far more song-oriented *Hotter Than July*, was a moment for Black folks, because of the King holiday, because of "Master Blaster," but it didn't have the same mainstream potency as the five unquestioned masterpieces he made across the early and mid-'70s. And his 1982 greatest hits set, *Original Musiquarium*, only had four new songs. But there was Eddie Murphy in 1983, telling everyone in *Delirious*, "Stevie Wonder is a musical genius!" For those of us who were somewhere between eight and fourteen at the time, who were sneaking and listening to the Eddie Murphy record out of our parents' earshot, what he said was law. And it gave Stevie Wonder a new lease on life, probably twenty-five more years when no one had to wonder who he was, because he was the guy from the Eddie Murphy routine. (Eddie did the same thing for James Brown—how many people from the early '80s, the time before "Living in America," knew James only from the Celebrity Hot

Tub sketch? You can estimate how many from their James Brown impressions. Are they imitating James or imitating Eddie imitating James?) Without that new lease on life, would Stevie Wonder really have been the go-to celebrity for the episode of *The Cosby Show* where the kids crashed into the limo of a star? It put the family in the studio with Stevie, but I can't imagine seven-year-old Rudy, or even teenage Theo, knowing who he was. The same is true now for Kanye West, who was anointed a genius by Jay-Z in the lyrics to "Lucifer," a distinction that should last him another forty-one months or so at least.

As for Rosa, she's still in the air. Early in 2020, Nicki Minaj released a standalone single, "Yikes," that included the line "All you bitches Rosa Parks, uh-oh, get your ass up." There were complaints on Twitter, of course. Thus far, though, no lawsuits.

1999

Two teenagers at Columbine High School in Colorado open fire on classmates and teachers, killing thirteen ○ John F. Kennedy, Jr., dies when the small plane he is piloting crashes; his wife, Carolyn Bessette, and her sister Lauren are also killed ○ Bill Clinton is acquitted by the U.S. Senate in his impeachment trial ○ Maurice Ashley becomes the first Black chess grandmaster ○ An unarmed twenty-three-year-old Guinean immigrant, Amadou Diallo, is fatally shot by four New York City plainclothes officers ○ The peer-to-peer file-sharing service Napster launches ○ The author Stephen King is badly injured when he is hit by a van ○ *SpongeBob SquarePants* debuts ○ Serena Williams wins the U.S. Open Women's Singles Tennis Championship in Flushing Meadows, becoming the first African American woman to do so since Althea Gibson's win in 1958

THINGS FALL APART

How should we understand our responsibility to the future versions of ourselves?

For 1999, I considered writing about "1999," the 1982 song in which Prince seemed to predict the end of the world. For a while, getting further from 1982 meant getting closer to 1999 (the year), which meant that "1999" (the song) was going to be put to the test. During those years of getting further but getting closer, Prince went through some changes. He started to feel ill-used by Warner Bros. for controlling his career and his catalog, began writing "Slave" on his face, and then left the label entirely. In 1999, still angry that one of his best and best-known songs was going to enrich a company he considered his enemy, he set out to rerecord "1999," to create a new master that would divert funds from his old master. The new version of "1999" was released in February of that year, and it was a throwback in more ways than one—even though Prince was still going by his other name, the unpronounceable symbol that looked like the male and female symbols intertwined, the song was credited to Prince and the Revolution, and on the cover of the EP he even wrote "Revolution" in mirrored letters, like it had been on the original LP seventeen years earlier. Prince used pieces of the original music but supplemented them with contributions from his band at the time, including new vocals by Rosie Gaines and Larry Graham. The result didn't sound as good as the original, not by a long shot. Why? Part of the answer was aesthetic. Much of it was, actually: the new vocals cluttered up the mix, especially when they were rap tags on the ends of lines; there were several flourishes that seemed unnecessary, extra synths that hurt the leanness of the thing; and the way the song was supposed to end, with the "Mommy, why does everybody have a bomb" chant, was all wrong, with a Latin piano section. It sounded like a cover version by someone who wasn't quite Prince. But that wasn't the only problem. It was out of context, or placed into a new context, not a distant and insistent warning of apocalypse by an up-and-coming young artist, but a self-advertisement by an older, established one. The next track, "Rosario: 1999," was better—it was a political monologue that Rosario Dawson read, backed not by "1999" at all but by the synth chords of "Little Red Corvette." But it didn't redeem the whole experiment.

• • •

For me, 1999 (the year) was about ends, but in a different way than "1999" (the song, either version) articulated. When I was a little kid, five or six, my parents would go on tour with their group, and when they left I would stay with my grandmother. That gave certain songs permanent associations of sadness or loneliness. I'd gravitate to sadder colors on certain days. The orchestral work of Clare Fischer on albums by Rufus, Switch, and the Jacksons made parting with my parents that much harder. (Rufus's "Magic in Your Eyes" is one. I go right back to being a sad little kid, watching my parents' backs as they go out the door.) Although it's a little different, for some reason—it brings up memories not of my parents leaving, but of being at my grandma's, listening to 8-tracks on her dingy old player, feeling sorry for myself—it couldn't compare to my dad's immaculate tubular stereo system with speakers all over the house, Sonos long before Sonos, not to mention that I had to bargain with her for any music-listening time at all.

For a while, the Sylvers's "New Horizons" also hung there as a marker of the sad six-year-old me, but what pushed it even further in the wrong direction was when it wound up on A Tribe Called Quest's *The Love Movement* in 1998. Tribe was one of the most important groups to me growing up and getting started as a musician. They had influenced everything from our fashion to our philosophy to my name. But *The Love Movement* was a hard record for me to get through. The romantic feelings I had for their music suddenly felt unrequited, and by the time I got to the middle of side two I realized it was just a disjointed record, with none of the magic I was looking for. I was in the car when I first heard it, riding with Tariq. We had a ritual around Tribe records, almost a religion. I remember hearing *People's Instinctive Travels and the Paths of Rhythm* back in 1990, *The Low End Theory* the year after that, *Midnight Marauders* in 1993. They were all so energetic. They energized both of us and our friendship, too. *The Love Movement* wasn't. Energy was leaking. By the time "Hot 4 U" appeared in the middle of side two, it was like the car was slowing down, like we were running out of gas. They had also done something with the Sylvers' sample, taken the bass, which was already low enough, and made it lower. It added another sad association to what was already a stack of them.

At the time, in fact, it felt like a death. Something that I had loved was no more. Over the years, I've allowed myself to analyze that record, and the one that came before it, which were the only two records Tribe made with J Dilla (depending on where you look, he's credited either as James Yancey or Jay Dee). The obvious take is that they made problematic albums when Dilla joined them, so Dilla ruined Tribe. It's not that simple. Tribe was at their best when they were sampling actual loops, when they had a repetitive pop melody that wouldn't leave your head. The records with Dilla didn't have those elements. They were more radical. But this is all critical thinking after the fact. The fact was that I was experiencing a loss.

And I was experiencing it on a day where I desperately needed to think in terms of gain. The day the record came out was the same day I finished mastering *Things Fall Apart*, the Roots' new record. The Tribe record shook me. There I was, a lifelong fan, reacting to them that way. What if people reacted that way to us? It was even more complicated, because we had come up in their wake, inspired by them, to some degree in their image (I'm still not convinced Tip doesn't believe I'm a sociopath who named himself after the group). If that was the death of the sound, would we die along with it? It was also the same day that *Aquemini* came out, which was possibly the birth of another sound. Not to mention the same day as the big photo shoot for *XXL* magazine that collected hundreds of hip-hop stars on the stoop of a Harlem brownstone (see 1986). September 29, 1998: a day that will live in infamy forever. I went in to master that record with all those things on my mind.

Which isn't to say they weren't already there. To me, we had to make a mark on history with this record, or else we weren't going to make a mark at all. Our previous album had gotten notice because of our "What They Do" video, which made a clear distinction between commercial hip-hop and left-of-center hip-hop, angering some people in the process (including Biggie, who said in an interview that if he saw us he was going to rush us). But it had sold somewhere in the middle, maybe 400,000 copies, which meant that this next record, what we thought of as our third real record, needed to push us up to the next level. We couldn't afford to have a bomb. I told everyone who would listen that if we didn't make it, we ran the risk of being Fishbone. What I meant by that is that I didn't want us to be the most brilliant band that no one ever heard of, and to remind myself (and whoever was listening), I took a sticker of the Fishbone logo and drew the Ghostbusters symbol over it.

The album opened with a snatch of movie dialogue taken from Spike Lee's *Mo' Better Blues*. Denzel Washington's character, the jazz trumpeter Bleek Gilliam, is lamenting that Black people often go for lowest-common-denominator entertainment. His sax player, Shadow Henderson (Wesley Snipes), offers a counterargument, which is that much of what artists do is just meandering navel-gazing under the cover of art. That scene stuck with me because it was exactly the set of questions that wore on me. What was meaningful artistic creation and what was meaningless commercial pandering? Is it better to reach a small number of people deeply or a much larger number much less deeply? The questions wore on me because I knew our talents, and our limits. It was easy for us to make these left-of-center artistic statements, ten-minute free-jazz think pieces that summed up our impressions of the world. But it was hard to make something like "Drop It Like It's Hot," a track that's so effective because it's so simple, a song that might not say much about history but becomes part of the historical record. That song wouldn't come out until 2004, so I wasn't thinking about it then. But I was thinking about those questions as we started the record, and they stayed with me right until the end—after all, wasn't that the kind of thing I had found lacking on *The Love Movement*?

When our album came out the following February, it did something almost magical, which was that it hit both sides of the equation at once. While we were making it, I would never have thought that more than a million people would love the record. That was my Bleek side. But my Shadow side would have appreciated what it accomplished, the fact that it expanded our platform and amplified our voice, that it let us play bigger venues.

The record is a record of its time. But it's more than that, I hope. We had a practice in the Roots of numbering our songs consecutively, of using our first indie record, *Organix*, as the starting point, tracks 1–17, and then moving forward from there. The tracks of *Do You Want More?!!???!* were numbers 18 to 33, and the ones from *Illadelph Halflife* were 34 to 53. *Things Fall Apart* continued that practice, with its songs taking their position as tracks 54 to 71. That was more than a gimmick. It was a way of reminding our audience—and ourselves—that every discrete chapter is part of a larger book. Things fall apart and come together. People are born and die. The same thing happens to bands, to trends, to technologies, to wars, to nations, to ecosystems and species. History stops and starts, but mostly it keeps on going.

How Do I View . . . Me?

Over the years, I've drummed on many songs, by many artists, in many genres. Some songs stick out in my mind, and in my heart, but for strange reasons. Going back through them is like mapping my own personal history within a larger musical history.

"THE CHARADE"
D'Angelo and the Vanguard

Black Messiah, 2014 [RCA]

D'Angelo, legendary for taking long stretches between albums, started *Black Messiah* to my knowledge around 2003, only a few years after *Voodoo*, but it took molasses time. In 2006 I went to Electric Lady to work on "Really Love," and I didn't get back there until 2009. At that point we hadn't talked in a while. It's not uncommon. The two of us often have our seasons where we fall out and don't talk to each other for a year or two. Some of it was the different schedules. I had just started at *The Tonight Show*, which meant a real workday, during the day, and he was still in the world where you go from 7:00 P.M. to 7:00 A.M. We worked the way we always had, all the way back to the beginning of *Voodoo*, him on keyboards, me on drums, just having fun jamming, but for the first two nights it was a struggle. If I ever get to the afterlife and I get to ask questions about certain moments, this is one of the conversations I want to go back to, because it wasn't a conversation at all. We didn't say a word to each other. Back in 1997, we were at Electric Lady and it was all about bouncing off each other: "You know this song?" "I can't believe you know this song." It was like falling in love. But in 2009, it was almost dead silent. The first night nothing happened. The second night, though, I was acutely aware of everything, thinking, *I'm giving you my best drums—why isn't that sparking an idea for you at all?* It just wasn't happening. The third night he had played me "Sugar Daddy," which was one of the songs on the album that I wasn't on, and instead it was James Gadson drumming. Inside I was jealous. *He's about to move on without me*, I thought. And not only without me, but with James Gadson, the guy who drummed with Bill Withers. You're going to take my idol and throw him back at me? I'm seeing the Soulquarian Polaroid with my image about to fade out with the knowledge that he found someone who could give him something interesting and new. And Gadson wasn't even drumming on "Sugar Daddy." The thing that made it so unique is that he was just sitting on the drum set and listening to the playback and hitting his knees. "We got it," D said. "What?" Gadson said. "I wasn't even drumming yet." "That was perfect. Slapping your knee was all the song needed." When I heard the song I knew that he was right. That led me to a second thought. There are songs on albums that aren't the hits, but they're purely eclipsed by them. I think of Sheila E and "A Love

Bizarre." Or more specifically I think of "Dear Michelangelo," which comes before it on the record. You don't exactly listen to it because you like it. You listen to it because it's the pre-song that's getting you up for *the* song. But I was going to outdo my theory. I'm going to make this pre-song just as good. All this rapid panic thinking took place in the break room, around three in the morning, and Nick at Nite was on and Carlton was dancing. The volume was down so I don't even know if it was Tom Jones playing or not, but it got me thinking about Eddie Murphy's joke about white people dancing and how in *48 Hrs.* he had a scene with Black people dancing to the BusBoys, which always seemed like a joke to me, making this point by using the whitest Black guys ever. I said to myself, OK, this is what I'm gonna do. I'm going to create a song that's going to authentically make people want to do the Carlton in a hip way, and it would come before "Sugah Daddy." I told D'Angelo, "Look, I want to create this song, the one that comes just before," and for this magical half hour we didn't struggle at all. I had an idea in my mind, sort of a Stevie Nicks "Stand Back" Part II, and the way it starts on the record is how it actually starts. It's very authentic. I didn't know where the one was. But then it all came together. I knew instantly that this was it.

"NOT ABOUT LOVE"
Fiona Apple

Extraordinary Machine, 2005 [Epic]

The studio was about an hour out of West Hollywood, where I was staying, and Ladybug Mecca had left me two tickets for that night's Digable Planets reunion. It was a big deal. I needed to make that show. We finished "Get Him Back," one of the other songs on the record, and I had my eye on the clock, which was at 7:30 already. I needed to get out of there to get to the show. "Would you mind doing one more song?" Fiona said. I hemmed and hawed. I couldn't say no, because Fiona only occurs, like, once every ten years. "Get Him Back" had been relatively simple. But when I heard "Not About Love," it had so many starts and stops. In my mind I was just like, *Fuck, man, I'm going to miss this reunion.* I decided I would execute it perfectly, that I would listen to the song three times in a row and map it and do it in one take. I had my coat on, which meant that time was a problem. I walked back to the drum set. I didn't take my jacket off. "Play it for me three times and I'm going to figure it out." I don't notate or write music myself, so I had to write my own gibberish. If there's a riff there I'm going to have to call it what I think it is, say that it's from this part in "Human Nature" or another thing that's a slower version of that other moment in "Fancy Dancer." Fiona sat at the piano, I sat at the drums, and we did it in one take and I was gone.

"DAILY BREAD"
Martin Luther

Daily Bread, 2004 [Good Vibe]

When we were making *The Tipping Point*, I requested some Sly and the Family Stone stems. We were redoing "Everybody Is a Star" for "Star/Pointro." But I also requested five other songs. One was "Can't Strain My Brain." What I quickly learned about Sly reels is that just because the fade happens doesn't mean the song ends. "Daily Bread" is the magic that happen after the fade.

"VALERIE"
Mark Ronson and Amy Winehouse

Version, 2007 [Columbia]

I first met Amy in Scandinavia. There was a festival where we both were playing, but it was in the summer, where the sun never set, and you had to pull the blackout curtains in your room, but even then there was enough light that it was hard to sleep. I went downstairs to get an early breakfast, and she was there too. I had said great things about her records, and Mark Ronson and I developed a friendship. I just wanted to be down with Amy. "I'll do anything," I said. "I don't care if it's finger snaps or getting coffee." About seven months later he called and said, "I'm working with Amy tonight—do you want to do something?" "Say no more," I said. I had just gotten my driver's license, and there was an ice storm that had the news saying everyone should stay off the road. Cut to me on the New Jersey Turnpike doing about 30 miles per hour driving up from Philly to New York. It took about four hours. When I arrived, the studio was small as shit. "Where's the drums at?" I said. "Oh no," Mark said. "You said finger snaps or hand claps. That's all we need." I'm like, you, you tryna tell me I drove four hours in the snowstorm just to put handclaps on this shit? I think I put more effort into that tambourine shakin' and snap clappin' than I did any Roots song and will let no humblebrag opportunity ("that's me you hear!!!!!!!!!") pass if the song is within earshot.

"INTERNATIONAL PLAYBOY"
Money Making Jam Boys

The Prestige, 2011 [mixtape]

I was trying to mess with "Peaches en Regalia," by Frank Zappa. It was one of the first joints I worked on for *Rising Down*, our eighth album. But the climate was bad back then: not in the studio but in the country. We were going through a financial recession, and Philadelphia had jumped into the top-five murder capitals in the country. Too much was going on in Philadelphia and the world for us not to talk about it. We would have been crazy rhyming for the sake of riddling. We took it off the record and it ended up somehow on the Money Making Jam Boys mixtape. But there's nothing I hate more than when you work hard on a song and it doesn't see the light of day.

2000

George W. Bush defeats Al Gore in the presidential election, following the U.S. Supreme Court's decision to end the recount in Florida ○ Al-Qaeda-linked terrorists bomb the U.S.S. *Cole* off the coast of Yemen, killing seventeen sailors ○ An Air France Concorde crashes during takeoff in Paris, killing 119 ○ Venus Williams wins the first of her five Wimbledon singles titles ○ Bob Jones University ends its ban on interracial dating ○ Vermont legalizes civil unions for same-sex couples ○ Charles Schulz dies and the final *Peanuts* strip is published ○ Elian Gonzalez is returned to Cuba ○ DeviantART, which will become the world's largest online art community, is founded ○ *Dora the Explorer* debuts ○ Montgomery Ward goes out of business after 128 years

THINGS COME TOGETHER

Each of us is surrounded by others, who in turn are surrounded by us.

Most of the history in this book, and much of the history in people's minds, revolves around discrete events. A spacecraft is launched and then explodes. A battle is waged on acres of farmland. A concert is held on acres of farmland. A man or woman is born, makes a mark in a certain discipline at a certain time, and later dies. I've written earlier about how this model of history can perpetuate inaccurate ideas about individual genius, or for that matter individual villainy, since usually the people who are foregrounded in these stories were working with a support network.

Sometimes, though, history and its tapestry of events arise out of scenes. This is clearest in the arts, perhaps, where we talk about Warhol's Factory, or the Brill Building, or the Des Moines hardcore scene, or Dafen, but there are also historians who look at similar groupings in technology, or architecture, or medicine. Each of those scenes is like a supercharged site: due to the high density of a certain kind of person, they generate a disproportionate number of similar or at least related events. The story of *Things Fall Apart*, which I told part of in the last chapter, was just as much about things coming together—particularly a scene.

You might think that it's about the scene around our recording of the record: the sessions at Electric Lady that overlapped with parts of other albums like *Voodoo* (D'Angelo's follow-up to *Brown Sugar*), *Mama's Gun* (Erykah Badu's follow-up to *Baduizm*), and *Like Water for Chocolate* (Common's major-label debut). Those records got grouped together, as did the artists in and around them—people called us the Soulquarians, a designation that was formalized by a picture in *Vibe* in 2000.

The part of the story I told in the last chapter was mostly about finishing *Things Fall Apart*. But there's a whole other story that started a few years before that, before we ever recorded a note. At a certain point, whenever we headed out of one album into the next one, Rich made sure that there was an idea stretching over us and protecting us from the elements, like an awning. Our records may have been concept albums, but they also grew out of highly conceptualized environments. The most extreme version of this came on *The Tipping Point*, released in 2004. For that record, Rich set up a kind of strip club/brothel that was a throwback to places we saw when we were barnstorming around Europe. In his mind, it let the band bond in ways we weren't able to otherwise, since we weren't touring as much anymore. Certain ideas couldn't happen without the proper environment, he thought, just as certain plants couldn't grow in the wrong kind of soil. *Things Fall Apart* was the birth of that kind of process. At the time, I had moved into a small house on St. Albans in South Philadelphia. Rich told our label at the time, MCA, that they had to pay for jam sessions at that house, and that the costs would include equipment, transportation, and food.

Rich's idea was that creative conditions would attract creative people, and he was right. We started with our core group—the Jazzyfatnastees, Kindred the Family Soul, Dice Raw, 3 7000 9—but soon enough people from all over Philadelphia (and beyond) started to drop by, hang out, sing, and play. There was a kid who was still in high school who had a unique singing style. There was an aspiring singer and songwriter who was working as a pizza-delivery guy. There was a woman from Atlanta who knew our high school mate Fatin Dantzler, who would occasionally come by with her acoustic guitar. There was an MC who came to our attention from Malik B. Over time, they would all turn into signed artists: Musiq Soulchild, Bilal, India.Arie, and Beanie Siegel, respectively. And once our sessions spawned a scene, that kind of thing became even more common. The more it happened, the more it happened. At some point, I remember someone in the room saying, "I have this friend who works in a denim store, a jeans place, on South Street. Can she come over?" Sure, we said. Why not? It seemed certain she'd end up being another star. The jeans-store woman ended up being Jill Scott. (As it turned out, we had met her before—she had come to a session for *Do You Want More?!!???!* with a friend of hers who sang on the record. Back then, she mostly sat on a couch and complained about a boyfriend who was cheating on her. I think she threatened to castrate him. I was scared of her back then, but it was great to see her when she showed up at St. Albans.)

There was music percolating all the time—and I mean all the time, until all hours of the night. I had to sometimes call the cops on myself, to sneak into a side room and report a noise complaint at my own address so that an officer would come and shut it down. But the scene kept throwing off sparks. When we went into the studio to make our record, and especially when we went off on tour, part of it splintered off and became the Black Lily collective, which emphasized the female artists in the bunch like the Jazzyfatnastees, Eve, the ladies of Floetry, Lady Alma, Ursula Rucker. Jill was the early star of that part of the movement.

She was on *Things Fall Apart*, sort of. We had picked one of the songs, "You Got Me," as our first single. We knew that it was our strongest contender. And the label agreed it had real potential. There was, however, a sticking point—the song had a sung hook, and they wanted a singer who had some measure of fame. In the studio, it had been sung by Jill, partly because she had co-written the song. But Jill wasn't a star yet. She wasn't even a solo recording artist. The label lobbied for Erykah Badu to sing the hook instead of Jill. I delayed, partly by asking all the uncomfortable questions. Who was going to break the news to Jill? Who was going to drop everything and go to Dallas to get Erykah's vocals? I don't remember who told Jill, but I remember that a bunch of us—me, Tariq, Rich, and I think Bob Power—went to Dallas. Erykah was happy to sing, but she said what everyone with ears said, which was that we were out of our minds to replace Jill. On tour, Jill spent months singing the part live. (We eventually released her version on the compilation *Home Grown! The Beginners Guide to Understanding the Roots, Vol. 1.*)

Jill became a solo artist soon enough, when her debut, *Who Is Jill Scott? Words and Sounds Vol. 1*, came out in 2000. "Love Rain" was, for me, the standout ballad, a poetic, playful, and at times painful account of a love affair. Right after that there's a short track called "The Roots (Interlude)," a bit of live audio taken from one of the tour stops. "What's your name, girlfriend?" Tariq says. Jill answers, spelling her name in song, and adding "Representing North Philly." So in a sense the Roots both followed "Love Rain" and preceded it.

"You Got Me" won us a Grammy. Collectives, done correctly, can find ways to correct the record.

• • •

I can't believe it's been twenty years since Jill's debut. In part of my mind, I'm still there in the studio making "You Got Me." How can it have slipped into the past, let alone enough years into the past that it's celebrating its platinum anniversary? (Though to be fair, the album did go double platinum.) But I know it's true, because Jill was supposed to go out in 2020 on a twentieth anniversary tour. She gave *Billboard* a quote where she explained the way she intended to split the difference between faithfully re-creating the original and giving herself enough freedom to reinterpret it:

> I'm going to be true to the album setlist. I'll do every song in the order of the album. My audience should bring their CD covers. Some may know the list by heart. I will create musical arrangements for the

songs' purposes with new energy but keep the integrity of the original songs they love. Expect theatre. Expect incredible musicianship. Expect love.

The pandemic canceled every tour, so it canceled that one, too. Maybe it'll get rescheduled. I'm curious to see how she does "The Roots (Interlude)."

2001

The 9/11 attacks: Two planes hijacked by terrorists fly into the World Trade Center, a third crashes into the Pentagon, and a fourth is brought down in a Pennsylvania field

THE BAD MINUS

One point is heavy enough to pull down the whole graph.

People talk about 9/11 like it was the only thing that happened in 2001, and in some sense it was. The chronology at the head of this chapter is a joke, but a grim and telling one.

Everyone—at least everyone who was in New York back then—has their own 9/11 story. We tell them to prove that we were part of history. Mine starts the night before, when the Roots were in downtown Manhattan working on a concert series. We were trying to get done early so I could go see the Michael Jackson tribute at Madison Square Garden, which was a celebration of his first thirty years in show business. But the rehearsal schedule started dragging because Meshell Ndegeocello was running late, and at some point it became clear that we weren't going to make it to the Garden. We closed up shop and went to the SoHo Grand, where we discovered that our hotel rooms didn't exist. Or rather, they existed, but they had been given away to other guests. I threw a little tantrum, which wasn't a common occurrence, then or now, but the events of the day—irritating delays, no Michael, and now no hotel—seemed to demand it. We got space at the Marriott right next to the World Trade Center. Great! But then the computers went down and when they came back up those rooms were gone. Less than great! Now the SoHo Grand split us up, sending some Roots to a Sheraton, some to a Howard Johnson's, and me and Tariq to the Bryant Park Hotel. We got there at who knows what time and went immediately to sleep. This was maybe two in the morning on September 11.

The noise of my phone woke me, not completely at first, but by the fourth or fifth time I wasn't able to roll back over and fall asleep. I checked and saw that I had multiple missed calls from my mom, which wasn't surprising, but also from multiple other people, which was. My first thought was that someone had died. When I checked my mom's messages, I found out how right I was. The planes had already crashed into the World Trade Center. I turned on the TV and watched as the South Tower collapsed. I couldn't believe what I was seeing, and yet there was no question it was true. Everyone else was seeing it, too, which I knew because they kept texting me. The texts weren't sophisticated. "Are you watching this?" "I don't understand." "I'm shaking." They were texts by human brains who had encountered a moment in history too large to process.

When I finally was able to move, I moved quickly. I checked with the front desk and extended my stay through the end of the week. Then I ran outside. Everything was dead quiet. I found a cab, gave him a hundred dollars, and asked him if he could take me just a few blocks to the Virgin Megastore. I don't know why I didn't walk. It didn't seem safe? It didn't seem right? There were people in the street, but they were moving slowly, stunned, looking around and usually up. It was like a zombie attack where the city itself had become a zombie. In the store, I bought a bunch of CDs, including whatever was new that day—it was Tuesday, which used to be the day that new records came out. I loaded them into my arms just to feel the weight of something familiar.

The day eventually ended, though it was hard to believe that it did. At some point that week I heard a guy talking. He was murmuring something, maybe to himself, maybe to me. I wasn't scared of him, though maybe in another time I would have been. I was curious what he was saying, so I stayed where I was standing until he got close enough to hear. "History is over," he said.

For a day or two after the attacks, the city was entirely paralyzed. But then things started moving again. Subways resumed operation, which meant that people could go to and from Manhattan, which meant that theaters could open again, and offices, and gradually airports as well. But the intensity of that day, the power of the experience, meant that it would remain in all of our minds forever, a place to go when we needed to access common history. The guy who was talking to himself was right and wrong. History wasn't over, not exactly. But at that moment, it seemed unlikely that anything would ever happen again that rose to that level of history.

● ● ●

I don't remember exactly which albums I bought at the Virgin Megastore. I know that Jay-Z's *The Blueprint* was among them, because it became my soundtrack for the rest of that week. But when I think about what song best represents that year, I think of the Bad Plus's cover of Nirvana's "Smells Like Teen Spirit." Nirvana has, if not a special place in my heart, at least a special part in my history. It was Kurt Cobain's death, remember, that caused the Roots to panic about our standing at Geffen Records, to hurry up and finish our first major-label album, *Do You Want More?!!???!*, and to get to London so that we could retrench and regain our strength and anticipate returning to the States with a new audience and increased momentum. Some of those things happened.

For much of that year, I closed my DJ set with the Bad Plus's version of Nirvana's most famous song. It was not exactly a crowd-pleaser. In a sense, it was the other shoe dropping, since I usually played the original earlier in the set, and it was a big highlight. The Bad Plus's "Smells Like Teen Spirit," then, was a callback, history repeating in a different form, a rethink pressed so close to the original thought that it almost went back in time little and changed the first one. It's not a normal cover. It's a slow piano version that, after the five-minute mark, becomes something else entirely. The melody returns to the song's first verse while the arrangement dissolves into a series of violent musical crashes. It is modulated into a lower key, which alone is a frightening choice. Normally, to make a song bigger, you go higher. Even before 9/11, that song was many things—it was a symbol of crashing, a symbol of falling, a symbol of violence, a symbol of fear. After 9/11, it was all of those things in the service of the one thing that the year suddenly was. That crescendo had another effect, too. It worked like a musical version of the neuralyzer—that's the flashing pen-type-thing from *Men in Black* that wipes out all recent memories. It was such a powerful piece, with such a fragmented closing, that it wiped away all that had come before it, just for a second, before the past started flowing back in. Before 9/11, it was a challenge, a way of seeing how much of the set I had just played would remain in people's minds. After 9/11, it was a relief. For the first time I could remember, history had delivered us all something that we couldn't forget, even for a second, but that we desperately wanted to pretend we could.

• • •

Two funny stories to cap off this grim reminiscence. The first starts long before the attacks and ends long after them. Public Enemy's great 1990 song "911 Is a Joke" is about the disparity in emergency-service response times in the Black and white communities. Flavor Flav is more concise: "So get up, get, get, get down / 911 is a joke in your town." In 2009, the group visited a shelter for homeless teens in Washington, D.C. Nice gesture, right? But in reporting the visit, the *Washington Post* misprinted the title as "9/11 Is a Joke." Which, in turn, led a number of readers to write in, outraged, about this anti-American hip-hop group that was mocking the nation's worst tragedy.

Was it the nation's worst tragedy? It's not a rhetorical question. It's a framing device for the second funny story, which is an actual joke by Michael Che, the comedian who currently holds down one of two anchor positions on *Saturday Night Live*'s Weekend Update. The joke comes not from the show, but from a stand-up special, during which Che discussed how the injuries done to Black Americans are minimized in favor of an insistence that things are improving:

> Why do black people always have to get over shit so quickly? Every time we bring some shit up. Slavery. "Oh, that was four hundred years ago." Segregation. "You guys got Black History Month out of it. We gave you February." Police shooting. "That was two weeks—come on, still?" 9/11. "Oh, never forget."

The special was originally released in 2016, but gained additional currency in 2020, when a series of police shootings of unarmed Black Americans led to numerous protests in cities across the country, even during the first months of the coronavirus pandemic. The bit asks, with genuine intellectual curiosity, without bitterness, who decides how long it takes for a historical event to pass into the painless past, and whether anyone can fairly set that schedule for anyone else. It's one of the largest questions of history, and one of the questions that I'll go out on, because I genuinely don't know the answer. I only know that it's a question that has to be asked over and over again. Che ends with a joke that I'll end with, too, which is that every September 11, he's going to wear a shirt that says "All Buildings Matter."

Last but (Not?) Least

Some people are looking for the ultimate experience. I'm looking for the penultimate. What I mean is that I like to end my experience with an artwork before the artwork ends. When I play Marvin Gaye's *What's Going On*, I rarely listen to "Inner City Blues." When I play Michael Jackson's *Thriller*, I rarely listen to "The Lady in My Life." When I play Public Enemy's *Fear of a Black Planet*, I rarely listen to "Fight the Power." I can handle them as singles, as songs, but not as the ends of albums. For me, those albums wrap up with "Wholy Holy," "P.Y.T.," and "Final Count of the Collision Between Us and the Damned." I don't know all the reasons I feel this way, only that I do. But when I pressed myself, I was able to come up with ten songs that I truly love/embrace as final moments on albums. I am putting them here, at the end of the book. What? It's not the end of the book? There's one chapter left? So be it.

"EGYPTIAN SONG"
Rufus

Ask Rufus, 1977 [ABC]

I have written elsewhere about the songs that I heard in my youth that saddened me because they represented a certain moment: that time when my parents went on tour and left me with my grandmother. "Egyptian Song" is one of those. It's so powerful to me. But the personal resonance is part of a larger principle, one that's at play in any album I love. Last songs are goodbyes, and saying goodbye is hard. You never know when you're going to get to say hello again.

"GOD LIVES THROUGH"
A Tribe Called Quest

Midnight Marauders, 1993 [Jive]

On the promo version of *Midnight Marauders*, and even on the vinyl version, the album ends on "The Chase." I'm not a huge fan of that. If it truly ended there I wouldn't consider it as powerful as I do, and certainly I wouldn't think of it as the equal of its predecessor, *The Low-End Theory*. But then there is "Lyrics to Go," and then there is "God Lives Through." I am grateful. They're treats that actually solidified the album for me. More than that: I consider them the greatest one-two punch of fast material on any record. You can argue for other kinds of ends, like "Purple Rain," say, which is the heart of the record, but most of those cases are about sweeping ballads or at least midtempo. This is faster, better, a completely successful final track that corrects the record.

"RAILROAD MAN"
Bill Withers

+'Justments, 1974 [Sussex]

I've said elsewhere that how people play records is almost as important as the records themselves. When my parents played *+'Justments* at first, they started with "Heartbreak Road,' which is the first song on side two, but to me it was side one. Because I didn't know that it was the last song, I didn't let my prejudice against last songs settle in, and by the time I got the real song order right, it was already in my good graces.

"MURDER BY NUMBERS"
The Police

Synchronicity, 1983 [A&M]

As I've said elsewhere, the Police are geniuses about balancing perspectives, alternating Sting songs with songs by Andy Summers or Stewart Copeland, usually on side two. This album works a little differently. Side two is straight Sting and straight hits: "Every Breath You Take," "King of Pain," Wrapped Around Your Finger." The true ending for this LP (the non-cassette or CD version) was "Tea in the Sahara," a downright mean trick of a song to end an already dark album. And then comes this, even darker, a co-write between Sting and Summers (there's an even more evil end to certain versions of the CD, "Once Upon a Daydream"). These jazzy numbers didn't bother me much . . . until Harry Connick, Jr., ruined it for me in the 1995 Quasi-of-the Lambsesque film *Copycat*, where it was used as a piece of evidence.

"ADDICTED"
Amy Winehouse

Back to Black, 2006 [Island]

On the one hand, this shouldn't count at all, because when I first heard the album, in its European configuration, it started with "Addicted," so that's what I was used to and what I considered the opener. The American version, weirdly enough, starts out on the song that I thought was the second song ("Rehab") and closes with the Euro opener. That's how powerful that album is: a noncreative damn near railroaded this album with an amateur mistake, and it *still* manages to work. I refuse to listen to the LP the way that Americans received it. I start it with the last song and then back up and start over again.

"RETURN OF THE B-BOY"
The Pharcyde

Bizarre Ride II The Pharcyde, 1992 [Delicious Vinyl]

Had the Roots made music the way I thought we were going to make music when we first started going to the studio, it would have been more akin to the Pharcyde and this record, the same thing that Dr. Dre was doing—half beats, half live drums. So this whole album was a game changer. I listened all the way through in this case, because I hadn't heard Prince samples used that way. Up until then it was mostly things like MC Hammer's "Pray," which Hammer-sampled "When Doves Cry," or Digital Underground's "Sex Packets," which used "She's Always in My Hair," or Kwame's "Skinee Muva," which quoted "Bob George" and was aiight. But this was a deeper cut—it was Madhouse, "Two"—and a better use. My use of Madhouse, "Four" on "What Goes On Pt. 7" from the Roots' *Do You Want More?!!!??!*, was an homage/answer to that. It was my way of saying, if you use Prince that way, I see you—and few other people do.

"WHENEVER, WHEREVER"
Minnie Riperton

Come to My Garden, 1970 [GRT]

I know albums need peaks and valleys in order to make their point. But I'm not always fully aware of how that works as I'm listening. I've written earlier (back in 1987) about Janet Jackson's *Control* and the way it ensured its own success—specifically, the way that it contained allegedly weaker songs that actually helped listeners to get to the allegedly stronger ones, and how this arrangement actually strengthened both the weaker songs and the entire album. *Come to My Garden* is a more understated version of that. Every song works so perfectly. Charles Stepney is flying under the radar. But it still needs this not-overwhelming end to put the others into relief.

"CED-GEE [DELTA FORCE ONE]"
Ultramagnetic MCs

Critical Beatdown, 1988 [Next Plateau]

This has the same effect on me as "Egyptian Song," for very different reasons. For starters, it doesn't have Kool Keith. He was, to me, the heart of the group, while Ced-Gee was always a good sidekick. So it's strange to end a record with the second name in the group, but it's also sort-of-welcome strange, as was the slower tempo. Add to that that they use a bridge/turnaround from Bob James's "Nautilus." That was my favorite part. Bob James music was something I always associated with Philly TV of my youth and the way they scored interstitials on the news—this community gathering announcement, that 8th Annual BBQ Jamboree. It was always a song like "Westchester Lady." So all my Bob James was public service TV, and hearing it used differently like this was worth noticing.

“THE PARASITE (FOR BUFFY)”
Eugene McDaniels

Headless Heroes of the Apocalypse, 1971 [Atlantic]

The end of the album is the only place for a song like this, a ten-minute-plus anthem about the mistreatment of Indians, dedicated to Buffy Sainte-Marie, that descends (or ascends) into absolute chaos at the eight-and-a-half-minute mark. In 2002, we did a bunch of dates with Lauryn Hill when her *Unplugged* record was coming out. I would always curate the front-of-the-house music. She hadn't yet entirely developed her interesting relationship to time, but it had started. I decided to spend forty-five minutes on energetic music, keeping the crowd up, but if she took longer I was going to play a different kind of thing. It was like a game of chicken. Would she delay long enough to get to the weird songs, to the disturbing ones? I figured she never would. I figured my last songs would be like the last songs I experience on records: unlistened-to. I put “The Parasite” in around the fifty-five-minute mark. Most of the time she got out there before it played. Twice, in Portland and Seattle, she did not. When I heard it starting from my tour bus—Ron Carter's bass is loud—I couldn't believe it. They let it get to this? I ran to the side of the stage. The song was about to get really crazy. I had to call my own bluff. Should I run to the front and put on some rap music? I let it go. You should have seen their faces when the chaos hit.

“PINOCCHIO”
Miles Davis

Nefertiti, 1968 [Columbia]

Nefertiti is, for me, a backward album. Like Kendrick Lamar's *DAMN,* it feels like the songs are sequenced in reverse order. I wrote, back in the 1971 chapter, about the title song, and how it was slow, exhausting, circular, Miles's farewell to an era of jazz. And that's the opener. “Pinoccho” holds as a last song because it doesn't sound like a last song. It has energy and momentum. It makes me happy.

2002 – PRESENT

OUR TWENTY-FIRST CENTURY

Let's break from the year-by-year organization now, partly because we got to a year that broke.

Prior to 9/11, I had not lived through any incident that I knew would be in every permanent record of not only this nation but this planet, probably for as long as I or anyone else lives. There were major moments, of course: Watergate when I was too young to care, the *Challenger* disaster, the fall of the Berlin Wall. But 9/11 felt like the first indisputable moment of History.

It was also the last, at least until now. I say that knowing full well that what's happening here in 2020 will be History eventually. No question. It's like wondering whether LeBron will make the Hall of Fame. But at this point, it's not yet there. It's right on top of us, more so than we're right on top of it. We can't see anything with perspective yet. To some degree, that's true for the entire twenty-first century. The Iraq War was no small potatoes. The 2008 financial crisis almost brought down the world's economy. But if I was teaching a history course—or writing a book that doubled as a strange version of one—I might not yet classify those events as history. We haven't been able to acquire perspective yet. This is a slippery slope and a blurry line and all other kinds of equivocal. I know that. When you're refusing to make a definitive statement on objects in the mirror because they're too close, what counts as too close? Five years? Ten? Twenty? Is it affected by how old you are, and how much history you passed through before this most recent period? Does that make you more qualified to make a snap judgment? Less qualified? These are all aspects of the argument. But what is history if not a series of arguments?

● ● ●

If this is true of history, it's also true of music. If I drop back into the past a little, I have a decent sense of which albums are classics. If I have heard them many times, over a period of time, and they still stick to the ribs of the mind, I feel confident about promoting them. I know which Stevie Wonder albums rise rather than fall away, which Prince albums do the same. I know what to do with Public Enemy or with Chaka Khan, with Minnie Riperton or Mavis Staples, with Michael Jackson and even most of Janet. But when you get closer to the present, the same cloud of uncertainty descends. Have I sat with this record long enough to render judgment? Do I understand completely what came before it and what came out of it? The last record I'm absolutely sure about is D'Angelo's *Voodoo*, from 2000. J Dilla's *Donuts*, from 2006, also gets classic status, but I know that my feelings about it aren't easily separated from my feelings about his early death.

And yet we have to keep our critical faculties sharp, whether we're talking about events from a hundred years ago, events that have been picked over by generations of academics and analysts, or events that happened this morning.

If you look at the hip-hop artists who have surfaced over the last few years, from Blueface to Tierra Whack to Saba to Noname to Injury Reserve to Leikeli47 to Megan Thee Stallion to (YBN) Cordae, the principle holds. Sorting them out isn't yet possible. You can make judgments, even forceful ones, but writing about Roddy Ricch is journalism, not history. There's a different but related problem for artists who rose to prominence five to eight years ago.

They're not right alongside the vehicle. They're a little back, in the blind spot. It's hard to see whether they'll eventually drift to a place where I can get a better look at them.

My point, metaphors aside, is that it's very hard to know what you think about things that you haven't thought about hard for very long. One of the best examples comes from around five years ago, though it starts twenty years ago, and it starts with me angry. There was a singer named Carl Thomas, signed to Bad Boy Records, who released his debut album, *Emotional*, in 2000. There was a good two weeks there where I was secretly mad at James Poyser, one of the Roots and a talented producer in his own right, because I was sure that he had gone sneaking off to make *Emotional*. In the same way that Prince thought Jimmy Jam and Terry Lewis secretly did "Keep On Lovin' Me" for the Whispers rather than Leon Sylvers, who actually did it, I assumed James had gone behind my back. And it stung, because the record sounded like something we would have—should have—done together. I wasn't sure, so I didn't confront him, but I was sure enough that I allowed myself to be passive-aggressive. Oh, you want a glass of water? Get your own water! I would have put my publishing up that he had done it.

He hadn't, of course. I found out the truth, that all the producers credited for that record (Gordon Chambers, Mario Winans, Ron Lawrence, Harve Pierre, Chucky Thompson) were real people with credits of their own. (Harve Pierre is a real person? I'm still a little suspicious.)

Now fast-forward to this century, to the last year or two of the Obama administration. James had done some work with Rihanna, played keyboards on "No Love Allowed." I wasn't sure whether that was a one-off or the beginning of a longer working relationship. In 2016, I heard "James Joint," a song from her new album. I mentioned it before, in a playlist, but I want to mention it again, because of how amazed I was by it. It was a short song, only a minute and fifteen seconds, but it was fully fleshed out, a complete musical story and a full narrative on top of that. Damn, I thought, James went and did this song without me. I could have worked on it with him. It was Carl Thomas all over again. For a week or so, he had to get his own water.

Time passed. I got more information. (There's an important takeaway here, too, about reacting to history too quickly, not just before you've had time to emotionally process what has occurred, but before you really know the facts of the matter.) I discovered that the song had been created with another James, James Fauntleroy. I forgave James Poyser. I may have even gotten him water.

The longer I sat with "James Joint," the more I became obsessed with the album it came from, *Anti*. I own every Rihanna album, but largely for DJ completeness. This was something different. The more time I spent with it, the more certain I was that I was listening to something that was art, plain and simple. It had layers and levels. Many albums represent a slight advance over the albums before them. This was way past that. It was leaps and bounds of growth. In the moment, I was certain that I had encountered a classic. I couldn't stop telling people. I did one tweet that went so over the top that I got word from the Roc Nation camp. They were concerned that my high praise was a form of saying that all of Rihanna's other albums were shitty. In their minds, it was like if someone loses a whole bunch of weight and you say, "Now you look good." I immediately destroyed the tweet.

Now, almost five years later, I look back on that and wonder if I was overreacting. I still love the record. I still think it's her finest hour. But I was so much in the moment, so overloaded with emotion (first, the frustration that James was running around behind my back again—"again," even though he hadn't the first time, then the relief that there was another James, then the pleasure of measuring this song against her catalog) that nothing I was saying belonged outside the moment. Check back in ten years, or twenty, when the centripetal pull of that moment has weakened. This is a note for myself, not for readers. I need to check back in with myself in ten years, or twenty, and see if *Anti* maintains its status.

And it's even more complicated than that. Everything is. The same year that Rihanna released *Anti*, Kanye West released *The Life of Pablo*. He worked right up to the deadline, as often happens. I remember having conversations with people (people in the know) on the Wednesday before the Friday that it was supposed to be delivered to streaming services, and Kanye (and his producers) were still adding samples and verses, smoothing transitions. It was a real nail-biter. But then the album came out. At which point, normally, we would have said that it entered the historical record. But streaming—well, streaming plus Kanye—upended that process. Even once the album was on streaming services, Kanye continued to tinker with it. He thickened the choir vocals on "Ultralight Beam" and added ad-libs from Chance the Rapper. He changed a lyric in "Famous" (goodbye, "She be Puerto Rican Day parade waving," hello, "She in school to be a real estate agent"). And on and on. Def Jam, his label, put out a statement: "In the months to come, Kanye will release new updates, new versions, and new iterations of the album. An innovative, continuous process, the album will be a living, evolving art project." Okay, I guess. Innovative and continuous, sure. But what does it do to history? What does it do to the album's status as history and the ability of the rest of us to read it as part of history? What if a famous painting continued to change while it was on the wall of the museum? Counterargument: it does, of course. Time makes itself known in every way. But we know how to think about historical artifacts being taken over by time. We know how to read deterioration and buildup. And counterargument to the counterargument: this only happens in one direction, to an agreed-on original version. This is the hand of the creator reaching back in and altering that original version. Technology permits that, and not just for music. So far, at least, this problem only applies to artifacts. Actual events can't be altered after the fact. Or can they? An article published in digital form (as most now are) can later be updated without a clear account of the changes. The original date stamp will still seem true but the contents will have changed, maybe in ways that affect our sense of events, which means that they will also be affecting events. Wow, that article predicted the score of that game exactly! Wow, that politician said something that seemed to suggest that he or she knew about that pharmaceutical company's research! So it seems like it's even more important both to track the way artifacts and events are initially put into the historical record and to let time pass before any long-view opinions are rendered. This paragraph was not in original versions of the book. It just appeared.

• • •

Changes combine to produce more changes. If, since 9/11, I have thought about history differently and about music differently, I have also thought about music history differently. The main place I articulate my ideas about music and history, other than this book, is in my DJ sets. I mentioned that throughout 2001 I closed my sets with the Bad Plus's version of "Smells Like Teen Spirit." That changed fairly quickly. It wasn't because of trauma, or at least it wasn't solely because of trauma. Technology played a role as well. In 2002 or so, I started to use Serato's DJ software. Before that, I needed some time for the switch-outs between songs, time to look for the next record and cue it up. Technology sped up those transitions and saved me maybe twenty seconds per song, which meant that I could not only build momentum in different ways—energy didn't leak at the seams—but include more records. I went from eighty songs in a three-hour set, maybe ninety if I was lucky, to more than a hundred. Before the new software, I was a human iPod. After that, I was a human with mastery over the contents of an iPod. Different closing songs started suggesting themselves, and I tried them on—for a while, I was ending with Harry Belafonte's "Day-O (The Banana Boat Song)."

After a few years of using the new technology and thinking about how it affected my DJ practice, I started to see that what I was doing was not only assembling a collage of the best recorded music, but building a real history that used those musical artifacts as its plot points. Over a few years, I felt myself shift from collector to curator. What mattered wasn't only having the right records and being able to bring them into the set, but being able to design and display a show consisting of those records. Increasingly, when people came to a DJ performance after 2002, they were stepping into a kind of museum, but 4D rather than 3D because I was also controlling the time element.

And the show I was hanging was not only a form of history, but a commentary on it. As I have said, I like new music. As a fan, as a pair of ears, I respond to it, whether it's "Stir Fry" one year or "The Box" the next. But I am also concerned (obsessed?) with looking at how the universe of music resolves into galaxies, and galaxies into constellations. And I want to build a night sky from what I know. There are so many connections in music that mean you can play Chet Baker just a few songs away from a sitcom theme and play that just a few songs away from M.I.A. American music is related to international music. Rock's related to soul. Punk's related to reggae. At some level, music is like one gigantic organism, flowing through people at different times, in different places. If you know enough, you can light up enough parts of its body to show that you're looking at a body.

Throughout this book, I've talked about how to read history, how to receive it and interpret it. DJing is more a matter of writing history. I build all the music I have into giant playlists, by theme, by era, by style. Once those big lists are in place, I start pruning and refining, moving things from here to there. This is a long process—it doesn't just take hours, but months. In the past, I used the calendar to discipline the process: around New Year's, I started to feel pressure, and over the first two or three months of the year, I worked to vent that pressure, making sure that I had new lists in place by March or so.

About five or six years after the innovations in DJ software came innovations in streaming platforms, and that forced me to reassess the process yet again. Now I could build giant playlists on servers, test them out, reorganize and replace, without even touching a real record. That opened up more intellectual possibilities, but it also made the entire idea of a playlist seem less consequential. History is filled with those kinds of compromises. Think of how much more quickly and comprehensively you can research with the Internet—you don't have to get on a horse and ride to Bobbio, Fulda, or Cluny anymore—but also how many more opportunities there are to run afoul of legitimacy. Or think of how many more primary images exist now thanks to the fact that there are camera phones everywhere, but how we have to be careful not to accept images at face value. I knew that I was looking at tools that made it easier to collect primary materials but potentially more difficult to write a history with authority. I did my best to strike a balance.

• • •

Why do people write history? I mean, what is the most common motivation? Some people just have that kind of personality. They want to set the record straight, and they don't care who knows it. But much of the time, history gets told when people are permitted (or even invited) to tell it—in other words, when someone who is already interested in telling a story is charged with doing so.

In 2008 or so, I was charged. The Roots, like many artists, were campaigning for Barack Obama. There was something about him that seemed culturally knowing, and something else that seemed curious about what he didn't know. I got word that he wanted me to build him a playlist, and I dove right in, creating a massive playlist that not only addressed different aspects of the human condition, but organized them in a way that told the history of the nation through the history of its music. I put it on an iPod. But as I was doing it, I realized that it was just a draft, not yet ready for Obama. I think I gave that one to Jay-Z. That process repeated another time, and then another.

Every time I had any contact with the president or anyone else from his administration, I was reminded—good-naturedly, without any sense that I wasn't turning in my homework, but still—that I owed them a playlist. "I'm up through P," I'd say. "By next year, maybe I'll be at U, and then I'm rounding into W." It wasn't that I wasn't interested in the task. During that time I was teaching a course at NYU. Music through history and history through music was exactly what I was doing. But something about the size of the playlist, or the person I was supposed to send it to, intimated me. I didn't want to do it until I could do it right.

Then word came through that it was too late. He was wrapping up his time in the White House. There would be no playlist for President Obama, though I was still welcome to deliver it when he was once again a private citizen. I had spent so long building my history mix that history had passed me by. It was like that story of a map that's as big as the country it's mapping. Who's that by again?

As a consolation prize, Obama invited me to DJ his final party at the White House in January 2017, weeks before he was scheduled to vacate. I hadn't delivered the playlist or the iPod, so I wanted to make sure that my DJ set did everything that it was going to do and more. I tried parts of the set out in my other gigs, including a party for the *Hamilton* cast. And then I was ready. I had seen other DJs play the White House, including D-Nice at a BET party a few years earlier, and I was amazed to hear his set, which was an arrow-to-the-bullseye Black music set, lots of trap, lots of gangster rap. It was liberating to see the Blackest of sounds fill the Whitest of Houses, especially with Obama as the resident. But I wanted to do something different. I wanted to represent through presenting, teach history through telling a story, walk my way back through everything from rock and disco and funk and soul and jazz and show tunes and everything else.

The set started off fine. People were dancing. Connections were being made. The music, selected and sequenced, was illuminating and elucidating. Obama suddenly appeared. "Great job," he said. He said it in the way that there's a "but" hovering in the air. Then it came: the younger kids wanted to dance. Suddenly I understood. My set, brilliant as it was, wasn't going to last out the night. My host—my president—was asking me to change course. He wanted me to switch away from the set I had built, with its meticulous historical construction, its intricacies and interrelations, and to play party music. And so I did. And the president was right. The kids came to dance. It was more than that: more than just the kids came to dance. Everyone, suddenly, was on the floor. And then I was just pandering. People started whispering suggestions to me—and I took them! I went on Spotify to see what the most popular songs of that week were—and I played them!

As good as it felt to please the crowd, that was exactly as bad as it felt to have abandoned my original plan. Even the best-laid plans sometimes had to bend to meet the moment. I had come in ready to make history by remaking History, but I had run into an event.

• • •

After I got back from Washington, I reassessed and paused on DJing for a while. Maybe there was a little self-pity in the mix. I hadn't told the story I wanted to, despite my best efforts. But the reassessment included some analysis. Did that change the story at all? Capital-H History still existed, and I had managed to capture it in a way that satisfied me. Wasn't it on me to find the right landing place for what I had made? Add to that the fact that I was at the point when artists often begin to look back over their body of work and reassess, to tangle themselves up in doubt and second-guessing. I knew what Stevie Wonder had done in the late '80s, what Prince had done in the mid-'90s. They had floundered.

I lost focus and I lost time, and by the time I got them back, Obama had left the White House. Trump had moved in. And with Trump came a number of ideas about immigrants and people of color. I won't say that they were new ideas. They were old ideas revived for purposes of separating people. One of the things I wondered immediately was how artists would respond to his election. Many were opposed, I knew. But how would they focus their opposition?

It wasn't that music couldn't go after the president effectively. I thought back to Reagan, and how so many songs took a stand against him, not just album tracks like Prince's "Ronnie, Talk to Russia" (see 1983) but big pop hits like INXS's "Guns in the Sky," which was supposedly about Reagan's Star Wars defense system, or Genesis's "Land of Confusion," which starred all those ugly Spitting Image puppets and ended with Reagan waking from a nightmare, drenched in sweat, and pressing the "nurse" button—except that he pressed "nuke" instead! I thought about Bonzo Goes to Washington again, and "Bonzo Goes to Bitburg," the Ramones song from 1985 about Reagan visiting a cemetery where Nazi soldiers were buried (instead of, say, a concentration camp). I thought about Reagan samples in songs by everyone from EPMD to Afrika Bambaataa, and then I thought about Gil Scott-Heron, who was hip-hop before there was a name for it. He had released a single called "B-Movie" back in 1981, expressing his disbelief that the country had elected a not-very-good actor to its highest office. In 1984, he was back with a sequel, "Re-Ron," seven minutes of politics and patter that talk about U.S. involvement in the Middle East and Central America with some real questionable rhymes ("up to his keisters with the Sandinistas").

The Trump songs started to appear. There was a first wave where artists either supported Hillary Clinton in the wake of her defeat (Le Tigre's "I'm with Her") or championed a humanism that everyone feared was being lost (Arcade Fire's "I Give You Power," which featured vocals by Mavis Staples). Then people started to zero in on the forty-fifth president. YG and Nipsey Hussle went right for the throat with "FDT" (the initials stand for exactly what you think they stand for). Fiona Apple recorded a short, sharp piece called "Tiny Hands." Eminem recorded a long, sometimes sharp piece called "Campaign Speech." Dozens of artists in every genre made their dissatisfaction known. But too few of the attempts seemed to stick. Why? Maybe Trump was resistant to art in the same way that he was resistant to satire—maybe he was in control of his own image, as objectionable as it was, to the point where it was hard to say anything about him that he hadn't already anticipated. Or maybe his statements and actions were so outrageous that artists were falling into the counterweight trap, making songs that were equally mindless but from the other side. Public Enemy's "STFU," which didn't arrive until 2020, was a version of that—a brilliant and historic rap group reduced to telling the president to shut the fuck up. I mean, many people wanted to say it, and maybe it had to be said, but still. Whenever Trump appeared before, back in the 1980s and '90s, he was depicted as a blowhard or a nouveau riche buffoon, like in the Coup's "Pimps (Free Stylin' at the Fortune 500 Club)."

The best answer came from an unexpected place, a place that I was sure was boarded up forever. In November 2015, the night of the Paris Bataclan attack, A Tribe Called Quest came on *The Tonight Show* to play "Can I Kick It?" Since they had broken up after *The Love Movement*, they had reunited a few times, mostly as a support act on Kanye West's *Yeezus* tour, but here they were appearing on the same show where I was employed. It was like having a concert in my office. That performance went better than they imagined, and Phife and Tip buried the hatchet and started working toward a new record. In March 2016, Phife passed away as a result of complications from diabetes. That November, the record they had been working on, *We Got It from Here . . . Thank You 4 Your Service*, came out. (The title, evidently, had been Phife's. No one understood it but he took the secret with him, and their only job was to use it.) The record was released on November 11, a Friday, but I came from an era when records were released on Tuesdays, so in a way I think of it as having been released on Election Day, November 8.

The following February, Tribe went on the Grammys to perform with Busta Rhymes. "I just want to thank President Agent Orange for perpetuating all of the evil that you've been perpetuating throughout the United States," Busta said. At that point, the relevant outrage centered on the Muslim ban and the border wall. The group then performed "We the People . . . ," the album's first single, which went through a list of all the people who, in this new America, "must go"—the Black people and the Mexicans and the poor people and the Muslims and the gays.

"We the People . . ." was not only a great anti-Trump song, but a song that reminded me that music could effectively wade into the waters of the society around it and sometimes even part them. It had been recorded months before the election and released right afterward, and had gained power every week since. By February, it was a searing reflection of what we were seeing in the headlines.

● ● ●

The Tribe song, and specifically their Grammys performance, made me think of the present, and in that it made me think of the past—not the Reagan era, but much earlier than that, back to the period in the early '70s when soul music seemed ready, willing, and able to take on issues of community awareness and social contract. In 1972, after the success of *What's*

Going On, Marvin Gaye started to compose an album of explicitly political songs keyed to that November's presidential election (which, in the spring of that year, probably looked like it would be Nixon, the incumbent, facing either Edmund Muskie or Hubert Humphrey). The first track from that set, and the projected title track, "You're the Man," was a warning to political candidates that their main skill, which was to create followers, amounted to little more than evil if they didn't have a plan for improving society. "I believe America's at stake," he sang.

During that year, Gaye recorded multiple versions of the song, and the differences are instructive. Take the way he handles busing. In one version, he names it as maybe the central question of the time:

> You know busin', busin' is the issue
> Ah, do you have a plan with you?

In another, it's just "an issue," one among many.

> Busing, busing is an issue
> Come on, lemme hear your plan, mister

He was working out his own platform, it seems. In either event, he is willing to cut to the heart of the matter, to discuss something even more elemental than policy. It's in a haunting refrain that he sings over and over again in the middle of the song: "Don't you understand / There's misery in the land."

Gaye had different politics than the Motown founder Berry Gordy, and Gordy didn't throw much support behind the "You're the Man" single, which came out in the summer—by that time, the Democratic race had shifted, and George McGovern had won the nomination. "Inner City Blues," Gaye's previous single, had gone number one on the R&B chart and Top Ten pop. "You're the Man" barely went Top Ten R&B and Top Fifty pop. The album was shelved.

Two decades later, long after Gaye's death and canonization as one of Motown's geniuses, tracks from the scrapped album started to appear on expanded versions of his early '70s records. Some of the songs were open-ended laments for society's shortsightedness (the heartsick/hopeful "Where Are We Going?"); others were more specific arguments about the dangers of controlling others ("Piece of Clay"), or the hypocrisy of objecting to sex in the face of so many other kinds of social pornography, from poverty to violence to pollution ("The World Is Rated X").

But the whole album was still a mystery—until 2019, when it was reconstructed and finally released. As I've said, I have had my own experience with reissues: the deluxe editions of *Things Fall Apart* in 2019 for its twentieth anniversary and *Do You Want More?!!!??!* in 2020 for its twenty-fifth anniversary. Those included the albums as they originally existed plus supplementary demos and remixes created at the same time intended to deepen, complicate, and elaborate upon history. I can't say whether they were revelatory. It's not for me to say. I can say that there's a whole range of effectiveness in the deluxe reissues of other bands. They can truly shine a light, like on the deluxe reissue of Fleetwood Mac's *Tusk*, where there are a half-dozen versions of "I Know I'm Not Wrong," a song Lindsey Buckingham couldn't seem to get quite right. Watching it crawl toward existence is like a trip to the Galápagos.

On the other hand, they can dim a light, like on the deluxe reissues of Prince's *1999* and *Sign o' the Times* that followed his death. Those sets fill out the portrait of Prince, certainly, and include lots of outtakes and demos I love, but for me they move my sense of him away from what I want it to be, which is a figure touched by greatness, and move it toward a sense of him as a more ordinary man, someone who wrote good songs and bad songs both. And given that even those deluxe sets are by no means comprehensive—they omit other outtakes, as well as concert soundchecks, which is where he was working out some of his most interesting ideas—that larger picture may not be a more accurate one. It's not always right for posterity to paint more of the portrait, especially when an artist is no longer around to explain or justify the choices made. The completist argument doesn't necessarily hold water, because artists leave things off finished records for as many reasons as they put things on the records, and the mere fact that a piece of music was created in the same time period isn't necessarily a justification for including it in the group shot. Does the same thing hold for histories that aren't about artistic creation? Is it important merely to shine a light on as many events as possible, without providing context or commentary? If Thomas Jefferson wrote a funny-angry letter to a friend while he was working on *Notes on the State of Virginia*, should it be included in an expanded edition? When history opens its mouth, how many teeth should you count? I'm not answering this question here, just asking it. But it is true that how you come to history has everything to do with how history comes to you.

The 2019 version of *You're the Man* approaches these questions from a slightly different angle. Rather than build out an existing structure, a *What's Going On* or a *Let's Get It On*, it buys an empty lot and builds something new. It's a forty-seventh-anniversary reissue of an album that never existed in the first place, an imaginative exercise, built from notes and notions, that inserts a work into history. It's not an accurate reflection of any statement by Gaye, since his statement at the time was to not make a statement, to pull the album before it could be pushed out into the market. And while some of the songs, especially the title track, have a whiff of prophecy, they also raise the depressing possibility that history just cycles through the same set of plots and problems, that we are looking at the same conflicts and conundrums as people a hundred years ago or a thousand, that time is a flat circle. That's from *True Detective* back in 2015, but it's also from Nietzsche in 1882. Eternal recurrence, he called it, almost certainly knowing that the idea itself would recur.

● ● ●

The failed DJ gig at the White House was still in my mind as the years passed. And then I had a chance at redemption, in the form of the Gold Party, the annual post-Oscars celebration hosted by Jay-Z and Beyoncé. Jay hired me for the 2020 party the day after the 2019 one, maybe because I had complained about it a little bit, told him that he had such a great thing going and that he deserved a DJ who was at the same level as the rest of the event. I put myself out there. "I don't think you want to do it," he said. I don't know whether that was honestly his opinion or if he was trying to motivate me, but for the next year, I took twenty minutes out of every day to build a set, went slowly and deliberately, and when the night came, I promised myself that I wouldn't come off course no matter what happened. The night of the event, it went like I had dreamed, and then some. People in the crowd started off with "He's a really good DJ," went to "Wait, what's he doing?" and ended up in the vicinity of "I understand now" or "This is art" or "I think I'm going to cry."

After the Gold Party, I finally was able to release the frustration and the tension that had built up over the years. I had written a history, not just in my head, but put it out in the world, made it public. I had taken thirty years of music knowledge and distilled them into one gig, and I didn't know what was left. I don't know what's left. In the wake of that triumphant night, I have found that it's hard to return to the same mindset as before, the same *CSI* approach to samples and chronologies and lyrical inspirations. It's not that I'm cavalier about music. I'm probably just as obsessive as ever. But after years of trying, I finally wrote a work of history in the form of a DJ set, and that produced such an unfamiliar charge that it's like one of those scenes in the movies where a character is electrocuted and still has electricity, green or blue, sizzling in his bones. It was either my last gig or the first real gig or the only gig of its kind, a one-off, not history in the making but history made.

• • •

The past dead-ends in the present. Now we skip forward again, but only a little. My last DJ set in person was February 2020. A month later, the COVID-19 pandemic became a factor in American lives. Then it became the dominant factor, which it has remained since then, infecting more than thirty million Americans, killing more than half a million. Those are the current numbers. They'll continue to rise.

My DJ gigs became virtual, like the rest of the world. I got to play music that I wouldn't ordinarily have played. I started doing more visual art, drawing with my girlfriend on Sundays and doodling most days, just as a way of opening up my mind. I tried to tune to the frequency of the quarantine. What I learned, or what I relearned, is that the majority of people live only for the past. I don't mean that they study the past. That makes sense. I've been doing it my whole life. I've been doing it my whole book. I mean that they boost the value of the past, look back with rose- (or otherwise-) tinted glasses. It's the case in politics, where we've been hearing for years about making America great again. It's the case in culture, where we've been hearing for years about how movies, or music, or literature, used to be one thing, and how they're now something else. I've even been guilty of that myself, often, in the way I hang on my *Soul Train* obsession, replay episodes in my mind, try to experience the same emotions I felt back then. It's true that the past is different from the present. But understanding those differences before broadcasting value judgments, that's the better goal. That's one thing I learned in the pandemic, as I've been thinking through the relationship between then and now, as I've been relearning how to sit comfortably in the now. I think of an introduction to a Jimi Hendrix live set. I think it might be one of his Maui shows. "Forget about tomorrow and yesterday," he says, and I know what he means, but also, do I? Forgetting about tomorrow can feel like sensible advice or a major chronological paradox, depending on where my head's at.

You want to do the things that matter now (or at least soon), to minimize the long game. But when you live too much in the moment, you can both block responsible memory (that's blowing out the retroactive) and fail to see the point of planning (that's blowing out the proactive). This year has felt that way sometimes. I said that 9/11 stopped history, or at least scratched history in ways that made it hard to play the record without skipping. That's happening again now, but in vastly different ways. As we've discussed, 9/11 happened at the expense of everything around it, at least in terms of mind share. The pandemic has not worked that way. It has hung over the year, a dark cloud getting darker, while life (and death) went on. It hasn't eclipsed other events. There have been so many other events: the protests this summer against police brutality, the election in November and the desperate claims of fraud that followed. Murder hornets. Hurricanes. Kobe Bryant's death, only a year ago, seems like ten years ago. But watching the way this year has been written and revised has made me rethink the way we write ourselves into history.

"Time is what keeps everything from happening at once." It's been that kind of year. That's a famous quote, attributed to Einstein, except when it's attributed to Mark Twain, though it seems both are misattributions. I looked around, and it seems like the idea was first articulated by a sci-fi writer named Ray Cummings, who started his career as an assistant for Thomas Edison. Remember Edison? Great Man. But so what if Ray Cummings said it? So much of history, the vast majority, is neither seen nor heard, and most things that have been said were said by no one—I mean, they were said by someone, but not Someone, not a person visible in history or even named within it. Just a person.

That's the truth, and that's the challenge, and that's the sinkhole that sits at the bottom of any act of writing history or any act of trying to understand what's been written about history. No matter how small the scale, no matter how fine the grain, there's simply no way to recover the past in all its richness and contradiction, just like there's no way to capture the present. And what about when the present becomes someone else's past? I don't envy the historians of the future who have to untangle this year—or build a playlist about it. But I have been thinking about them. How will history view this period? When the books are written in fifty years, or a hundred, what will be the one-liner, the two-liner, the paragraph? A year and a half ago I would have guessed that it would be Trump, his unpredictable rise and surprising staying power, the sad fact that populism was revived as a Trojan horse for racism, and that it was never populism at all but rather demagoguery. A year ago I might have said all that, but also felt that his legacy was being softened by what looked like a strong economy, and that people were going to cut him slack for pocketbook gains. Then I thought it would all be swept away by the pandemic, the way that it changed nearly everything about American life and did it so rapidly. Education, privacy, dating, working, mourning: it's all been remade, and who knows if we'll ever get back to what we were. And then, like everyone else, I watched as 2020 ended and we moved into what people were certain would be a calmer 2021. It wasn't. Within a week, the Capitol was stormed by a violent mob, and then Trump was impeached again, and many social media platforms banned him, and the face of the nation changed again. Now I think the last year will be told primarily as a story of the pandemic, which we're still in the midst of, but that it'll have a close-second story, which is how the pandemic changed voting, and how voting brought in Biden, and how Trump's fragile ego couldn't handle it, and how the lies about the results of the election stirred up a population that has been battered by the pandemic and confused by propaganda, and how that population remained stirred up in the days before Biden's inauguration, which is where we are now.

You know, I could be wrong. I know I could be wrong. That's the excitement of it, or the terror. It's like walking into a room without any real sense of what's in there. Later they'll come and take pictures of the room, and they'll figure out what happened here. But I gotta go.

INDEXES

EVERY SONG IN THIS BOOK

EVERY SONG IN THIS BOOK, BY ARTIST

INDEX

ABOUT THE AUTHOR

QUESTLOVE is a five-time Grammy Award–winning musician, bandleader, producer, director, culinary entrepreneur, DJ, and the musical director for *The Tonight Show Starring Jimmy Fallon*. He is the author of the *New York Times* bestsellers *Mo' Meta Blues* and *Creative Quest*, the Grammy-nominated audiobook *Creative Quest*, *Soul Train: The Music, Dance and Style of a Generation*, the James Beard Award–nominated *somethingtofoodabout*, and, most recently, *Mixtape Potluck Cookbook*. He recently made his directorial debut with *Summer of Soul*, winner of the Grand Jury Prize and the Audience Award at the Sundance Film Festival.

Ben Greenman is a *New York Times* bestselling author who has published both fiction and nonfiction, including collaborations with Brian Wilson and George Clinton. He has previously collaborated with Questlove on *Mo' Meta Blues* and *Creative Quest*, among other works.

Creative Director: Alexis Rosenzweig
Cover Design: Reed Barrow

ABRAMS:
Editor: Holly Dolce
Designer: Heesang Lee
Managing Editor: Lisa Silverman
Production Manager: Anet Sirna-Bruder

Library of Congress Control Number: 2021932568

ISBN: 978-1-4197-5143-1
eISBN: 978-1-64700-184-1
Extended Remix Edition ISBN: 978-1-4197-6071-6

Portions of some chapters appeared in different form in *New York* magazine ("1974: The Payback," "1978: Disco Tech," "1990: Return of the Impressed")

Printed and bound in the United States
10 9 8 7 6 5 4 3 2 1

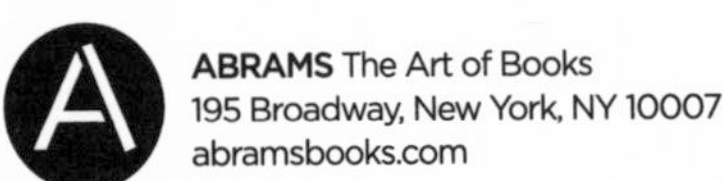
ABRAMS The Art of Books
195 Broadway, New York, NY 10007
abramsbooks.com